Publisher

Marie Butler-Knight

Managing Editor

Elizabeth Keaffaber

Product Development Manager

Faithe Wempen

Acquisitions Manager

Barry Pruett

Development Editor

Seta Frantz

Production Editor

Michelle Shaw

Copy Editor

San Dee Phillips

Cover Designer

Karen Ruggles

Designer

Barbara Webster

Indexer

Bront Davis

Production Team

Gary Adair, Dan Caparo, Brad Chinn, Kim Cofer, Lisa Daugherty, Jennifer Eberhardt, Mark Enochs, Beth Rago, Bobbi Satterfield, Kris Simmons, Greg Simsic, Carol Stamile, Robert Wolf

Special thanks to C. Herbert Feltner for ensuring the technical accuracy of this book.

Contents

INTRODUCTION

Well, you've finally mastered the basics of using WordPerfect for Windows 6.0, which is no mean trick. You can type a letter or a memo, spell check it, and get it printed without much of a problem. But you have this nagging feeling that you should be able to do more with a program that's cost you more than a few hundred dollars.

It'd be nice to fiddle around and create a good-looking fax cover letter, or some personalized mailing labels, but who has the time? Actually, no one does, but with the step-by-step instructions you'll find inside this book, you won't be wasting any time choosing the wrong options or changing things around to get the look you want. Without any real effort at all, you'll create hundreds of useful items, such as sales brochures, invoices, thank-you cards, bulletin board notices, posters, calendars, and more.

YEAH, BUT IS THIS BOOK FOR ME?

This book is for *anyone* who uses WordPerfect for Windows 6.0, whether it's around the office, home, or school. There are projects for families, professionals, and even projects just for kids. You'll learn how to make sale flyers, résumés, newsletters, bookmarks, restaurant menus, report covers, and party games, to name just a few examples. If you have WordPerfect for Windows 6.0, you can complete any of the project ideas in this book.

OKAY, SO WHAT DO I NEED TO KNOW TO USE THIS BOOK?

Only what you already know about WordPerfect for Windows 6.0. Just follow the instructions and the carefully detailed figures, and you'll easily create any of the items you find in this book. If you'd like more help with a feature that's new to you, there's a basic skills section in Part VII (called Basic Kitchen Skills) to tell you what you need to know.

WHAT WILL I FIND INSIDE?

Just browse through the many different sections in this "cookbook" of ideas:

- **Appetizers**   Recipes for correspondence and communications, such as customized letters, envelopes, business cards, fax covers, résumés, and more.

- **Main Dishes**   Recipes for reports and presentations, such as report covers, report designs, bibliographies, footnote pages, term papers, transparencies, and more.

- **Fruits**   Recipes for advertising and publicity, such as brochures, flyers, newsletters, signs, bulletin board notices, and more.

- **Vegetables**   Recipes for forms, such as credit, employment, and membership applications, permission slips, purchase orders, invoices, sales proposals, time sheets, and more.

- **Bread**   Recipes for planning and organizing, such as auto maintenance logs, home inventory sheets, address books, things-to-do lists, travel itineraries, and more.

- **Desserts**   Recipes just for fun, such as party games, bumper stickers, Christmas cards, party decorations, gift tags, and more.

Once you find a project you like, just follow the simple step-by-step instructions that tell you exactly what to do. Along the way, you'll encounter:

 Chef's Tip   Tips from the experts on how to make your project more special.

 Cook's Caution   Cautions to help you avoid trouble spots.

Look for this heading . .

VARIATIONS

. . . and you'll find variations for changing each project to fit your style.

Best of all, everything is presented in easy-to-follow recipe format that includes level of difficulty, step-by-step instructions, and lots of pictures to show you how each project was made. Using a little imagination and the power of your computer, you'll be amazed at the variety of creations available at your fingertips. You'll never think of WordPerfect for Windows as an ordinary word processing program again! But don't take our word for it—grab an apron, turn on your computer, and let's get cookin'!

ACKNOWLEDGMENTS

I'd like to thank Sherry for all her help. Your artistry inspired me to higher levels of creativity. Who knew WordPerfect could do so much? I'd also like to thank my husband Scott, who put up with me through this whole process. Creative books, such as this one, can sometimes be more stressful, and I appreciated his patience and thoughtful suggestions. — *Jennifer Fulton*

I'd like to extend special thanks to Marie Butler-Knight, Faithe Wempen, Seta Frantz, and Mary Rack for all of their "preheating" of ideas and directions; and an extra scoop of thanks to Jennifer, for her support and comradery that helped make this book so much fun to write. — *Sherry Kinkoph*

PART ONE

APPETIZERS: CORRESPONDING AND COMMUNICATING

From the day we are born, we communicate. Our first cry sends an unmistakable message: "How'd I get here? What am I doing naked? Put me back in!" Probably the main reason you bought WordPerfect for Windows was to create some *communication*. I mean, can we talk?

But how do you create a letter, memo, or fax that won't get lost in the communications shuffle? How do you write the perfect résumé, create a perfect envelope, present the perfect business card? With the recipes in this section, you'll learn how to do all this and more—perfectly.

10 min.

Moderate

BUSINESS CARDS

Guy Hamilton
Product Manager

The Sky's the Limit
2450 Sunnyside Drive
Indianapolis, Indiana   46290
(317) 581-8181

If you work out of your home, or if you'd like to advertise a side-line business venture, create your own customized business cards. It's a great way to cut costs on a necessary expense. With a nice logo, you can create matching stationery, too. See the letterhead and logo recipes in this section for more ideas and the steps to create a logo.

PREPARATION

Create a business card paper size.

1. Select Layout. • Select Page. • Select Paper Size. • Click Create.

2. Enter Business Card under Paper Name. • Size: 3.5" by 2". • Select Wide Form. • Click OK.

3. Choose Business Card from the list. • Click Select.

4. Select Layout. • Select Margins. • All margins: .25". • Click OK.

Insert your logo.

 5. Click on Figure button. • Select your logo. • Click OK.

6. Resize logo as necessary (see the next figure). • Drag logo into place.

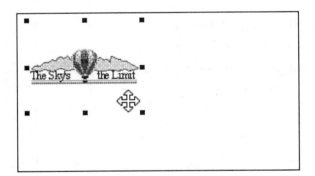

7. Click on the Border/Fill button. • Border Style: None. • Click OK.

Enter your name and address.

 8. Font Face: Times New Roman. • Font Size: 10. • Click on Bold button. • Type your name. • Turn off bold. • On next line, type your job title.

 9. Press Enter four times. • Click on Bold button. • Type your company's name. • Bold off. • Type company address and phone number.

 Cook's Caution If necessary, use the Ruler to reset left margin so lines of type are even.

10. Save your business card file. • Take your completed art to a printer to have your business cards professionally printed.

VARIATIONS

No Logo? *You can easily create a logo, such as the initial logo shown here, with one of the recipes in this section. Or you can create a free-form piece of art with WordPerfect Draw and use it instead.*

Coming Out? *Calling cards are making a comeback, so create cute, personalized cards for your children. Start with the BUTERFLY graphic, and then add a name by printing it with the Freeform tool, using a larger line width.*

EMERGENCY PHONE LIST

Emergency Telephone List

The Fultons
1016 West 116th
Indianapolis, In
356-4991

NAME		Address	Phone
Dr. Brown	Family Physician	10 West Medical Drive	544-0231
Dr. Caiser	Eye	2345 South 16th Street	678-9090
Dr. Barrie	Pediatrician	5802 East 56th Street	879-0231
Betsy Wilson	Babysitter	6709 West 116th	356-9089
The Whitmers	Aunt Pat and Uncle Bill	5790 North Keystone	456-7878
The Wilsons	Aunt Beth and Uncle Bob	6123 Evanston	477-4819
The Flynns	Grandpa and Nana	5820 Hillside	253-1234

I keep all my important numbers in a day planner, which is okay when I'm at work and it's conveniently on my desk. But when I go home, it's a pain to call someone unless I happen to have the number memorized. With this recipe, you'll use a WordPerfect template to create an emergency phone list of important numbers you can keep handy (at home or near the car phone).

PREPARATION

Select the Phonelst template.

1. Click on Templates button. • Select Phonelst. • Click OK. • Select the company information, and replace with your family's name, address, and phone number.

Begin with a slight make-over.

2. Click inside Name column. • Click on Tbl Insert button. • Click on Columns: set to 1. • Click After. • Click OK.

3. Click inside Ext. column. • Click on Delete Tbl button. • Select Columns. • Click OK. • Repeat for Fax column (see the next figure).

Telephone List

The Fultons
1016 West 116th
Indianapolis, Indiana 46290
3584991

NAME	DEPARTMENT	PHONE

Chef's Tip You can drag to select both Ext and Fax columns, and then delete both at once.

4. Select the Name heading cell and the cell to the right. • Click right mouse button. • Select Join Cells (see the next figure).

Telephone List

NAME		

Joined cell

Personalize it.

5. Add the word "Emergency" in front of "Telephone List."

6. To enter data, click inside first cell. • Press Tab to move from cell to cell. • To insert more rows, press Tab from the last cell in the table.

Print your listing.

7. Save and print your phone list.

VARIATIONS

Keep It Handy: *Seal your phone list in self-stick plastic, and keep it near the phone. Make sure your kids know where to find it and how to give emergency personnel your address.*

Dial 911! *Add this little reminder to your phone list, next to your address. There are many stories on TV about little kids saving their parents, grandparents, or guardian by knowing to call 911 in an emergency.*

ENVELOPE TO MATCH ANY LETTER

Alphabet Soup

201 West 103rd Street
Indianapolis, Indiana 46290

Scott Anderson
La Margarita Restaurant
345 NW 103rd
Oklahoma City, Oklahoma 73132

For the "perfect ensemble," create a matching envelope for any of the letterhead or letter recipes in this section. Add the customized envelope to your letter or letterhead template, so you can use it over and over again. With WordPerfect doing most of the work, it's easy. See later recipes in this section on how to create a letterhead template.

PREPARATION

Open your template.

1. Click on Open button. • Select your letterhead template. • Click OK.

Envelope, please.

2. Click on Envelope button. • Enter your return address. • Select Print Return Address.

3. If you want, change the address fonts to match the style of the logo. • Click on Append to Doc.

Copy your customized logo to the envelope.

4. Select the customized logo from page one of your letterhead template (see the next figure). • Click on Copy button.

5. Move insertion point back to envelope. • Click on Paste button.

6. Drag to resize logo, as necessary. • Place logo above the return address (see the next figure).

7. Click on Exit Template button. • Click Yes. When you use your template later, the recipient's address will automatically be added to your envelope, so it will be ready to print.

VARIATIONS

Placement Is Everything: *For a different look, place the logo beside the return address. If you want to place the return address exactly, you may want to cut and paste the text into a text box, as shown in the Arrowhead sample. Just select the address, click Cut, click on the Text Box button, double-click in the text box, and click Paste.*

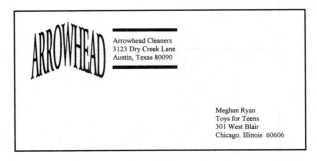

No Logo? *Copy the font style from your letter to make your return address match. Or to create a logo, see the logo recipes later in this section.*

FAX COVER SHEET WITH BORDER AND CHECK BOXES

Alphabet Soup

Finest Gifts for the Most Discriminating Tastes
201 West 103rd Street
Indianapolis, Indiana 46290
(317) 581-3500
Fax: (317) 581-8181

FAX TRANSMISSION COVER SHEET

Date: May 18, 1994

To: Meghan Ryan

Fax: (312) 555-5001

Subject: March Sales Event!

Sender: George Vasser

YOU SHOULD RECEIVE 3 PAGE(S), INCLUDING THIS COVER SHEET. IF
YOU DO NOT RECEIVE ALL THE PAGES, PLEASE CALL (317) 581-3500.

People receive so many faxes in this bustling world of the information superhighway. So you don't want yours to fall into the dreaded "circular file," especially if it's important and you need an answer soon. With this recipe, you'll modify the Fax3 template and add a border and some check boxes that will scream at your recipient to answer it right away. At the very least, your fax will really stand out in the in-basket, if and when the recipient ever goes through it.

PREPARATION

Select the Fax3 template.

 1. Click on Open button. • Change to Template directory. • Select Fax3. • Click OK.

 Cook's Caution Select Save As from the File menu and enter another name, such as FAXCHECK.WPT. Be sure to save your copy to the Template directory.

Run for a border.

 2. Click on GrphPgBrdr button on Design Tools Button Bar. • Select Starburst border. • Click OK.

Add check boxes you make yourself.

 3. Click on Draw button.

4. Select File. • Select Page Layout. • Width: 11", Height: 1.50". • Page Color: light gray. • Click OK.

 5. Click on Rectangle tool.

 6. Fill Color: white. • Line Color: black. • Draw small square or "check box."

 7. Click on small square/check box. • Select Edit. • Select Duplicate. • Drag new check box off first check box, and place it far enough to right so there's room to add text later.

8. Repeat step 7 for third and final check box.

Time to add some text.

 9. Select Text. • Select Font. • Font Face: Times New Roman. • Font Size: 36. Click on Text tool. • Click next to first square. • Type: Urgent! (see the next figure). • Press Enter.

10. Click next to second check box. • Type: Reply Requested (see the last figure). • Press Enter.

11. One more time! Click next to third check box. • Type: For Your Review (see the last figure). • Press Enter.

12. Click on Select tool. • Move text boxes to make room for their check boxes.

Save your template.

13. Select File. • Select Exit and Return to Document. • Click Yes.

14. Click on the check box figure to select it. • Drag check boxes to the middle of the page.

15. Click on Exit Template button. • Click Yes. For tips on how to use your template, see the "Basic Kitchen Skills" section in the back of this book.

VARIATIONS

Got a Long Message? *Drag the check boxes into an unused area, near the sender information.*

Fax Cover Sheet
with Logo

facsimile
TRANSMITTAL

to: Donald Tempest
fax #: (312) 555-5001
re: New Product!
date: May 18, 1994
pages: 1, including cover sheet.

I've got a new product line to demonstrate for you! See you on Tuesday!

From the desk of...

Alice Pendleton
Product Manager
Alphabet Soup
Finest Gifts for the Most Discriminating Taste
201 West 103rd Street
Indianapolis, Indiana 46290

(317) 581-3500
Fax (317) 581-8181

It seems these days that everything has a logo or a symbol—even things that don't need one, like grocery store breads and rolls, K-Mart underwear, and luxury sedans. Well, if your business, school, or organization faxes stuff and has a logo, why not put the two together? With this recipe, you'll learn how to add a graphic image (the already designed logo) to one of the premade faxes. If you don't already have a logo (sniff), don't fret; just turn to the middle of this section, and you'll find a good recipe.

PREPARATION

Select the Fax2 template.

1. Click on Open button. • Change to Template directory. • Select Fax2. • Click OK.

 Cook's Caution   If you don't want to modify the Fax2 template, select Save As from the File menu, and enter another name, such as FAXLOGO.WPT. Be sure to save your copy to the Template directory.

Insert the logo.

2. Click on Figure button.

3. Select your logo file. • Click OK. • Click Close.

Make necessary adjustments.

4. Resize logo if necessary. • Move logo into place, just above the "From the desk of" area (see the next figure).

From the desk of...

Alice Pendleton
Product Manager
Alphabet Soup
Finest Gifts for the Most Discriminating Taste
201 West 103rd Street
Indianapolis, Indiana 46290

(317) 581-3500
Fax: (317) 581-8181

5. Click on Exit Template button. • Click Yes. For tips on how to use your template, see the "Basic Kitchen Skills" section in the back of this book.

VARIATIONS

Make a Mark: *You can place your logo as a watermark, which appears behind text as a faint image. Follow the graphic variation in the recipe, "Fax Cover Sheet with Watermark."*

FAX COVER SHEET WITH WATERMARK

RUSH

To: Scott Jameston

Fax: (406) 876-9011

From: Murphy Green

Date: May 18, 1994

Pages: 1, including cover sheet.

I will be in your area next Thursday, and I'd like to stop by and demonstrate our latest products. How about 2:00 p.m.? Let me know by phone or fax today. Thanks!

RUSH

fax

RUSH

From the desk of...

Murphy Green
Product Manager
Alphabet Soup
Finest Gifts for the Most Discriminating Taste
201 West 103rd Street
Indianapolis, Indiana 46290

(317) 581-3500
Fax: (317) 581-8181

RUSH

WordPerfect comes with four fax templates, but that shouldn't stop you from "making your own mark." A watermark is an image placed within the fibers of hoity-toity, expensive paper. WordPerfect can help you recreate this effect so everyone will be duly impressed. With this recipe, you'll insert a watermark called "Rush" into the Fax1 template and save it as a new fax template you can use whenever you're in a hurry for a reply.

PREPARATION

Select the Fax1 template.

 1. Click on Open button. • Change to Template directory. • Select Fax1. • Click OK.

2. Select File. • Select Save As. • Enter a new name, such as RUSHFAX.WPT. • Be sure to save your copy to the Template directory.

Insert the watermark.

 3. Click on GrphWtrmrk button on Design Tools Button Bar. • Click on Graphic, Watermark A. • Click OK.

4. Select Rush from watermark list. • Click OK.

 Chef's Tip WordPerfect offers many premade text watermarks, such as "Confidential" and "Reply Requested." Some of these watermarks flow along the left-hand side of the page (as does our Rush watermark), while others are centered. See Appendix E of your WP manual.

Make necessary adjustments.

5. Drag "From the desk of" box up to reveal last "Rush" watermark (see the next figure).

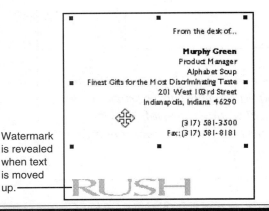

Watermark is revealed when text is moved up.

6. Drag "Fax" box up, out of the way of third "Rush" watermark (see the next figure).

Watermark is revealed when text is moved up.

Save your work.

7. Click on Exit Template button. • Click Yes. For tips on how to use your template, see the "Basic Kitchen Skills" section in the back of this book.

VARIATIONS

Get Graphic: *Instead of a text watermark, add a graphic image. In step 3, click on the Watermarks button. Click Create, and then click Figure. Select a graphic (such as a silhouette), and then click OK. The image will appear, centered on the page. Click on Close twice to return to the document.*

20 min.

Moderate

LABELS

 Alphabet Soup
201 West 103rd Street
Indianapolis, Indiana 46290

 Alphabet Soup
201 West 103rd Street
Indianapolis, Indiana 46290

 Alphabet Soup
201 West 103rd Street
Indianapolis, Indiana 46290

 Alphabet Soup
201 West 103rd Street
Indianapolis, Indiana 46290

 Alphabet Soup
201 West 103rd Street
Indianapolis, Indiana 46290

 Alphabet Soup
201 West 103rd Street
Indianapolis, Indiana 46290

 Alphabet Soup
201 West 103rd Street
Indianapolis, Indiana 46290

 Alphabet Soup
201 West 103rd Street
Indianapolis, Indiana 46290

 Alphabet Soup
201 West 103rd Street
Indianapolis, Indiana 46290

 Alphabet Soup
201 West 103rd Street
Indianapolis, Indiana 46290

You can customize mailing labels and/or return-address labels to match your stationery. With WordPerfect's label feature, it's easy. Then, you can print them out on your laser or dot-matrix printer. If you're up to doing some mail merge, you can create a dummy label form complete with logos, and merge it with your address data file (this almost makes learning to use a computer worthwhile). If you don't have a logo, see the recipes later in this section.

PREPARATION

The set up.

1. If you want to perform a merge to create mailing labels, first create your data file. See the "Mail Merge" section in Part 7 of this book for more information.

2. Select Layout. • Select Labels. • Choose your label style. • Click Select.

 Cook's Caution All label types are listed. To list only laser or dot-matrix labels, click on one of these options at the top of the dialog box.

Add a logo, logo, logo to the label, label, label.

 3. Click on Figure button. • Select a logo. • Click OK.

4. Resize the logo. • Drag it into place. • Click on Border/Fill button. • Border Style: None. • Click OK. • If you're creating return address labels, type your address (see the next figure). (I used Times New Roman 10 pt. text for the sample shown here.)

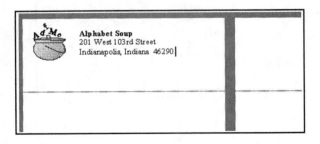

5. If you're creating more than one label, copy logo to other labels in set (see the next figure). • If you're creating return address labels, copy your return address as well. • Save your label file.

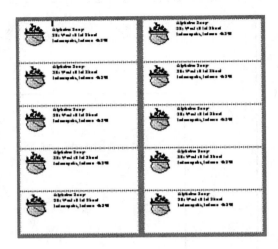

6. If you're creating mailing labels and you have a merge data file, insert data fields and perform the merge. • Print the labels.

VARIATIONS

1001 Uses: *You can use your labels for more than just mailing; for example, create custom labels to identify mystery boxes, files, and so on. Print labels for your garden to mark what you've planted. (Protect these with self-stick plastic covers.)*

LETTER WITH FOOTER

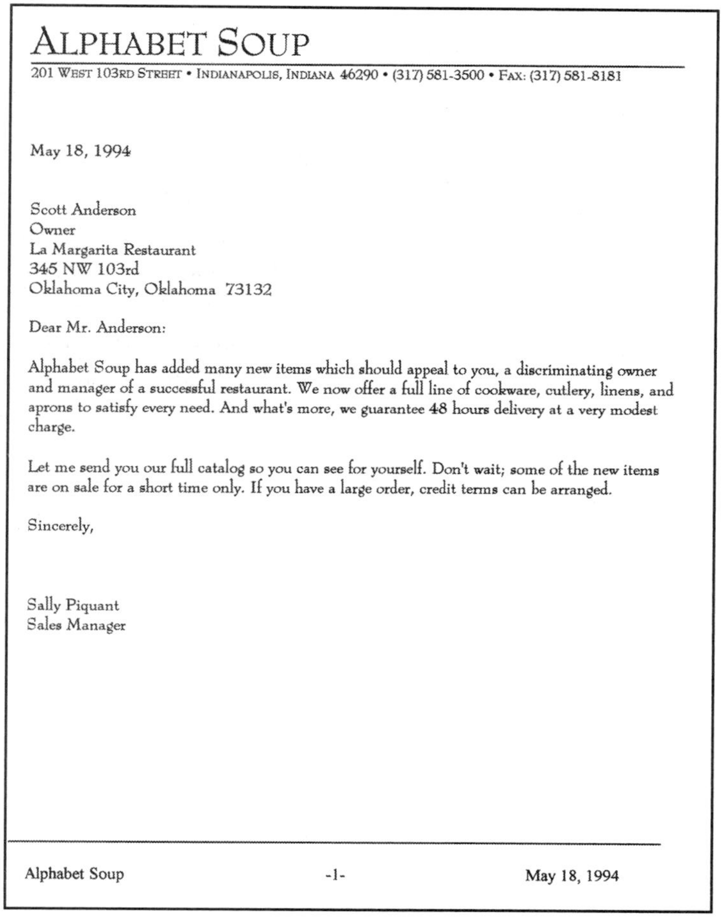

ALPHABET SOUP
201 WEST 103RD STREET • INDIANAPOLIS, INDIANA 46290 • (317) 581-3500 • FAX: (317) 581-8181

May 18, 1994

Scott Anderson
Owner
La Margarita Restaurant
345 NW 103rd
Oklahoma City, Oklahoma 73132

Dear Mr. Anderson:

Alphabet Soup has added many new items which should appeal to you, a discriminating owner and manager of a successful restaurant. We now offer a full line of cookware, cutlery, linens, and aprons to satisfy every need. And what's more, we guarantee 48 hours delivery at a very modest charge.

Let me send you our full catalog so you can see for yourself. Don't wait; some of the new items are on sale for a short time only. If you have a large order, credit terms can be arranged.

Sincerely,

Sally Piquant
Sales Manager

| Alphabet Soup | -1- | May 18, 1994 |

WordPerfect comes with five nice letter templates, but that shouldn't stop you from adding your own touches. For example, I hate it when I get a letter and read it, then file it away (usually under some other "important" stuff), and when I dig it out later, the pages are all mixed up and I don't know what order they belong in! Adding a footer to a letter template takes care of that little problem quite nicely. With this recipe, you'll add a footer to the LETTER1 template, and save the result so you can use it over and over.

PREPARATION

Select the Letter1 template.

1. Click on Open button. • Change to Template directory. • Select Letter1. • Click OK.

Add a footer.

2. Select Layout. • Select Header/Footer. • Select Footer A. • Click Create. • Font Face: Times New Roman. • Font Size: 12. • Type your company or organization's name, and press Tab four times.

3. Type: – (a hyphen) (see the next figure). • Click on Number button. • Select Page Number. • Type : – (hyphen).

Alphabet Soup   -1-

4. Press Tab four more times. • Select Insert. • Select Date. • Select Date Code.

5. Click on Line button. • Select Single Line Style. • Click OK. • Drag the line above footer text (see the next figure). • Click Close.

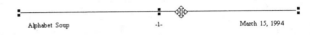

Alphabet Soup   -1-   March 15, 1994

6. Click on Exit Template button. • Click Yes.

VARIATIONS

And What Is This Regarding? *Add a short description to the letter as part of the footer. In step 2, type your description instead of the company name. In other letters you create from this template, select Header/Footer from the Layout menu. Select Footer A, and click on Edit. Type your description, and click on Close.*

5 min.

BUSINESS   ORGANIZATION   HOME   SCHOOL

Easy

LETTER WITH MODIFIED BLOCK STYLE

From the Desk of Jennifer Fulton

3456 Race Car Drive ● Indianapolis, Indiana 46290 ● (317) 581-3500 ● Fax: (317) 581-8181

March 7, 1994

Beth Wilson
2456 West 103rd
Indianapolis, Indiana 46232

Dear Beth:

Hi! Sorry I haven't written for so long. A lot has happened since I saw you at my wedding last October. First of all, the honeymoon was terrific! We had great weather the whole time. St. John's is a perfectly romantic spot - and I guess a lot of other folks agree, since almost everyone there was a honeymooner too!

Scott and I have settled into a nice two bedroom apartment. We'd like to have you and Bob over soon for dinner so you can see the place. It's small, but it's ours! We plan on looking for a house next spring.

So how are you and the kids? How does Meghan like her first year in junior high? Does Ryan still play tennis and soccer? Write soon and let us know how you are doing.

Love and miss you,

Jennifer

With a few simple changes to any of the letter templates, you can go from a formal to a more casual look. Simply indent the date and signature lines of a letter to duplicate the Modified Block style, suitable for all occasions. With this recipe, you'll modify the LETTER2 template.

PREPARATION

Select the Letter2 template.

 1. Click on Open button. • Change to Template directory. • Select Letter 2. • Click OK.

Make a dent with an indent.

2. Select the date line. • Select Layout. • Select Paragraph. • Select Format. • Enter 3.5 for Left Margin Adjustment. • Click OK. The date is now indented (see the next figure).

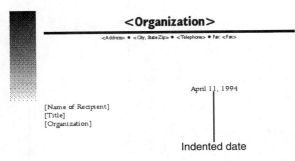

<Organization>

<Address> • <City, State Zip> • <Telephone> • Fax: <Fax>

April 11, 1994

[Name of Recipient]
[Title]
[Organization]

Indented date

Make some more dents.

3. Select "Sincerely" and the name and title holders. • Select Layout. • Select Paragraph. • Select Format. • Left Margin Adjustment: 3.5. • Click OK (see the next figure).

Sincerely,

<Name>
<Title>

4. Click on Exit Template button. • Click Yes. For help using your template, see the "Basic Kitchen Skills" section at the back of this book.

VARIATIONS

Go for the "Laid-Back" Look: *If you want a letter template for personal use, make it more casual. After step 3, add a "From the Desk of" line, and replace "Sincerely" with something like "See you soon" or "Love." Sign with just your first name.*

LETTER WITH WATERMARK

May 18, 1994

Meghan Ryan
Toys for Teens
301 West Blair
Chicago, Illinois 60606

Subject: New Product Catalog

Dear Ms. Ryan:

It's spring at last here at The Sky's the Limit! We've got a lot of new gifts
to offer you, the discriminating buyer. For your teen shoppers, may I
suggest our new line of hip-hop clothes, jewelry, and colognes? Place your
order soon – many of our customers are sure to snap these up!

Sincerely yours,

Barry Lingwart
Product Manager

THE SKY'S THE LIMIT

2456 Sunnyside Drive ◆ Indianapolis, Indiana 46290
(317) 581-3500 ◆ Fax: (317) 581-8181

You can dress up any of the letter templates with a watermark made from your own logo. (I think this was the first time I was glad to get "water" on something I'd just spent ten minutes typing!) If you don't have a logo, create one. (This section contains several recipes for logos.) With this recipe, you'll add a logo watermark to the LETTER4 template.

PREPARATION

Select the Letter4 template.

1. Click on Open button. • Change to Template directory. • Select Letter4. • Click OK.

Make your mark with a watermark.

2. Click on Watermark button. • Select Watermark A. • Click Create. • Click on Figure button on the Watermark Feature Bar. • Select your logo file. • Click OK.

3. Click Close (see the next figure).

4. Click Close.

5. Click Exit Template button. • Click Yes.

VARIATIONS

Modify Your Logo: *For a good-looking watermark, modify your logo to make the best use of the vertical space on a page. The resulting "vertical version" of the logo can then be used as a watermark, while the original "horizontal version" can be used as a letterhead. To modify your logo, insert it into a document, then double-click on it. Make your changes, then select Save Copy As from the File menu. Give the modified logo a new name.*

LETTERHEAD WITH LOGO

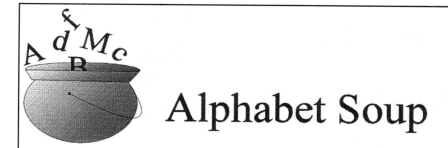

A letterhead is like a doorbell: it announces your arrival. What better way to do that than to use your own logo? With this recipe, you'll learn how to change your logo into a professional-looking letterhead (see other recipes in this section).

PREPARATION

Insert your logo.

1. Prepare your logo using a recipe from this section. • Save logo as a graphics file.

2. Select Insert. • Select File. • Select your logo. • Click OK. • Resize logo as necessary.

3. Click on Border/Fill button. • Border Style: None. • Click OK. • Click Close.

Add your address.

4. Click under logo. • Select Graphics. • Select Custom Box. • Select User. • Click OK.

5. Resize address box. • Drag it into place (see the next figure). • Click on Border/Fill. • Select Custom Style. • Select Bottom side only. • Line Style: Double. • Click OK.

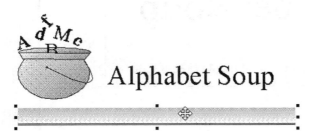

6. Fill Style: Gradient 2. • Click OK.

 Chef's Tip If you are using a colorful logo, you may want to select a matching foreground color under the Fill Style in step 6.

 7. Double-click inside address box. • Font Face: Arial. • Font Size: 12. • Click on Bold button. • Type the address (see the next figure).

8. Click Close. • Select File. • Select Save As. • Type: LETTRHD1.WPT. • Change to Templates directory. • Click OK.

VARIATIONS

Return to Sender: *Create a matching envelope for your letterhead. See the many recipes for tasty envelopes in this section.*

LETTERHEAD WITH REVERSE TEXT

Alphabet Soup

201 West 103rd Street ● Indianapolis, Indiana 46290 ● (317) 581-3500

For a dramatic letterhead, you can't beat the effect of white text on black. And best of all, it's surprisingly easy to do! With this recipe, you'll use WordPerfect Draw to create a dramatic headline and top it off with a text figure for the address.

PREPARATION

Get out your drawing board!

 1. Click on Draw button.

Change the background.

2. Select File. • Select Page Layout.
   • Width: 11". • Height: 3". • Page
   Color: Gradient. • Center Color: almost
   black. • Outer Color: white. • Angle:
   35. • Click OK.

Add your name.

3. Select Text. • Select Font. • Font Face:
   Arial. • Font Size: 72. • Click on Bold
   button. • Click Attributes. • Foreground Color: white. • Click OK.
   • Click OK again.

4. Click on Text tool. • Click inside your
   letterhead box. • Type your company
   or organization name. • Press Enter.

5. Click on Select tool. • Drag text into
   place (see the next figure).

6. Select File. • Select Exit and Return to
   Document. • Click Yes.

Don't forget to add the address!

7. Select Graphics. • Select Custom Box.
   • Select User. • Click OK. • Resize user
   box. • Place user box under name box.

8. Double-click on user box. • Select
   Layout. • Select Font. • Font Face:
   Arial. • Font Size: 12. • Click on Bold
   button. • Click OK.

9. Type your street address. • Press Ctrl
   and W. • Select Typographic Symbols
   character set. • Select first character,
   a black circle (see the next figure).
   • Select Insert.

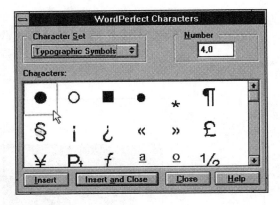

10. Click inside document; type your city,
    state, and ZIP code. • Select Insert and
    Close to insert another black circle.

11. Type your phone number.

Add the finishing touches.

12. Click on Border/Fill button. • Select
    Customize Style. • Select Bottom side
    only. • Line style: Thin/Thick 1 (see
    the next figure). • Click OK. • Click OK
    again.

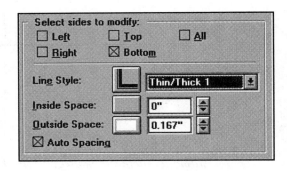

13. Click Close. • Select File. • Select Save
    As. • Type: LETTRHD2.WPT. • Change
    to Templates directory. • Click OK.

LETTERHEAD WITH
SIDEWAYS TEXT

Gwen Harding

Looking for something a bit unusual? Try a simple, yet striking, letterhead created with TextArt. With this recipe, you can create a personalized letterhead to use for personal and professional purposes.

PREPARATION

Start with TextArt.

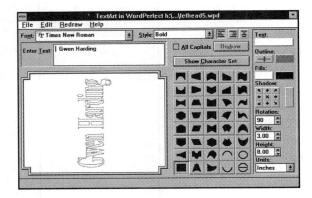

1. Click on TextArt button.

Enter your name.

2. Select Times New Roman. • Click on Text. • Select White. • Type your name.

Change direction.

3. Rotation: 90 (see the next figure). • Width: 3". • Height: 8".

Make a quick exit.

4. Select File. • Select Exit & Return to WordPerfect. • Click Yes.

5. Click on TextArt and drag it into place.

Change the background.

6. Select Graphics. • Select Edit Box. • Click on Border/Fill button. • Fill Style: 100% Fill. • Foreground Color: gray (see the next figure). • Click OK.

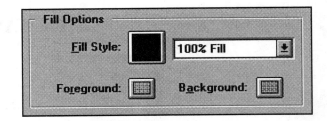

7. Click Close.

Save it for another day.

8. Select Save As. • Type: LETTRHD3.WPT. • Change to Templates directory. • Click OK.

VARIATIONS

Envelope Please: *Create a matching envelope for your letterhead with one of the many recipes for envelopes in this section.*

LETTERHEAD WITH TEXTART

Arrowhead Cleaners
3123 Dry Creek Lane
Austin, Texas 80090

Serving your dry-cleaning needs for a quarter of a century.

WordPerfect comes with TextArt, a program that enables you to bend and twist text into interesting shapes. With TextArt, it's easy to create Cinemascope letterhead paper for work, school, or home. Using this recipe, you can create your own TextArt letterhead—3-D glasses not included.

PREPARATION

Start with TextArt.

 1. Click on TextArt button.

Now enter some text.

2. Font Face: Arrus BT. • Type your company or organization name.

Get into shape.

3. Click on a shape.

> **Chef's Tip** Sometimes, text looks better in all capital letters. Click on All Capitals and decide for yourself.

Time to make for the exit.

4. When you've found a shape you like, select File. • Select Exit & Return to WordPerfect. • Click Yes.

5. Resize your graphic. • Drag it into place (see the next figure).

Add a border line.

6. Select Graphics. • Select Custom Box. • Select Text Box. • Click OK.

  7. Double-click on Text Box. • Click on Italics button. • Font Face: Times New Roman. • Font Size: 18. • Type a company logo or motto, such as "Serving your needs for over a quarter of a century." • Click Close.

Add the finishing touches.

 8. Drag text box into place under TextArt logo (see the next figure). • Resize to fit the margins. • Click next to TextArt logo. • Font Face: Times New Roman. • Font Size: 12. • Type your address.

ARROWHEAD

Serving your dry-cleaning needs for a quarter of a century.

9. Save your document as a template.

VARIATIONS

Matched Set: *Create a matching envelope for your letterhead for a complete ensemble. See the many recipes for tasty envelopes in this section.*

Get Lined Up: *If you want a snazzier look, place the company address in a text box similar to the one used for the motto.*

BUSINESS   ORGANIZATION   HOME   SCHOOL

LETTERHEAD WITH WORDPERFECT GRAPHIC

From the dezk of

Caitlin Tasker

Create a casual letterhead for business or personal use with one of the WordPerfect graphics. With this recipe, using a butterfly graphic, you'll create a letterhead for a little girl.

PREPARATION

Start WordPerfect Draw.

1. Click on Draw button.

2. Select File. • Select Page Layout.
   • Width: 11". • Height: 3". • Click OK.

Add the butterfly graphic.

3. Click on Figure tool. • Draw an area for the butterfly (see the next figure). • Select BUTERFLY.WPG. • Click Retrieve.

Add your child's name.

4. Select Attributes. • Select Line. • Line Width: .08. • Click OK.

5. Click on Freehand tool. • Carefully print From the desk of.

Chef's Tip For a more childlike appearance, you may want to reverse the "s" in desk.

6. Select Text. • Select Font. • Font Face: Times New Roman or a fancier font, such as ShellyVolante. • Font Size: 58. • Click on Bold button. • Click OK.

7. Click on Text tool. • Click in the letterhead window. • Type your child's name. • Press Enter.

8. Click on Select tool. • Drag text into place.

Add the finishing touches.

9. Select Attributes. • Select Line. • Line Width: .10. • Click OK.

10. Click on Freehand tool. • Draw a line under the butterfly graphic and the name (see the next figure). • Select File. • Select Exit and Return to Document.

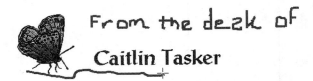

Make some last minute adjustments.

11. Click on the letterhead. • Select Graphics. • Select Edit Box. • Click on Size button. • Width and Height: Size to content. • Click OK. • Click Close.

12. Save your letterhead as a template.

VARIATIONS

Congratulations, It's a Business! *To adapt this recipe for a casual business letterhead, consider one of the silhouettes, woman figures, or GROUP.WPG.*

LOGO WITH DRAWN ARTWORK

Alphabet Soup

If you can't find any predrawn art that fits your corporate image, don't fret; with just a little skill (and lots of patience), you can create a masterpiece of your own. With this recipe, you'll create a soup kettle for a company called Alphabet Soup.

PREPARATION

Get out the ol' drawing board.

 1. Click on Draw button.

Soup's on!

2. Select Attributes. • Select Fill. • Click on Gradient. • Center Color: white. • Outer Color: medium blue. • Angle: 35. • Click OK.

 3. Click on Ellipse tool. • Draw the kettle.

 4. Click on Polygon tool. • Draw the kettle rim (see next figure).

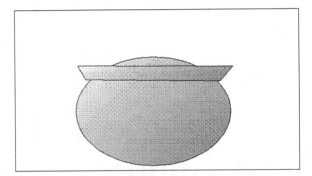

 Chef's Tip Remember to click at each corner, and double-click to close the polygon.

 5. Click on Ellipse tool again. • Draw the inside of the kettle.

 6. With Select tool, place inside piece just over rim (see the next figure). • Click on the rim. • Select Arrange. • Select Front.

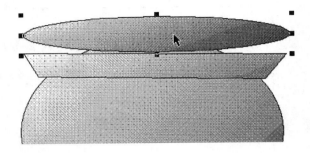

Get a handle on it.

 7. Click on Fill Color tool. • Fill Color: medium blue. • With Ellipse tool, draw a small circle for handle ring. • Click on Select tool, then move ring into place on kettle.

 8. Use Curved Line tool to draw handle. Start at handle ring, and swing around to right edge of kettle (see the next figure).

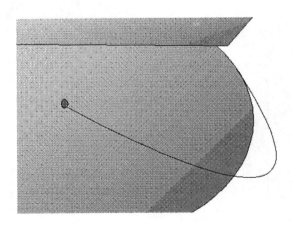

Chef's Tip   Remember to click at the turning point in the curve, and double-click to end the curve.

Say your ABC's.

 9. Click on Text tool. • Click where you want to start typing. • Type: A. • Press Enter. • Type the rest of the letters shown, pressing Enter after each one so each letter is in its own text box.

10. Click on Select tool. • Drag each letter into place. • If you want, select Edit, and select Rotate to rotate a letter (see the next figure).

11. Select Text. • Select Font. • Font Face: Times New Roman. • Font Size: 50. • Click OK.

12. Click on Text tool. • Type: Alphabet Soup. • Press Enter.

13. Select File. • Select Save Copy As. • Give your masterpiece a name, such as ARTLOGO.WPG.

14. Select File. • Select Exit and Return to Document (if you want to place your new logo in the current document), or select Close and Return to Document (if you don't). • If you chose Exit, select Yes to update the document. To get help using your logo, refer to the "Basic Kitchen Skills" section at the back of this book.

VARIATIONS

Twist and Shout!   *Since you're doing your own artwork, there are endless variations to this recipe. You may want to try to curve the company name. First, draw a curve using the Curved Line tool. Next, press Shift as you click on both the text line and the curved line. Select Effects from the Arrange menu, then select Contour Text. Click OK.*

LOGO WITH INITIAL

One way to add class to letters, memos, and faxes is to add a customized label. Armani did it to suits, Georgio did it to perfume, and Calvin Klein did it to underwear—and look how much they get paid! With this recipe, you can create your own initial logo.

PREPARATION

Start up WordPerfect Draw.

 1. Click on Draw button.

Make a square.

2. Select Attributes. • Select Fill. • Click on Gradient. • Center Color: light magenta (or some other light color). • Outer Color: magenta (or some other medium color). • Angle: 90. (Don't close that dialog box yet!)

3. Click on Line. • Line Color: black. • Line Width: .05. • Click OK.

 4. Click on Rectangle tool. • Draw a square.

Make that two squares.

5. Select Attributes. • Select Fill. • Center Color: medium shade of magenta. • Outer Color: darker shade. • Click on Line. • Line Width: .01. • Click OK.

6. Click on Rectangle tool. • Draw a second, smaller square on top of the first square (see the next figure).

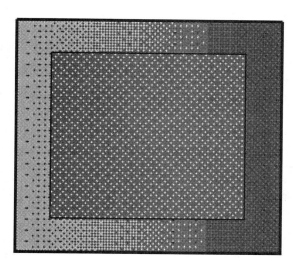

Get your lines crossed.

 7. Click on Line tool. • Draw two diagonal lines from corner to corner of the bigger square (see the next figure).

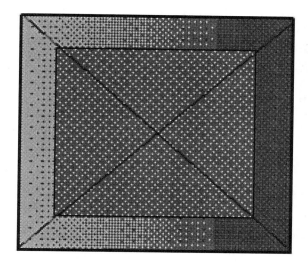

 Cook's Caution Remember to double-click to end the first line before starting the second.

 8. Click on Select tool. • Select the smaller square. • Select Arrange. • Select Front.

Initial it.

9. Select Text. • Select Font. • Font Face: Times New Roman or Arrus Blk BT. • Click Attributes. • Select a contrasting color for your initial. (I used Cyan—that's a fancy name for turquoise.) • Click OK. • Click OK again.

 Chef's Tip You may want to select bold to make your initial stand out.

A 10. Click on Text tool. • Click in middle of smaller square • Type your initial. • Press Enter.

11. Click on Select tool. • Resize the initial; put it in place.

Time to go home!

12. Select File. • Select Save Copy As. • Enter a name for your logo, such as LOGO1.WPG. • Click Save.

13. Select File. • Select Exit and Return to Document (if you want to place your new logo in the current document), or select Close and Return to Document (if you don't). • If you chose Exit, select Yes to update the document. If you need help using your new logo, see the "Basic Kitchen Skills" section at the back of this book.

VARIATIONS

Make It Gray: *If you don't have a color printer, you might get better results by using gray shades in the creation of your logo. But personally, I like to see the colors on-screen, and they seem to convert to a truer shade of gray when printed.*

Get Real Fancy: *Use both, or even all three, of your initials, instead of just one.*

Logo with WordPerfect Graphic

Sometimes an initial is not enough. I guess that's why at birth we're given a first and a last name, to anchor that bare middle initial. Anyway, if you want to try a more impressive logo than the previous one, here's one you can sink your teeth into. With this recipe, you can mix text with one of WordPerfect's pieces of art to create a high-flying logo.

Start at the drawing board.

 1. Click on Draw button.

Pick out a balloon.

 2. Click on Figure tool. • Select HOTAIR.WPG. • Click Retrieve. • Double-click on the figure. • Click on a balloon you like. • Select Edit. • Select Cut.

3. Select File. • Select Clear. • Click OK.

4. Select Edit. • Select Paste. • Move balloon to center of the drawing board (see the next figure). • Select File. • Select Page Layout. • Width: 10. •Height: 4. • Click OK.

Name it.

5. Select Text. • Select Font. • Font Face: Times New Roman. • Font Size: 58. • Click OK.

 6. Click on Text tool. • Type "The Sky's" on left side of balloon. • Press Enter. • Type "the Limit" on right side of balloon. • Press Enter.

 7. Click on Ruler button on Drawing Button Bar. • Click on Select tool. • Align the two Text Boxes evenly on either side of balloon (see next figure).

Line them up.

8. Select Attributes. • Select Line. • Select light cyan. • Line width: .03. • Click OK.

 9. Click on Line tool. • Press Shift as you draw a straight line about the same length as the art (see next figure).

 Chef's Tip You'll want to use an area of the drawing board that's kind of out of the way, so you can easily manipulate the lines. When you're done, you can move the group of lines into place.

 10. Click on Select tool. • Click on the line. • Select Edit. • Select Copy. • Select Edit. • Select Paste. • Move second line into place below first (see the next figure).

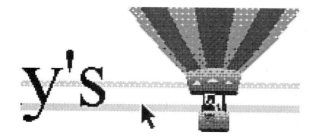

11. Click on Line Style tool. • Width of second line: one or two sizes wider. • Click on Line Color tool. • Select a slightly darker shade of cyan.

12. Select Edit again. • Select Paste. • Move third line into position. • Select Line Color and Line Style tools. • Darken and widen the line slightly.

13. Repeat step 12 for fourth and final line.

14. Click on Select tool. • Click on first line. • Press and hold Shift key as you select each of the other three lines, forming a group. • Move this group into position within the artwork.

15. With the group still selected, select Arrange. • Choose Back command.

16. Select File. • Select Save Copy As. Name your masterpiece, such as FIGLOGO.WPG. • Click Save.

17. Select File. • Select Exit and Return to Document (if you want to place your new logo in the current document), or select Close and Return to Document (if you don't). • If you chose Exit, select Yes to update the document. • To use your logo in other documents, see the "Basic Kitchen Skills" section at the back of this book.

VARIATIONS

Cut It Out!   You can, of course, cut out any part of a WordPerfect graphic to use in your logo, so get creative!

Get Your Head in the Clouds: Use the Closed Curve tool to add clouds on either side of the balloon, and send your logo soaring! For best results, just click to change direction often. Remember to double-click to close the curve.

MEMO WITH LOGO

To:	Pat Wooten
CC:	
From:	Michelle Taylor-Lee
Date:	May 19, 1994
Subject:	L'Orio's Marinara Sauce

memo

L'orio's is being featured in our spring catalog, which shipped out to restaurants on Monday. Regular price is $25.00 for a case of four 10# cans. Discount price is $19.50, effective through the end of this month. Please let everyone on your staff know about this new item.

Because it will be on sale, I want to be sure that we have a good supply on-hand. Keep tabs on inventory, and be generous on your replenishment amounts.

from the desk of...

Michelle Taylor-Lee
Sales Manager
Alphabet Soup
201 West 103rd Street
Indianapolis, Indiana 46290

(317) 581-3500
Fax: (317) 581-8181

The company president will know who the memo's from if it contains your personalized logo. If you don't have a logo, don't fret. Just create one with a recipe from this section. With this recipe, you'll add your logo to the Memo1 template.

PREPARATION

Select the Memo1 template.

1. Click on Open button. • Change to Template directory. • Select Memo1. • Click OK.

Insert your logo.

2. Select Insert. • Select File. • Select your logo file. • Click Insert. • Click Yes.

3. Drag logo into place above the "From the desk of . . ." area (see the next figure). • Click on Close button.

Save the template.

4. Click on Exit Template button. • Click Yes. • If you need help using a template, see the "Basic Kitchen Skills" section at the back of this book.

VARIATIONS

Logo-Mania: *If you like your logo, insert it as a watermark. For more help, see the "Memo with Watermark" recipe.*

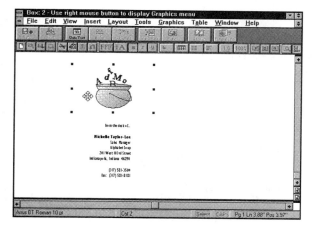

MEMO FROM SCRATCH

To: Scott Wilson
From: Caitlin Trask

Regarding: June picnic

May 19, 1994

The annual company picnic will be held at Waterford Country Club on Saturday, June 18. As usual, the picnic will start at 11:30 with our annual softball game. Spouses and children are welcome.

The barbecue will start at 12:30 and last until 2:00. Hope to see everyone from Marketing! Please inform all of your employees.

The best pies, cakes, and cookies are made from scratch, so why not the best memo? You can design a memo to fit your unique style if you start from scratch. And don't frown; with WordPerfect for Windows, "scratch" is not as hard as it sounds.

PREPARATION

Run for a border.

1. Click on Figure button.

2. Select Bord15P. • Click OK. • Click on Size button. • Width and Height: full. • Click OK. • Click OK again.

3. Click on Wrap button. • Select No Wrap. • Click OK. • Click Close.

Take a memo.

4. Click on TextArt button. • Select a fancy font face, such as ShelleyVolante BT. • Text Color: black. • Height: 1". • Width: 2.5". • Type: Memo.

5. Select File. • Select Exit & Return to WordPerfect. • Click Yes.

Add some color to the memo box.

6. Drag memo box into place (see the next figure). • Select Graphics. • Select Edit Box. • Click on Border/Fill button. • Border Style: Single. • Fill Style: Gradient 2. • Foreground Color: light blue. • Click OK.

7. Click Close.

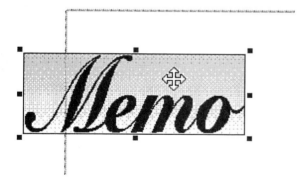

Just a few more things.

8. Select View. • Select Ruler Bar. • Adjust Left and Right margins using Ruler (see the next figure).

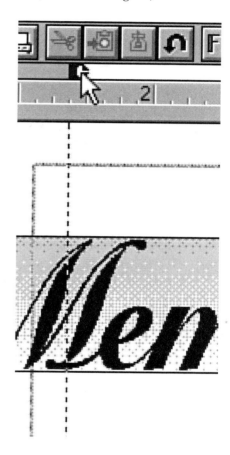

9. Press Enter enough times to move cursor along side of memo box (see the next figure). • Font Face: Times New Roman. • Font Size: 14. • Click on Bold button.

To:

From:

Regarding: |

10. Type labels: To:, From:, and Regarding: (see the last figure).

11. Press Enter four more times. • Select Insert. • Select Date. • Select Date Code.

12. Select File. • Select Save. • Type: MEMO1.WPT. • Change to the Templates directory. • Click OK.

VARIATIONS

Borderline: *WordPerfect offers many border styles to choose from. So if feathers aren't your thing, select from those you'll find in Appendix E of the Reference manual.*

5 min.   Easy

MEMO WITH WATERMARK

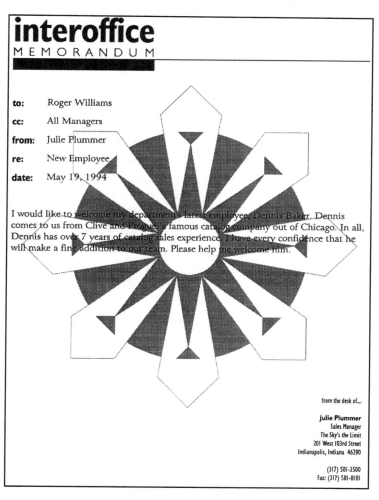

Your memos will be treated like gold when they're printed on watermarked paper. A watermark is a faint image placed in the fibers of expensive paper. So what if your boss says to count paper clips—you can still create an elegant (yet inexpensive) image with a WP watermark. With this recipe, you'll insert a watermark into the Memo2 template.

PREPARATION

Select the Memo2 template.

1. Click on Open button. • Change to Template directory. • Select Memo2. • Click OK.

Insert the watermark.

2. Click on Watermark button. • Click Create. • Click on Figure.

3. Select Ender03 from the watermark list. • Click OK (see the next figure). • Click Close twice to return to document.

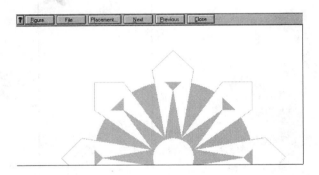

Chef's Tip   There are many other watermark designs to choose from. See Appendix E of your WP manual.

Save your new memo template.

4. Click on Exit Template button. • Click Yes. For tips on how to use your template, see the "Basic Kitchen Skills" section in the back of this book.

VARIATIONS

Word Up!   *Instead of a graphic watermark, add some well chosen text, such as "Confidential" or "Final Copy." Click on the GrphWtrmrk button on the Design Tools Button Bar. Click on Graphic, Watermark A, and then click OK. Select a premade text message for your watermark.*

Make Your Own Statement: *If you want to type your own text message instead of choosing one of WordPerfect's, click on the GrphWtrmrk button on the Design Tools Button Bar. Then click on Text, Watermark A, and then OK. Type your message. Press Ctrl+Enter to type more than one line. Click OK. Change font and any other attributes if you want.*

MESSAGE PAD

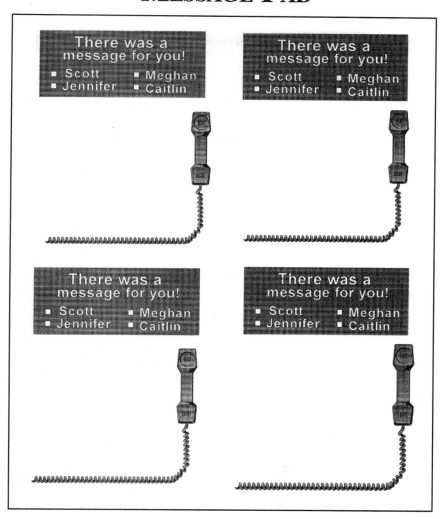

WordPerfect comes with its own message pad template, but it's a bit formal for home use. Why not create your own message pad, customized with the names of family members? With this recipe, you use a WordPerfect graphic to give your message pad the right touch.

PREPARATION

Change the margins to allow for the most room.

1. Select Layout. • Select Margins. • All margins: .25. • Click OK.

Insert the telephone graphic.

2. Click on Figure button. • Select TELEREC.WPG. • Click OK. • Resize graphic, and place it in the upper left corner.

3. Click on the Border/Fill button. • Style: None. • Click OK.

4. Select the graphic. • Click on Copy button. • Click in document. • Click on Paste button. • Drag second graphic into lower right-hand corner. • Repeat for other graphics (see the next figure).

5. Click Close.

Create a customized message box.

6. Click on Draw button.

7. Select File. • Select Page Layout. • Width: 3". • Height: 1.23". • Page Color: light gray. • Click OK.

8. Select Text. • Select Font. • Font Face: Arial. • Font Size: 36. • Click on Bold button. • Click Attributes. • Font Color: white. • Click OK. • Click OK again.

9. Click on Text button. • Click where you want to start typing. • Type: There was a. • Press Enter. • Type: message for you! • Press Enter again. • Drag two text boxes into place.

10. Select Text. • Select Font. • Font Size: 24. • Click OK. • Click Text button again. • Type name of a family member. • Press Enter. • Repeat for additional family members. • Drag each name into place (see the next figure).

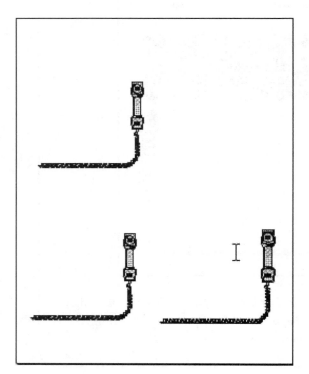

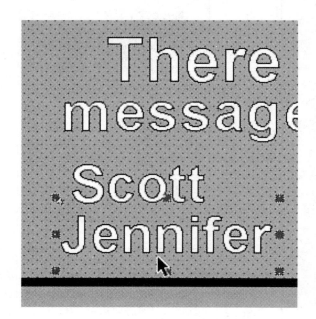

Create some check boxes.

11. Select Fill Color tool. • Set: white.
• Select Line Color tool. • Set: black.

12. Click on Rectangle tool. • Draw a small square.

Cook's Caution WordPerfect Draw does not default to black and white, so be sure you complete this step carefully, or you'll end up with bright blue squares.

13. Click on Select tool. • Click on the check box. • Select Edit. • Select Duplicate. • Drag new check box off first check box; place in front of another name (see the next figure). • Repeat for each name.

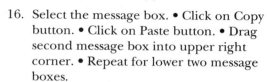

14. Select File. • Select Exit and Return to Document. • Click Yes.

Finishing up.

15. Resize the message box as necessary, and drag it to the upper left corner.

16. Select the message box. • Click on Copy button. • Click on Paste button. • Drag second message box into upper right corner. • Repeat for lower two message boxes.

17. Save your message file and print it.

VARIATIONS

Colorize It! *Take your message sample to the printer and have it printed on bright paper and cut and bound into message pads.*

NOTEPAD WITH BORDER

There's never a notepad around when I need one—even when I stash them away everywhere! So, try this for revenge: create your own notepad with WordPerfect, and it'll always be there when you need to dash off a note. With this recipe, you create a notepad using one of the WordPerfect borders and a customized paper size.

PREPARATION

Create a notepad paper size.

1. • Select Layout. • Select Page. • Select Paper Size. • Click Create.

2. Enter Notepad under Paper Name. • Width: 5". • Height: 8". • Click OK. • Choose Notepad from list. • Click Select.

Add a border.

3. Select Insert. • Select File. • Select BORD16P.WPG file. • Click Insert.

4. Click on Size button. • Width and height: Full. • Click OK. • Click OK again.

5. Click on Border/Fill button. • Border Style: None. • Click OK.

6. Click on Wrap button. • Select No wrap. • Click OK.

7. Click Close.

8. Select View. • Select Ruler Bar. • Use Ruler to reset left and right margins so they are inside the "borders" of the graphic (see the next figure).

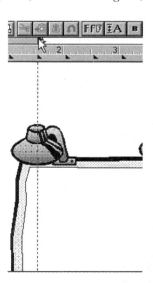

Now for some TextArt.

 9. Click on TextArt button. • Font Face: Brush738 BT, Banff, or similar font. • Type: Notes.

10. Select File. • Select Exit & Return to WordPerfect. • Click Yes.

11. Resize TextArt as necessary; drag into place under painter's brush (see the next figure).

12. Save and print your notepad.

VARIATIONS

Get a Pad: *Print your masterpiece and take it to a professional printer, who can print you up a nice bound set of notepads. You could even have it printed on colored paper.*

Run for the Border: *WordPerfect offers many border styles you can substitute for the one used here. See Appendix E of the Reference manual for details.*

NOTEPAD WITH WORDPERFECT GRAPHIC

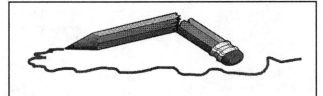

Take Note!

Notepads are easy to create, and fun, too. Let your imagination run free, and customize a different notepad for each aspect of your life: work, home, personal, and social. This recipe provides another way to create customized notepads: with a WordPerfect graphic and a little imagination.

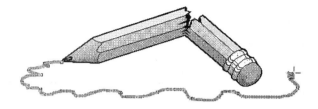

PREPARATION

Create notepad paper size.

1. Select Layout. • Select Page. • Select Paper Size. • If there is no Notepad paper definition, go to step 2. If Notepad is in the list, skip step 2 and go on to step 3.

 Cook's Caution If you created a notepad paper size for another recipe, it will be in the Paper Definitions list, so you won't need to create one as described in step 2.

2. Click Create. • Enter Notepad under Paper Name. • Size: 5" by 8". • Click OK.

3. Choose Notepad from Paper Definitions list. • Click Select.

4. Select View. • Select Ruler Bar. • Use ruler to reset left and right margins to .5".

Start WordPerfect Draw.

 5. Click on Draw button.

6. Select File. • Select Page Layout. • Width: 4.5". • Height: 1.5". • Click OK.

Add the pencil graphic.

 7. Click on Figure tool. • Draw an area for the pencil. • Select PENCILBR.WPG. • Click Retrieve.

Add a freehand border.

 8. Click on Line Style button. • Select a thin line, about .03 inch.

 9. Click on Freehand tool. • Start at the pencil point and draw a meandering line (see the next figure).

10. Select File. • Select Exit and Return to Document. • Click Yes.

Add some TextArt.

 11. Click on TextArt button.

12. Width: 5". • Height: 1.5". • Font Face: Ribbon 131 BT, Freeport or similar font. • Type: Take Note! • Click on a shape you like (I used the third shape in the sample).

13. Select File. • Select Exit & Return to WordPerfect. • Click Yes. • Drag the TextArt into place at the bottom of the notepad.

14. Save and print your notepad.

 Chef's Tip Have your notepads printed and bound at a print shop, or check your local art supplies store for a special glue that will allow you to bind the pads yourself.

VARIATIONS

Check It Out: *Add small check boxes you create with WordPerfect Draw, and make it easy to leave the notes you write most often, such as "Be back in ten minutes," "Let me know ASAP," and "For Your Information."*

Fund-Raiser Idea: *Create some customized notepads to sell as a fund-raiser for your school, church, or bazaar. The cost to make several designs would be very modest, and the profits would be large.*

RÉSUMÉ FROM SCRATCH

Bob Slacker
201 West 10th Street
Indianapolis, Indiana 46290
(317) 584-3708

Objective: *A high-paying job with lots of perks such as a big fat car and a home on the beach. Short hours (such as one or two per day) are also desirable.*

Professional Experience

Tanners of America   **March 1985 to September 1986**
Orlando, Florida
    Tan guard
    Patrolled local beaches to protect the best tans. Dispensed tanning lotions
    where necessary. Posted tan warnings. Voted "Best Tan" 1985 and 1986.

Beach Bums of California   **September 1986 to Present**
San Diego, California
    President
    Organize beach parties, volleyball games, and cookouts. Responsible for over
    25 beach bums like myself.

Education

Blah University   **1976 to 1982**
Boring, South Dakota
    Bachelor of Science, Boredom
    Captain of the Party Team

Blah-Blah University   **1982 to 1984**
More Boring, North Dakota
    Doctorate, Wasting Time

Organizations

TANNERS CLUB OF AMERICA   FLORIDA REGION
PROCRASTINATORS UNITED   WASHINGTON, D.C.

REFERENCES AVAILABLE UPON REQUEST.

It's a tough world out there for the unemployed, so use WordPerfect for Windows to gain an edge over all those other job seekers cranking out identical résumés. Make yours an original by starting from scratch. Follow this recipe, or copy one you like from a good job-search book.

PREPARATION

Enter the ol' name and address.

1. Justification: Center. • Click on Bold button. • Font Face: Times New Roman. • Font Size: 14. • Type your name. • Press Enter.

2. Turn bold off. • Type your address. • Turn bold back on. • Type your phone number. • Press Enter twice.

Make your objective clear.

3. Justification: Left. • Font Size: 12. • Type your name and address. • Press Enter twice.

4. Type: Objective:. • Click on Italics button. • Type your objective. • Press Enter two times.

Create a sense of style.

5. Select Layout. • Select Styles. • Click Create. • Enter "Coname" for style name. • Enter "Company Name" for description. • Select Layout. • Select Font. • Font Face: Times New Roman. • Font Size: 14. • Select Bold. • Click OK.

6. Select Layout again. • Select Line. • Select Tab Set. • Click on Clear All. • Under Type, select Right. • Position: 6.5. • Click OK. • Under Enter Key will Chain to, select None. • Click OK.

7. Click Create again. • Enter "Position" for style name. • Enter "Position Held" for description. • Select Layout. • Select Font. • Font Face: Times New Roman. • Font Size: 14. • Click OK. • Select Layout. • Select Paragraph. • Select Indent. • Under Enter Key Will Chain

to, select None. • Click OK. • Click Close.

Add sections.

8. Click on Draw button.

9. Select File. • Select Page Layout. • Width: 6.5"; Height: 1". • Page Color: black. • Click OK.

10. Select Text. • Select Font. • Font Face: Arial. • Font Size: 36. • Click on Bold button. • Click Attributes. • Foreground Color: white. • Click OK. • Click OK again.

11. Click on Text tool. • Click, and then type: Professional Experience.

12. Select File. • Select Exit and Return to Document. • Click Yes.

13. Resize the header as necessary, and drag it into position under the Objective. • Click on Copy button. • Click inside document. • Click on Paste button. • Drag copy into place, leaving room for text between these headings. • Repeat for additional headings.

14. Double-click on second heading. • Click on Text tool. • Replace "Professional Experience" with "Education". • Select File. • Select Exit and Return to Document. • Click Yes. • Repeat for additional headings.

Enter your professional experience.

15. Type a company name. • Press Tab. • Enter dates you were with that company. • Press Enter. • Type city and state where the company is located. • Press Enter. • Type your job title. • Press Enter. • Type list of your accomplishments and responsibilities (see the next figure).

```
Tanners of America        March 1985 to September 1986
Orlando, Florida
Tan guard
Patrolled local beaches to protect the best tans. Dispensed tanning lotions where
necessary. Posted tan warnings. Voted "Best Tan" 1985 and 1986.
```

16. Repeat step 15 for additional companies.

Enter other information.

17. Repeat steps 15 and 16 for additional sections, such as Education, Organizations, Hobbies and Interests, and so on.

Add styles.

18. Place cursor in a company name heading, such as "Tanners of America." • Select Layout. • Select Styles. • Select Coname. • Click Apply. • Repeat for additional company, university, or similar names (see the next figure).

```
Tanners of America              March 1985 to September 1986
Orlando, Florida
    Tan guard
    Patrolled local beaches to protect the best tans. Dispensed tanning lotions
    where necessary. Posted tan warnings. Voted "Best Tan" 1985 and 1986.
```

 Chef's Tip To copy a style quickly from one paragraph to another, place the cursor in the first paragraph (such as "Professional Experience"), click on the QuickFormat button, and then drag the cursor over additional headings. To turn it off, click on the QuickFormat button again.

19. Place cursor in a description, such as a job title or job description. • Select Layout. • Select Styles. • Select Position. • Click Apply. • Repeat for additional descriptions.

Add the finishing touches.

 20. Click on Italic button. • Add the line, "References available upon request" to the end of your résumé.

21. Save and print your résumé.

VARIATIONS

Look Expensive: *Since your résumé represents who you are, why not look and feel expensive by printing your résumé on high-quality paper using a laser printer?*

Keep It Simple: *Most personnel directors spend less than one minute on each résumé, so keep yours uncluttered and easy to scan. Place pertinent information where it can be found easily. Don't feel you have to include your life history; save something for the interview.*

RÉSUMÉ FROM TEMPLATE

BOB SLACKER

201 West 10th Street • Indianapolis, Indiana 46290 • Telephone: (317) 584-3708

Insert photo here.

OBJECTIVE

A HIGH-PAYING JOB WITH LOTS OF PERKS SUCH AS A BIG FAT CAR AND A HOME ON THE BEACH. SHORT HOURS (SUCH AS ONE OR TWO PER DAY) ARE ALSO DESIRABLE.

EDUCATION

BLAH UNIVERSITY
Boring, South Dakota
Bachelor of Science, Boredom, 1982
Captain of the party team.

Blah-Blah University
More Boring, North Dakota
Doctorate in Wasting Time, 1984

EXPERIENCE

TANNERS OF AMERICA
Tan Guard, March 1985 to September 1986
Voted "Best Tan", 1985 and 1986

BEACH BUMS OF CALIFORNIA
President, September 1986 to Present
Organize beach parties, volleyball games, and cookouts. Responsible for over 25 beach bums like myself.

SKILLS

- Great tan.
- Skilled in numerous ways to waste time, yet still look busy.
- Can really "party down".

It's the most important form of communication, upon which rests all your hopes and dreams of getting that great job where you get to lie at the beach all day, raking in millions. So, now that you know what's at stake, make your résumé the best it can be, with the help of this recipe and a WordPerfect template.

PREPARATION

Select the Resume template.

1. Click on Open button. • Select Resume template. • Click OK.

Change the _Section Style.

2. Click on Styles button. • Select _Section style. • Click Edit. • Double-click on LftMar marker. • Left: .5. • Click OK. • Click Close.

Insert a box for your photograph.

3. Select Graphics. • Select Custom Box. • Select Figure. • Click OK. • Click Close.

4. Resize the figure box. • Drag it into place (see the next figure).

Final touches.

5. Click on Exit Template. • Click Yes.

Chef's Tip   Have your résumé professionally printed, with a scanned copy of your photograph added where the figure box is located. Have your photograph taken by a professional for best results.

VARIATIONS

Age Before Beauty: *Emphasize your strong points by placing them first. So if you have a lot of work experience, place that before the education section on your résumé.*

Bottom Line: *Add a line at the bottom that reads, "References available upon request." Type up your references and have them printed at the same time, on the same high-quality paper, so they will be ready when needed.*

RÉSUMÉ COVER LETTER

Bob Slacker
201 West 10th Street • Indianapolis, Indiana 46290 • Telephone: (317) 584-3708

March 11, 1994

Scott Wilson
Personnel Director
Our Jobs R EZ
1223 West 116th
Indianapolis, In. 46240

Dear Scott,

I am applying for the job of "Car Jockey," as advertised in the Indianapolis Star, March 6th. I am an expert at being lazy, so I feel confident that I will fit right in with your organization. In fact, I have over 8 years of experience at being lazy.

My most recent experience sums it up rather nicely. I am currently the President of the Beach Bums of California. In this position, I am responsible for organizing beach parties and volleyball games. In addition, I organized several large cookouts and was responsible for the $35.00 Bum Bank. Thank goodness I am responsible for over 25 beach bums, to whom I could pass the buck.

As a Car Jockey for your organization, I would bring my 8 years of lazy experience. Furthermore, I work and play well with others and am very experienced in vehicular transportation, especially motorcycles and dune buggies. Please keep this inquiry confidential, because I don't want the other Bums to find out. I will call next week to arrange a convenient time for an interview. Thank you for your consideration.

Sincerely,

Bob Slacker

Create a good impression with a cover letter to match your résumé. Follow this recipe, or copy an example cover letter from a job-search book. If you haven't created a résumé yet, turn back a few pages, and follow the recipes.

Preparation

Copy your style.

 1. Click on Open button. • Select your résumé file. • Click OK.

 2. Select your name and address on résumé. • Click on Copy button.

 3. Click on New File button. • Select Window. • Select Document1. • Click on Paste button.

Type your cover letter.

4. Select Insert. • Select Date. • Select Date Text. • Press Enter twice. • Type personnel director's address. • Press Enter twice. • Type your greeting.

5. Press Enter twice. • Type body of letter. • Press Enter twice. • Type your closing, leaving room for a signature.

6. Select closing and your name (see the next figure). • Change left margin with the Ruler.

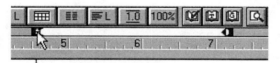

bring my 8 years of lazy experience.
and am very experienced in vehicular
buggies. Please keep this inquiry
is to find out. I will call next week to arrange
for your consideration.

Sincerely,

Bob Slacker

7. Save your letter and print it.

Variations

Matched Set: *Print your résumé cover letter on high-quality paper that matches your résumé.*

Keep It Pertinent: *Be sure to emphasize the skills you can bring to the company. Explain simply how the advertised job was designed with you in mind.*

THANK YOUS

Show your appreciation for a special someone by creating a thank-you card. And best of all, you can take the hassle out of going to a card store on some made-up holiday, such as "Sweeeeetest Day."

PREPARATION

Tell someone you care.

1. Select Graphics. • Select Custom Box. • Click User. • Click OK.

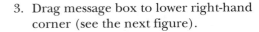

2. Font Face: ShelleyVolante. Font Size: 24. • Type your message. • Click Close.

3. Drag message box to lower right-hand corner (see the next figure).

Upside-down thanks.

4. Click on TextArt button. • Font Face: Brush738 BT, Brush Script, or similar font. • Rotation: 180. • Type: Thanks! • Select File. • Select Exit & Return to WordPerfect. • Click Yes.

5. Drag the TextArt to the upper left-hand corner (see the next figure).

A rose is a rose.

6. Select Insert. • Select File. • Select ROSE.WPG. • Click Insert. • Click Yes.

7. Click on Wrap button. • Select No Wrap. • Click OK.

8. Click on Tools button. • Click on Brightness button (see the next figure). • Select a faint image.

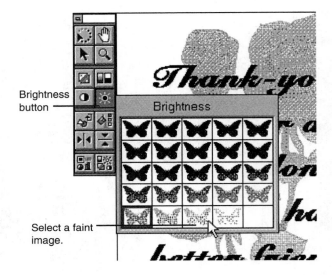

Brightness button

Select a faint image.

Cook's Caution Image (rose) will print darker than it appears on-screen.

9. Click on Border/Fill button. • Style: Hairline Border. • Click OK.

10. Click Close.

Finishing touches.

11. Save and print your card. • Fold card in half horizontally, and then fold in half again, this time vertically. The word "Thanks" should be in front, with the message inside.

WEDDING ANNOUNCEMENTS

Mr. & Mrs. Robert Wilson
6110 Evanston Ave.
Indianapolis, Indiana 46210

Like most people, my husband and I opted for traditional engraved wedding invitations. After the package arrived, we were so excited! That is, until we sat down to address all those envelopes (and why is there an inner and an outer envelope to address? So your fingers will really go numb?). Before we panicked (and before I practically sprained my wrist trying to do calligraphy), we hit on the idea of using mail merge to do all the work. In this recipe, I'll show you how it's done.

PREPARATION

Create a wedding database.

1. Select Tools. • Select Merge. • Click on Place Records in a Table. • Click Data. • Click OK.

2. Type: firstname. • Click Add. • Repeat for each field you need to add: "lastname," "address," "city," "state," and "zipcode." • Click OK (see the next figure).

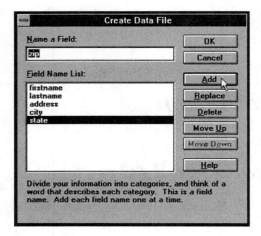

Enter your guest list.

3. Type the information for first guest or family. • Press Enter to move to next field. • When record is complete, click on New Record. • Repeat for all people to be included in list.

4. When all guests are entered, click Close. • Click Yes. • Enter file name, such as WEDDATA.WPD. • Click OK.

Create a merge envelope.

5. Click on Merge button. • Click Form. Click OK. • Type file name for your data file, such as WEDDATA.WPD. • Click OK.

6. Select Layout. • Select Envelope. • Deselect Print Return Address option. • Click Create New Definition. • Type: Wedding Envelope. • Enter size dimensions. • Click Wide Form if necessary. • Deselect Rotated Font. • Click OK.

7. Click inside Mailing Addresses box. • Click Field. • Select firstname. • Click Insert. • Spacebar. • Select lastname. • Click Insert. • Press Enter to move to next line. • Repeat for additional fields, adding spaces or punctuation as needed (see the next figure).

8. Mailing Addresses Font: ShelleyVolante BT. • Click OK. • Click Append to Doc.

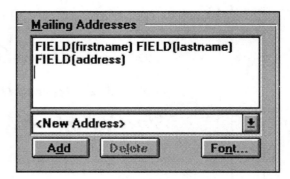

Print your envelopes!

9. Click Merge. • Click on Merge button. • Click OK.

10. Print your envelopes.

VARIATIONS

What About Those Darn Inner Envelopes?
In step 2, add a field called "guestnames." Follow the rest of the directions to print the outer envelope. To print the inner envelopes, select Merge from the Tools menu. Click on Form. Follow the directions for step 6, selecting Wedding Envelope, or creating new dimensions if necessary. In step 7, insert the guestnames field. Follow the rest of the directions.

PART TWO

MAIN DISHES: REPORTS AND PRESENTATIONS

We've all had it: the dream where you're standing in front of a huge audience, about to give a speech, when you notice that something's missing. Clothes. And when you're up in front of a bazillion people, believe me, they notice every little flaw. Even a small thing like your see-through suit.

With the recipes in this section, you present only your most flattering side. The "bare-bones" instructions will help you create professional-looking reports, report covers, transparencies (no pun intended), and handouts. Need to write a term paper that includes a table of contents, bibliography, footnotes page, glossary, or index? No problem with the recipes you find here. Have to teach a class? You'll find the instructor's manual and training evaluations very enlightening. Remember, presentation is everything, so if it looks good, so do you (even in your birthday suit).

AGENDA

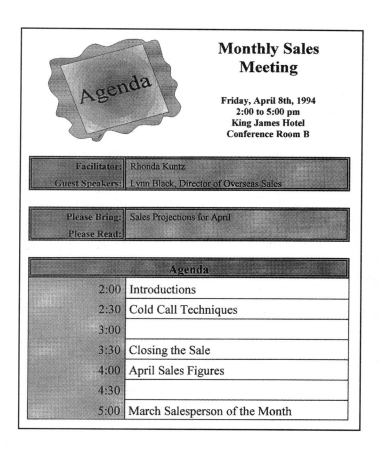

Monthly Sales Meeting

Friday, April 8th, 1994
2:00 to 5:00 pm
King James Hotel
Conference Room B

Facilitator:	Rhonda Kuntz
Guest Speakers:	Lynn Black, Director of Overseas Sales

Please Bring:	Sales Projections for April
Please Read:	

Agenda	
2:00	Introductions
2:30	Cold Call Techniques
3:00	
3:30	Closing the Sale
4:00	April Sales Figures
4:30	
5:00	March Salesperson of the Month

Before you call your next meeting to order, make sure everyone has their thoughts "in order." Get the most from your meetings by distributing an agenda beforehand, so folks can prepare their questions. You'll be able to whip through everything you want to cover, confident that everyone is prepared, and not thinking about the coffee and donuts in the back of the room. With this recipe, you'll create an agenda you can use over and over.

PREPARATION

Create a table.

1. Click on Table Create button. • Drag to set Columns: 2; Rows: 20.

2. Select View. • Select Ruler Bar. • Drag right edge of first column to 3" mark.

3. Select cells in first row. • Click right mouse button. • Select Join Cells (see the next figure).

Joined cell

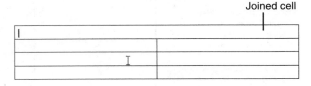

Enter meeting info.

4. Click on Bold button. • Font Face: Times New Roman. • Font Size: 24. • Justification: Center. • Type name of your meeting, such as Monthly Sales Meeting. • Press Enter twice.

5. Font Size: 12. • Type rest of meeting information, such as the date, time, and location.

Snazz up your agenda.

6. Click on Draw button.

7. Select File. • Select Page Layout. • Width and height: 2.5". • Click OK.

8. Select Attributes. • Select Fill. • Fill Type: Gradient. • Center Color: light gray. • Type: Rectangular. • Click OK. • Click on Rectangle tool. • Draw a square.

Chef's Tip Hold the Shift key while dragging with the Rectangle tool to draw a perfect square.

9. Select the square. • Select Edit. • Select Rotate. • Drag to rotate square (see the next figure).

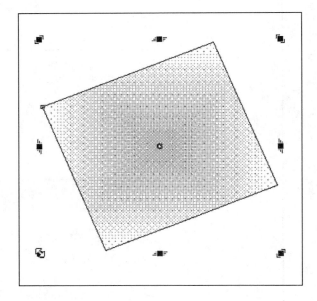

Add the text.

10. Click on Text tool. • Click inside box. • Type: Agenda. • Press Enter. • Select the text box. • Select Edit. • Select Rotate. • Drag text to match angle of tilted square.

Add some frills.

11. Select Attributes. • Select Fill. • Select Pattern. • Foreground Color: medium gray. • Click OK.

12. Click on Closed Curve tool. • Draw a freehand shape around the square (see the next figure). • Select the freehand shape. • Select Arrange. • Choose Back.

13. Select File. • Select Exit and Return to Document. • Click Yes. • Click on figure and drag it into place.

Add a bit of color.

14. Font Size: 14. • Type "Facilitator" and "Guest Speakers" into their respective cells.

15. Select the Facilitator and Guest Speakers cells. • Click on TblLineFill button. • Outside: Thick Double. • Inside: None. • Fill Style: 90% Fill. • Foreground Color: light gray. • Click OK.

16. Select the cells to right of Facilitator and Guest Speakers cells. • Click on TblLineFill button. • Outside: Thick Double. • Inside: None. • Fill Style: 90% Fill. • Foreground Color: lighter gray. • Click OK.

17. Repeat steps 15 and 16 for the Please Bring and Please Read cells.

18. Select first two cells in the Agenda section. • Right-click, then select Join Cells. • Click on TblLineFill button. • Outside: Thick Double. • Inside:

None. • Fill Style: 90% Fill. • Foreground Color: light gray. • Click OK.

19. Select the time cells. • Click on TblLineFill button. • Inside: None. • Fill Style: 90% Fill. • Foreground Color: lighter gray. • Click OK.

Got the time?

20. Click on the Agenda cell. • Font Size: 18. • Justification: Center. • Type: Agenda.

21. Justification: Right. • Type the times covered by the meeting.

Chef's Tip   To add more rows for additional time slots, press Tab from the last cell in the table.

Mine's a blank.

22. Select the cells in a row between sections. • Click on TblLineFill button. • Outside and Inside: None.

Finish line.

23. Save your agenda template.

VARIATIONS

Where Am I?   *Use WordPerfect Draw to create a simple map to your meeting, and add it to your agenda.*

Registration Table: *Add a simple registration form to the bottom of your agenda for keeping attendance.*

5 min.

Moderate

ARTICLE

Pat Whitmore
P.O. Box 5413
Indianapolis, Indiana 46245
(317) 576-1016

© The Word Factory   Total Number of Words: ____

(Place Title Here)

by

Pat Whitmore

Start article here.

© The Word Factory   Page 1

If you've been waiting to submit The Great American Article to "National Big-Time Magazine with the Super Huge Circulation," wait no longer. Send it off in style with this recipe.

PREPARATION

Create a heading.

 1. Click on Draw button. • Select File.
• Select Page Layout. • Width: 10".
• Height: 3". • Page Color: Gradient.
• Center Color: light gray. • Outer Color:
white. • Click OK.

 2. Select Text. • Select Font. • Font Face:
Times New Roman. • Font Size: 24.
• Click OK. • Click on Text tool. • Click
inside text area. • Type your name.
• Press Enter. • Repeat for your address
and phone number (see the next
figure). • Drag these text boxes into
center of page.

Pat Whitmore
P.O. Box 5413
Indianapolis, Indiana 46245
(317) 576-1016

 3. Click on Text tool. • Click in lower left-
hand corner of the Draw page. • Select
Text. • Select WP Characters. • Select
Typographic Symbols. • Select copyright symbol (see the next figure).
• Click on Insert and Close. • Type
your company name. • Press Enter.

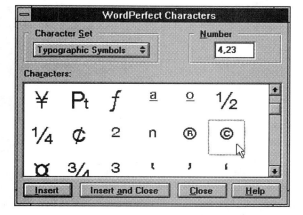

 4. Click on Text tool. • Click in right-hand
corner of Draw page, leaving room for
text and a small box, as shown. • Type:
Total Number of Words. • Press Enter.

 5. Click on Fill Color tool. • Select white.
• Click on Rectangle tool. • Draw a
small box after "Total Number of
Words" text. • Press Enter.

6. Select File. • Select Exit and Return to
Document. • Click Yes. • Click on
figure and drag it into place.

7. Select Graphics. • Select Edit Box.
• Click on Border/Fill button. • Border
Style: Thick Top/Bottom. • Click OK.
• Click Close.

 Chef's Tip   To determine the number of
words in your finished document, select
Grammatik from the Tools menu. Select
Statistics from the Options menu. Click on
Start.

Time for titles.

 8. Press Enter five times. • Click on Bold
button. • Justification: Center. • Font
Face: Times New Roman. • Font Size:
18. • Type your article title (see the
next figure).

(Place Title Here)

by

Pat Whitmore

Start article here.

9. Press Enter twice. • Type: by. • Press Enter twice again. • Type your name (see the preceding figure).

 10. Press Enter five times. • Justification: Left. • Font Size 12. • Type: Start article here.

Add a footer.

11. Select Layout. • Select Header/Footer. • Select Footer A. • Click Create.

12. Select Insert. • Select Character. • Select Typographic Symbols. • Select copyright symbol. • Click Insert and Close button. • Type the name of your company.

13. Press Tab to move to right-hand side of footer. • Type: Page. • Press Spacebar. • Click on Number button. • Select Page Number. • Click Close.

14 Save your article template.

VARIATIONS

Need Data: *Some magazines require more information in your header, such as the date the article started, date the article completed, draft number, editor name, and name of feature. Add these to the header with WordPerfect Draw.*

5 min.

Easy

BIBLIOGRAPHY

Bibliography

Flanders, Linda. *10 Minute Guide to Quicken 6*. Carmel: Alpha Books, 1992.

Flynn, Jennifer. One Minute Reference WordPerfect 5.1. Carmel: Alpha Books, 1993.

———. *20th Century Computers and How They Worked, The Official Starfleet History of Computers*. Carmel: Alpha Books, 1993.

Fulton, Jennifer. *The Complete Idiot's Guide to Ami Pro*. Carmel: Alpha Books, 1994.

———. *The Complete Idiot's Guide to DOS*. Carmel: Alpha Books, 1993.

Kraynak, Joe. *Show Me PCs*. Carmel: Alpha Books, 1993.

———. *The Complete Idiot's Guide to PCs*. Carmel: Alpha Books, 1993.

Kinkoph, Sherry. *The Print Shop Idea Book*. Carmel: Alpha Books, 1993.

Tyson, Herb, rev. Kelly Oliver. *10 Minute Guide to OS/2 2.1*. Carmel: Alpha Books, 1993.

Bibliography   (Title of Article)   Page 1

A bibliography is a listing of the sources you consulted during the creation of The Great American Article, term paper, thesis, or novel. A bibliography can be a complete or a selected listing of major sources, whichever is the most appropriate (i.e., whatever you have time to do). Use this recipe as a guide for creating a bibliography for your life's work.

PREPARATION

Create a heading.

1. If you want to include the bibliography in your document file (instead of in a separate file), move to the end of your document. If necessary, press Ctrl+Enter to start the bibliography on a new page.

2. Justification: Center. • Font Face: Times New Roman. • Font Size: 24. • Type: Bibliography.

3. Select Graphics. • Select Horizontal Line. • Drag line into place under Bibliography title.

Now add a footer.

4. Select Layout. • Select Header/Footer. • Select Footer A. • Click Create.

 Chef's Tip If you added the bibliography to the end of your document file, you can skip steps 4-7.

5. Click on Bold button. • Type: Bibliography. • Press Tab to move to center of footer. • Type title of your article, report, thesis, or whatever. • Press Tab to move to right-hand side of footer. • Type: Page. • Press Spacebar. • Click on Number button on Header/Footer Feature Bar. • Select Page Number.

6. Click on Line button. • Select Double style. • Click OK. • Drag the line into place above footer text (see the next figure).

Bibliography   (Title of Article)   Page 1

7. Click Close.

List your sources.

8. Font Face: Times New Roman. • Font Size: 12. • Justification: Left.

9. Select View. • Select Ruler Bar. • Drag left-hand paragraph markers to 1.5" mark (see the next figure). • Press Shift. • Drag First Line marker back to 1" mark to create hanging indent.

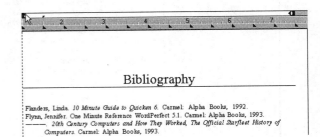

10. Enter your sources, using this example as a guide (see the next figure).

Bibliography

Flanders, Linda. *10 Minute Guide to Quicken 6.* Carmel: Alpha Books, 1992.
Flynn, Jennifer. One Minute Reference WordPerfect 5.1. Carmel: Alpha Books, 1993.
———. *20th Century Computers and How They Worked, The Official Starfleet History of Computers.* Carmel: Alpha Books, 1993.
Fulton, Jennifer. *The Complete Idiot's Guide to Ami Pro.* Carmel: Alpha Books, 1994.
———. *The Complete Idiot's Guide to DOS.* Carmel: Alpha Books, 1993.
Kraynak, Joe. *Show Me PCs.* Carmel: Alpha Books, 1993.
———. *The Complete Idiot's Guide to PCs.* Carmel: Alpha Books, 1993.
Kinkoph, Sherry. *The Print Shop Idea Book.* Carmel: Alpha Books, 1993.
Tyson, Herb, rev. Kelly Oliver. *10 Minute Guide to OS/2 2.1.* Carmel: Alpha Books, 1993.

11. Save and print your bibliography.

VARIATIONS

Protect Your Sources—Not! *If you just can't say enough about your sources (thereby completely ruining all chances of a career in journalism), you can even annotate your bibliography with your own comments. Just add them to the end of the bibliography entry.*

5 min.

Easy

BOOK REPORT

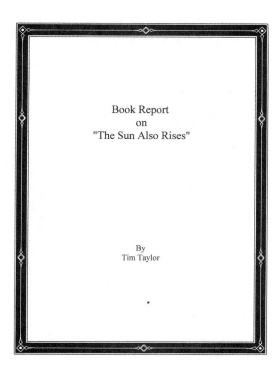

Character Profiles:

Enter character profiles here.

Summary of Plot:

Enter summary of plot here.

Conclusions:

Enter conclusions here.

Tim Taylor   Book Report on "The Sun Also Rises"   Page - 1

Book Report
on
"The Sun Also Rises"

By
Tim Taylor

Okay, so the book report's due tomorrow. Maybe you only read half of the book or maybe you just rented the video. But with the help of a guy named Cliff and this fancy template, no one needs to know.

PREPARATION

Run for a border.

 1. Click on GrphPgBrdr button on Design Tools Button Bar. • Select Classic. • Click OK.

Time for a title.

 2. Justification: Center. • Select Layout. • Select Page. • Select Center. • Select Current Page. • Click on OK.

 3. Font Face: Times New Roman. • Font Size: 24. • Type: Book Report. • Press Enter. • Type: on. • Press Enter. • Type name of book.

 4. Press Enter 10 times. • Font Size: 18. • Turn off bold. • Type: By • Press Enter. • Type your name. • Press Ctrl+Enter to insert page break.

Enter some impressive headings.

 5. Click on Bold button. • Justification: Left.

 6. Select View. • Select Ruler Bar. • Drag left margin marker to 1/2" mark (see the next figure). • Type your first heading, such as Character Profiles. • Press Enter two times. • Drag left margin marker back to 1" mark. • Enter a description of each of the book's major characters. • Press Enter two times.

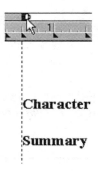

7. Repeat steps 5 and 6 for additional sections, such as Summary of Plot and Conclusions.

Get your footer in the door.

8. Select Layout. • Select Header/Footer. • Select Footer A. • Click Create. • Type your name. • Press Tab to move to center of page. • Type "Book Report on" followed by name of book (see the next figure). • Press Tab to move to right-hand edge. • Type: Page - (see the next figure). • Click on Number button. • Select Page Number.

Tim Taylor	Book Report on "The Sun Also Rises"	Page - 1

9. Click Close.

Number, please.

10. Select Layout. • Select Page. • Select Numbering. • Click Value. • Increase page number by 1. • Click OK. • Click Close.

11. Save and print your book report.

VARIATIONS

State of the Union: *This recipe is easily adapted for any type of report, such as a sales report, status report, or even the state of the union address.*

Bold Is Better: *If you like a bolder look, use WordPerfect Draw to create some outstanding headers, such as solid black with white text.*

FOOTNOTES PAGE

Notes

1. Quotations from Jennifer Fulton's works are cited in the text with the following abbreviations:

   L: *Love Poems for Today*, ed. Scott Wilson (Chicago, Brown & Weber, 1993).
   B: *Parade of Chickens*, ed. Meghan Ryan (Chicago, Brown & Weber, 1994).

2. Jennifer Flynn, *A Diary of Our Times*, ed. Mike Whitmer (London, Olgorthorpe Press, 1991), 113-120.

3. Ibid, 134-135. Jennifer often included analogies to birds in her poetry. This collection in particular is full of such references.

4. Mike Whitmer, "Editing a Master Poet," *Poetry Readers Monthly* 63 (June 1993), 28-29.

5. Most likely a reference to her husband Scott, whom Jennifer often referred to as "the great eagle" in her poems.

Notes	(Title of Article)	Page 2

Footnotes are a great way to convince your readers (and the teacher) that you spent lots and lots of hard-earned time creating this, your masterwork. Your reader will think, "Hey, here's a footnote interrupting my thoughts. Let me go see what amusing information it can offer me." In WordPerfect, footnotes are printed at the bottom of the page in which the reference occurs. Endnotes are a collection of these footnotes, printed at the end of a document. With this recipe, you can create an "endnotes" page to put at the end of your document.

PREPARATION

Create the endnote page.

1. Move to the last page of your document. • Select Insert. • Select Endnote. • Select Placement. • Select Insert Endnotes at Insertion Point. • Click OK. WordPerfect creates a new page on which to place the endnotes.

 Chef's Tip Endnotes usually appear just before a bibliography, and just after any appendices.

Enter your endnotes.

2. Type your text (see the next figure). • When you come to the end of a sentence to which you want to attach an endnote, select Insert. • Select Endnote. • Select Create. • Type your note. • Click Close on Footnote/Endnote Feature Bar.

particular is full of such references.

4. Mike Whitmer, "Editing a Master Poet," *Poetry Readers Monthly* 63 (June 1993), 28-29.

5. Most likely a reference to her husband Scott, whom Jennifer often referred to as "the great eagle" in her poems.

Format your endnotes page.

3. After you're done, move to the endnotes page at the end of your document.

 4. Justification: Center. • Font Face: Times New Roman. • Font Size: 24. • Type: Notes.

5. Select Graphics. • Select Horizontal Line. • Drag line into place under Notes title.

Now add a footer.

6. Select Layout. • Select Header/Footer. • Select Footer A. • Click Create.

 7. Click on Bold button. • Type: Notes. • Press Tab to move to center of footer. • Type the title of your article, report, thesis, or whatever. • Press Tab to move to right of footer. • Type: Page. • Press Spacebar. • Click Number on Header/Footer Feature Bar. • Select Page Number.

8. Click Line. • Style: Double. • Click OK. • Drag the line into place above footer text (see the next figure). • Click Close.

| Notes | (Title of Article) | Page 2 |

9. Save and print your document with its endnotes page.

VARIATIONS

AnNOTEtate! *For a more casual look, annotate your endnotes with your own comments. Just add them to the end of the endnote entry.*

10 min.

BUSINESS   ORGANIZATION   HOME   **SCHOOL**

Moderate

GLOSSARY

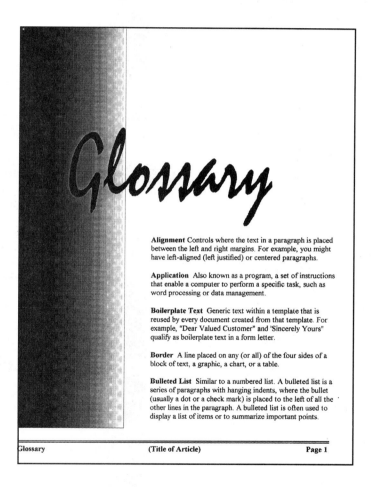

A glossary is like a miniature dictionary at the end of an article or book that contains all those "big words" that were placed in the document to impress the reader. Why not impress them more with the glossary itself? With this recipe, you'll create a handsome glossary to place at the end of your document.

PREPARATION

Create a footer for your glossary.

1. Move to the end of your document.
   • Press Ctrl+Enter to start the glossary on a new page.

Chef's Tip A glossary is usually placed just after any appendices and the endnotes section, and just before the bibliography and index.

2. Select Layout. • Select Header/Footer. • Select Footer A. • Click Create.

Cook's Caution If your document already has a footer, you can skip steps 2–6. However, if you want to change the footer for the Glossary section of your document (to make it say "Glossary" instead of whatever it says now), feel free to complete steps 2–6 anyway.

3. Font Face: Times New Roman. • Font Size: 10. • Click on Bold button. • Type: Glossary. • Press Tab to move to center of footer. • Type title of your article, report, thesis, or whatever.

4. Press Tab to move to right-hand side of footer. • Type: Page. • Press Spacebar. • Click on Number button. • Select Page Number.

5. Click on Line button. • Select Double. • Click OK. • Drag the line into place above the footer text.

6. Click Close.

Create a column.

7. Click on Draw button.

8. Select Attributes. • Select Fill. • Select Gradient. • Center Color: black. • Outer Color: white. • Angle: 90. • Click OK.

9. Click on Rectangle tool. • Draw a large rectangle on the left-hand side of the Draw page (see the next figure).

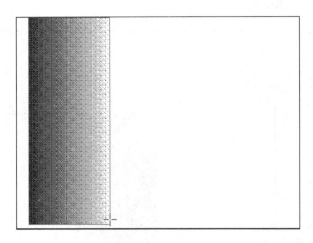

10. Select Text. • Select Font. • Font Face: Brush738 BT, Brush Script, Mystical, or similar font. • Font Size: 72. • Click OK. • Click on Text tool. • Click where you want to start typing. • Type: Glossary (see next figure). • Press Enter.

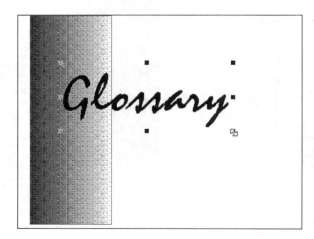

Adjust your graphic.

11. Select File. • Select Exit and Return to Document. • Click Yes.

12. Select Graphics. • Select Edit Box. • Click on Size button. • Set both dimensions to Full. • Click OK.

13. Click on Wrap button. • Select No Wrap. • Click OK.

14. Click Close.

Make your Glossary entries.

15. Press Enter until the cursor is below the word "Glossary." • Select View. • Select Ruler. • Drag left-hand paragraph marker so it's beyond edge of rectangle graphic (see next figure).

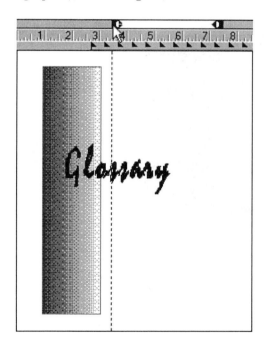

16. Make your glossary entries. You might want to bold the terms to make them stand out.

17. When text flows onto second page, move backwards to first letter on page two. • Press Ctrl+Enter. • On Ruler, move left-hand paragraph marker back to its original position at 1".

18. Click on Columns button. • Select 2 columns. This will give you a two-column layout on the second page.

19. Save and print your glossary with your document.

VARIATIONS

Teacher, Teacher! *You could also add a glossary to the handouts for a training session, covering the new terms that were used in the class.*

HANDOUTS

Course #1101 - Getting the Most Out of WordPerfect

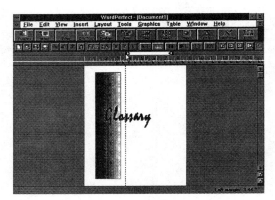

Drag one edge of the WordPerfect Draw graphic, until it fills a page.

Handout #1-15

Students remember more if they see something as they listen to an explanation of a complex procedure or concept. If they can see, hear, and do something during the learning process (such as adding their own notes to your handouts), they remember even more. So your handouts play an integral part in the learning process and should look attractive. With this recipe, they will.

PREPARATION

Create a header for your handouts.

1. Select Layout. • Select Header/Footer. • Select Header A. • Click Create.

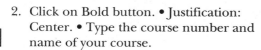

2. Click on Bold button. • Justification: Center. • Type the course number and name of your course.

3. Click on Line button. • Thickness: .022. • Click OK. • Drag the line into place below header text (see the next figure). • Click on Close button.

Course #1101 - Getting the Most Out of WordPerfect

Create a matching footer.

4. Select Layout. • Select Header/Footer. • Select Footer A. • Click Create.

5. Press Tab to move to right-hand side of footer (see the next figure). • Type: Handout #. • Click on Number button. • Select Chapter Number. • Type: - (hyphen). • Click on Number button. • Select Page Number. • Click Close.

Handout #1-15|

Chef's Tip   As you move through your document, increase the chapter number (section number) by selecting Page from the Layout menu, and then selecting Numbering. Click on Value. Increase the chapter number by 1. Reset the page number to 1. Click OK. Click Close.

6. Type your handout information on each page, or print a blank page and attach your drawings.

7. Save and print your handout template. • Make set of handouts for each participant.

VARIATIONS

Bullet-in: *This just in. For a simple yet effective handout, insert large bulleted text. Click on the Bullets button or use the Insert Character command to insert an interesting arrow.*

Course #1101 - Getting the Most Out of WordPerfect

Tips For Handling Graphics:

➡ To move a graphic, click on it and hold down the left mouse button. Continue to hold the left mouse button down as you drag the graphic to its new location.

➡ To resize a graphic, drag an edge. To resize a graphic proportionately, drag a corner.

➡ To save time when working with graphics, don't display them on-screen. Select Graphics from the View menu to turn this option off and on.

Handout #1-16

Get the Picture?   *If you'd like to include a screen shot for a computer class you're teaching (as shown in the first example), you'll need a screen capture program. There are many such programs available; we used Collage for Windows to capture the screen shots for this book.*

INDEX

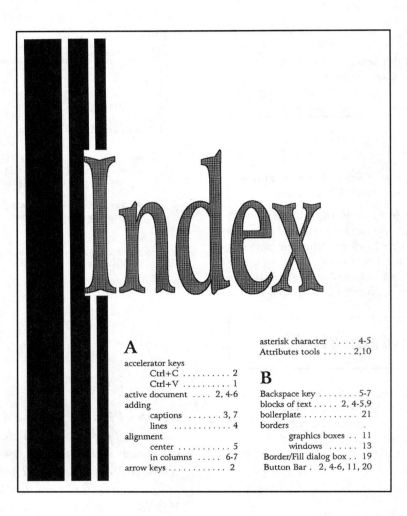

A

accelerator keys
    Ctrl+C 2
    Ctrl+V 1
active document 2, 4-6
adding
    captions 3, 7
    lines 4
alignment
    center 5
    in columns 6-7
arrow keys 2

asterisk character 4-5
Attributes tools 2,10

B

Backspace key 5-7
blocks of text 2, 4-5,9
boilerplate 21
borders   .
    graphics boxes . . 11
    windows 13
Border/Fill dialog box . . 19
Button Bar . 2, 4-6, 11, 20

Every good book, report, or article requires an equally good index. Use this recipe to create a great-looking index to grace any document.

PREPARATION

Create a heading for your index.

1. Move to end of your document. • Press Ctrl+Enter to start new page.

 Chef's Tip An index is usually placed just after the bibliography at the very end of a document.

2. Select Graphics. • Select Custom Line. • Click Vertical. • Click Line Styles. • Click Create. • Style name: Double Thick/Thin. • Width: .072". • Click Add. • Width: .038". • Click Add. • Width: .022". • Click OK.

3. Select the line • Click OK. • Widen the line by dragging to resize it (see the next figure).

Add the Index title.

 4. Click on TextArt button. • Text color: gray. • Outline: gray. • Font Face: Arrus Blk BT. • Type: Index.

5. Select File. • Select Exit & Return to WordPerfect. • Click Yes. • Click on figure and resize. • Drag it into place (see the next figure).

Generate your index.

6. Go through your document and mark index entries. Select Tools. • Select Index. • Select a term or word. • Click inside Heading box on Index Feature Bar and type a subheading if you want. • Repeat for additional terms, as needed. • Click Close.

 Chef's Tip Instead of marking your index entries by hand, create a simple text file with terms you want in the index. Type each term on a separate line, then save the file. Select Index from the Tools menu. Click on the Define button. Enter the file name for your index file. Click OK.

7. After marking all entries, return to Index page. • Press Enter to move the cursor below the word "Index." • Click on Generate.

Apply the finishing touches.

8. Click on Columns button. • Select 2 Columns. • Select View. • Select Ruler Bar. • Drag column margins into place (see the next figure).

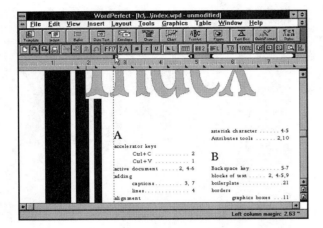

9. Move to beginning of second page of index. • Press Ctrl+Enter. • Use the Ruler to move column margins so they divide entire page. • Move back through index, adding a single letter to mark each alphabetical section. For example, move back to start of index and add an "A" in 24-point text.

10. Save and print your index along with your document.

VARIATIONS

Put Your Foot in It: *You can create a separate footer for your index, as shown in the glossary, notes, and bibliography recipes in this section. That way, the reader can easily see that he is in the index part of the book. Follow the directions in any of those recipes to create your unique Index footer.*

Get Bold: *Go through your index and bold page numbers that contain a picture or a definition of a term. This identifies for the reader the most important occurrence of that term.*

Figure Index: *If there are many figures in your document, consider adding a separate index listing figures with their captions. This helps a reader who has read the text, but needs to find a particular illustration.*

10 min.

BUSINESS ORGANIZATION HOME **SCHOOL**

Moderate

INSTRUCTION MANUAL

Course #1101 - Getting the Most Out of WordPerfect

Handout 4-1 **Flipchart 4-1**	**Working with graphics boxes.**

1. Think of a graphics box as a container for a WP graphic. They are like islands that allow text to flow around them.

2. Figures, clip-art, and text can all be placed within a WP graphics box.

3. Graphics boxes are separate within the document and they can be manipulated on their own. For example, they can be moved, copied, and resized without affecting the surrounding text (except that the text will change its flow around the new size of the graphic).

4. Click on a graphic to select it, and handles appear.

Adding a figure to a document.

Handout 4-2
Reference Manual pg. 240

1. Adding a pre-existing figure (clip-art) to a document is like opening a file.

2. Select Figure from the Graphics menu.

3. Change to the directory in which the graphic is stored. WP stores its graphics in the \Graphics directory.

4. Click on the graphic you wish to insert.

5. Click on OK or press Enter.

Handout 4-3   **The Graphics Box Feature Bar**

Working With Graphics   4 - 1

Teaching someone to do something right can give you a nice feeling, but who teaches the teacher so he teaches it right every time? If you are in charge of presenting the same type of class over and over, organize your thoughts into a training manual. That way, you can go to Florida for a well-earned vacation and leave the training to someone else.

PREPARATION

Get a new layout.

1. Select Layout. • Select Page. • Select Paper Size. • Choose Letter Landscape. • Click Select.

Create a header.

2. Select Layout. • Select Header/Footer. • Select Header A. • Click Create.

3. Justification: Center. • Click on Bold button. • Font Face: Times New Roman. • Font Size: 12. • Type course number and title.

4. Click on Line button. • Line Style: Thin/Thick 1. • Click OK. • Drag the line above the footer text (see the next figure). • Click Close.

Create a footer.

5. Select Layout. • Select Header/Footer. • Select Footer A. • Click Create.

6. Click on Bold button. Font Face: Times New Roman. • Font Size: 12. • Type name of this section of your manual. • Tab to right-hand margin. • Click on Number button. • Select Chapter Number. • Type: - (hyphen). • Click on Number button again. • Select Page Number.

 Cook's Caution To change the footer for the name of each section, repeat steps 5 and 6 later in the training manual file. To update the section number, select Page from the Layout menu, then select

Numbering. Click on Value, and increase the section number by 1. Click OK, then click OK again.

7. Click on Line button. • Line Style: Double. • Click OK. • Drag line into place above footer text. • Click Close.

Create two-column text.

8. Click the Columns button. • Select 2 Columns. • Select View. • Select Ruler Bar. • Change the column margins to make the column on right larger (see the next figure).

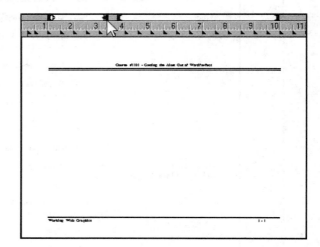

9. Font Face: Times New Roman. • Font Size: 12. • Type your notes into first column (such as handout, flipchart, or reference manual numbers). • Press Ctrl+Enter to move to right-hand column. • Enter instruction steps.

10. Save and print your manual.

VARIATIONS

More Columns, Please: *Insert a column for notes between the two columns shown here.*

INSTRUCTION SHEET

Fool-Proof Copying

✎ Enter your department number and press the "A" button.

✎ Select the paper size bin, and the output bin. To collate, press the Collate button.

✎ Change the lightness or darkness value if necessary. If you're copying a picture, press the Picture button for the best light/dark value.

✎ Enter the number of copies needed.

✎ Lay the originals in the automatic feed bin. If the originals are stapled or of low quality, you may want to place them on the glass one page at a time, or feed them into the manual feed bin.

✎ If the copier jams, follow the on-screen instructions.

People say that forgetfulness is one of the first signs of growing old, but it's really the first sign of common sense. With all the information an adult is bombarded with in the course of a normal day, a certain amount has to fall through the gray matter, or we'd all go insane. With this recipe, you'll create an instruction sheet for using the copier (or some other task you do just often enough to forget how to do it).

PREPARATION

Type a title.

1. Click GrphPgBrdr on Design Tools Button Bar. • Select Pencils. • Click OK.

2. Font Face: Swiss721 BlkEx BT. • Font Size: 24. • Justification: Center. • Type instruction sheet title, such as Fool-Proof Copying.

Enter the instruction steps.

3. Justification: Left. • Select Layout. • Select Paragraph. • Select Hanging Indent.

4. Select Insert. • Select Character. • Select Iconic Symbols. • Choose pencil icon (see the next figure). • Click Insert. • Click Close.

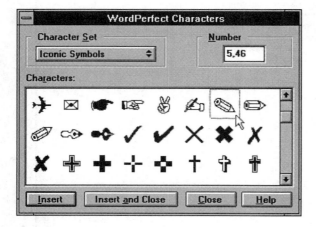

5. Press Tab. • Font Face: Arial. • Font Size: 18. • Type instructions for the first step.

6. Repeat steps 3–5 for additional instructions.

7. Save and print your instruction sheet.

VARIATIONS

Protect Your Investment: *Place your instruction sheet in a plastic cover if lots of people will use it.*

Make a Bold Statement: *For more pizzazz, use WordPerfect Draw or TextArt to create a bolder title with white text on black, bent text, or something else that's eye-catching.*

MARKETING FACT SHEET

SF 2000 PC

MARKETING FACT SHEET

Specs

- Intel Pentium 60 Mhz CPU
- 8 MB RAM
- 245 SCSI hard disk
- 14" SVGA monitor
- 3.5" 1.44 MB floppy drive

Insert picture here.

Buyer Info

Projected Retail Price: $2,100
Projected Wholesale Price: $1,795
Projected Sale Price: $1,995

Buyer Segment: Male 21-35 41%
Number of Units Produced: 40,000
Number of Units for Quota: 35,000

When your company releases a new product, it has to get the information into the salesperson's hands ASAP. Then the salesperson can ignore the facts and tell the buyer anything he wants. But that's none of your affair; your business is to present the facts, just the facts.

PREPARATION

Create a product "logo."

 1. Click on the TextArt button. • Font Face: Arrus Blk BT, Amerigo BT, or similar font. • Text color: black. • Type product name. • Choose a shape (see the next figure). • Select File. • Select Exit & Return to WordPerfect. • Click Yes.

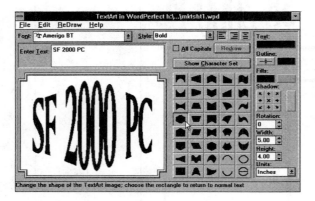

2. Click on TextArt and resize. Drag it to the upper right-hand corner.

Insert a title.

 3. Click on Text Box button. • Click inside text box. • Font Face: Arrus Blk BT. • Font Size: 24. • Type: MARKET-ING FACT SHEET.

4. Resize text box to stretch from left margin to right. • Drag it into place under logo (see the next figure).

Add your facts.

 5. Press Enter until the cursor's underneath the Fact Sheet title. • Click on Bullet button. • Select the triangle style. • Select New Bullet or Number on ENTER. • Click OK. • Font Face: Arrus BT. • Font Size: 18. • Type your list of specs.

Add the Specs marker.

 6. Click on Draw button. • Select File. • Select Page Layout. • Width: 1". • Height: 3". • Select Solid. • Color: light gray. • Click OK.

 7. Select Text. • Select Font. • Font Face: Arrus Blk BT. • Font Size: 36. • Click OK. • Click on Text tool. • Click where you want to start typing. • Type: Specs. • Press Enter.

 8. Click on Select tool. • Click on text box. • Select Edit. • Select Rotate. • Rotate text 90 degrees (see the next figure). • Select File. • Select Exit and Return to Document. • Click Yes. • Click on Specs box and drag in front of bulleted list.

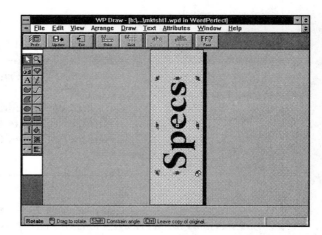

Add a placeholder for a figure.

9. Click on Text Box button. • Type: Insert picture here. • Click on Border/Fill button. • Border Style: Thick/Thin 1. • Click OK.

10. Resize text box. • Drag it to right of bulleted list. • Click Close.

Create a Buyer Info section.

11. Click on Specs box. • Click on Copy button. • Click inside document. • Click on Paste button. • Drag second Specs box just below first box.

12. Double-click on second Specs box. • Click on text box. • Select text. • Replace text with Buyer Info. • Select File. • Select Exit and Return to Document. • Click Yes.

13. Click on Buyer Info box and drag into place at left-hand side, under the Specs box. • Click just after last bulleted list item. • Press Enter enough times to move cursor to Buyer Info section (See next figure). • Font Face: Arrus BT. • Font Size: 18. • Type buyer's information.

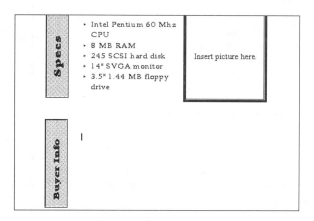

14. Save and print your marketing fact sheet.

Need More Data? *Add sections on market share, competitive products, sales projections, and so on.*

MEETING MINUTES

School Board Meeting Minutes

March 22, 1994
Minutes taken by: Jane Johnston

Time:	By:	Action:
7:00 pm		Meeting called to order.
		Reading of last month's minutes.
		Review of tonight's agenda (See attached).
7:10 pm	George Schnider	Motion to review driver's ed curricula, in view of last week's accident. Motion seconded by Sally Brown. Motion carried by a vote of 15-2.
		George to form a three person committee which will prepare a report on the current curricula, and recommendations for the board.
		Report by George's group will be presented at the next meeting.
7:30 pm	Sally Bowles	Finance committee recommends that a fence be installed around the parking lot to discourage teens from congregating there after hours. The cost would be $7,000, which could be added to next year's budget. The work could be completed during summer break.
		Discussion tabled until the complete financial report is presented in the May meeting.
8:15 pm	Mrs. Edwards	Enrollment levels for next year may be a concern. Early recruitment of freshman appears to be down by 10% over last year.
		Open Campus Day for freshman is scheduled for April 14th. Will need volunteers to act as guides.
	Pat Wilson	Recommends including a notice to this effect in the Church bulletin. Pat will prepare the notice and see that it gets over to the rectory to make the deadline.
8:35		Break

Page 1

Whether your group follows Robert's Rules of Order (or no order at all), you'll need an accurate record of what goes on. Having a set of minutes is good for those members who have to miss a meeting (home watching the game). With this recipe, you can create a minutes template to use over and over again.

PREPARATION

Type a title.

1. Font Face: OzHandicraft BT. • Font Size: 36. • Type: "Meeting Minutes" and press Enter.

2. Select Graphics. • Select Custom Line. • Line Style: Thick/Thin 1. • Click OK. • Shorten line (see the next figure).

School Board Meeting Minutes

3. Font Face: Arial. • Font Size: 12. • Click on Bold button. • Press Enter twice. • Click on Date Text button. • Press Enter. • Type: Minutes taken by: and add the appropriate name (see the next figure). • Press Enter.

School Board Meeting Minutes

March 22, 1994
Minutes taken by: Jane Johnston|

Create a table.

4. Click on Table Create button. • Choose 3 columns and 20 rows. • Select View. • Select Ruler Bar. • Drag right edge of the first two columns to make them smaller (see the next figure).

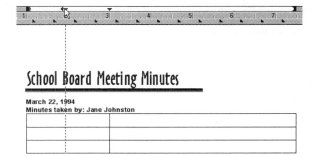

5. Type headings in first row: Time, By, and Action. • Click on TblLineFill. • Select Table. • Line Style: None. • Click OK.

Add a footer.

6. Select Layout. • Select Header/Footer. • Select Footer A. • Click Create. • Type: Page. • Press Spacebar. • Click Number button. • Select Page Number.

7. Click on Line button. • Line Style: Single. • Click OK. • Drag line into place above footer text. • Click Close.

8. Save your minutes template, or print it so minutes can be taken by hand. To enter minutes later, type them into the table.

 Chef's Tip Press Tab or use the arrow keys to move from cell to cell in the table.

VARIATIONS

Too Stuffy? *For a less formal look, create a two column table, and leave the "By:" column out.*

That's My Line: *Add a line to separate the "Action" text from the other two columns. Select the last column, click the right mouse button, and select Lines/Fill. Select a line style for Left, then click OK.*

PRESENTATION NOTES

Jacob Cannon Library Proposal/Slide Presentation

PRESENTATION NOTES/page 1
_____

SLIDE 1
_____

This morning, we would like to present our latest proposal for the Jacob Cannon Library Building project. It is with great excitement that we approach this opportunity to construct a building that identifies with the community, provides an avenue for discovery, and stands forth as a landmark for our citizens.

_____

SLIDE 2
_____

It is our intent to create a building that makes the most of the natural settings of the city's landscape. Yet, we also desire this structure to be a prominent source of civic pride, attracting the arts. But our main focus is to provide a structure that houses a great source of materials for learning and growing ourselves and our children.

_____

SLIDE 3
_____

We began with a 750,000 square foot base that houses a large entrance, and three sub-entrances. Covered with marble panels and limestone blocks, the building exterior slowly rises from the base to reveal recessed windows that make use of natural southern lighting.

_____

SLIDE 4
_____

The stairs that ascend to the main entrance, also composed of marble and limestone, will rise up from a grand entry drive that also readily connects to the parking lots. Multiple statuary guards the stairway from bottom to top. Landscaping features in this area include evergreen shrubberies and Japanese maple trees.

_____

SLIDE 5
_____

From a bird's-eye view, the building itself is surrounded by three main parking areas, all of which connect with the main driveway in and out of the facility. The driveway loops around the building itself, as well as forming a drop-off area in front of the main entrance.

For most people, giving a speech is nerve-racking. Trying to imagine everyone in the audience wearing just their underwear is a good relaxation trick, but having some good solid notes in your hands is much better. With this recipe, you can create a set of notes for your next presentation.

PREPARATION

Type a title header.

1. Select Layout. • Select Header/Footer. • Select Header A. • Click Create.

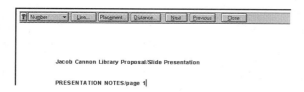

2. Font Face: Arial. • Font Size: 12. • Click on Bold button. • Type name of your presentation.

3. Press Enter three times. • Type: "PRESENTATION NOTES/page" (see the next figure). • Click Number on Header/Footer Feature Bar. • Select Page Number. • Click Close.

Jacob Cannon Library Proposal/Slide Presentation

PRESENTATION NOTES/page 1

Enter the slide notes.

4. Select Graphics. • Select Horizontal Line. • Press Enter. • Click on Bold button to deselect it. • Type: SLIDE. • Type slide number. • Press Enter two times. • Type text for slide. • Press Enter three times (see the next figure).

SLIDE 1

This morning, we would like to present our latest proposal for the Jacob Cannon Library Building project. It is with great excitement that we approach this opportunity to construct a building that identifies with the community, provides an avenue for discovery, and stands forth as a landmark for our citizens.

5. Repeat step 4 for each slide.

6. Save and print your presentation notes.

VARIATIONS

Out of Order? Mark your slides with the same number you use in your notes, so if you drop that tray . . . well, you get the picture.

REALTY OFFICE
PROPERTY FACT SHEET

One of the really nice things about WordPerfect templates is that you can fold, spindle, and mutilate them to do whatever you need, and most of the work's already done. In this recipe, you'll fold, spindle, and mutilate the Cost Analysis template and transform it into a fact sheet template for a real estate company.

PREPARATION

Fold and spindle a copy of the cost analysis template.

1. Click on Template button. • Click Options. • Click on Create Template.
   • New Template Name: REALESTA.
   • Template to Base On: COSTANYL.
   • Click OK.

Insert the title text.

2. Double-click on Font Face button.
   • Font Face: Arrus Blk BT, Hobo-WP, or similar font. • Font Size: 35. • Click OK.
   • At top of document, replace "Project Cost Analysis" with your company name (see the next figure). • Press Spacebar to move cursor near right margin.
   • Type your company phone number.

Project Cost Analysis

3. Font Face: Arial. • Font Size: 24. • Click the Italics Button. • Type: Real Estate Fact Sheet.

Insert the graphic border.

4. Click after <Organization>. • Click on Figure button. • Select BORD13L.WPG. • Click OK. • Resize border (see the next figure). • Drag it into place. • Click on Border/Fill button on the Graphics Feature Bar.
   • Border Style: None. • Click OK.

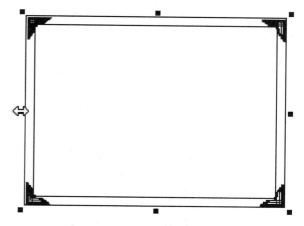

Prepare the property description panel.

5. Font Face: Arial. • Font Size: 10. • Click on Bold button. • Justification: Left.
   • Delete "Organization" text in table.
   • Replace it with property information, such as address, house highlights, and so on.

Complete the information table.

6. Font Face: Arial. • Font Size: 14. • Click on Bold button. • Replace "Estimated Costs" with "House Features" (see the next figure). • In table, enter information about the house.

House Features

1 story ranch, with brick exterior
3 bedroom
Great room
Dining room
Kitchen, with eat-in nook

Cook's Caution You may need to adjust the table portion. To insert or delete rows, place the cursor inside the table, then click on either the Tbl Insert or the Delete Tbl button. To change the format or appearance of cells, highlight the cells to be changed, and click on the TblLineFill button.

7. Click Exit Template button. • Click yes.

VARIATIONS

Not in Real Estate? *This format is easily adapted to a homeowner's policy data sheet for an insurance office.*

Lost House: *If you've lost your home, this sheet would make a great flyer to hand out at supermarkets. Seriously, though, you could use this format as an advertising sheet for selling not only your home, but also, say, a vintage restored automobile or any other item.*

10 min.

BUSINESS   ORGANIZATION   HOME   SCHOOL

Moderate

REPORT COVER WITH GRAPHIC LINES

Lansing & Stern

Environmental Controls on U.S. Manufacturing

September 1995

Professional typesetters know how to use graphic lines to draw the reader's eyes toward important elements, such as a report title. With this recipe, you, too, can create eye-catching covers for your business, school, or organization reports. Readers may be so impressed they won't even need to read the report!

PREPARATION

Create a text box for the title.

 1. Click on Text Box button.

2. Click on Border/Fill button on Graphics Box Feature Bar. • Click on Customize Style. • Select sides to modify: All. • Line Style: Thick Single. • Drop Shadow Type: lower right (see the next figure). • Click OK twice.

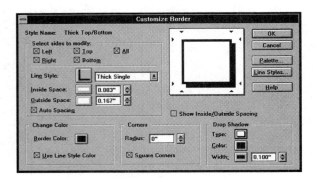

Enter the title text.

 3. Font Face: Times New Roman. • Font Size: 12. • Click on Italic button. • Justification: Center. • Type your company name in the text box. • Press Enter.

4. Font Size: 18. • Type the report title. • Press Enter twice.

5. Font Size: 12 . • Type the report date.

Position the text box.

6. Drag text box to the lower right corner of the page.

 Cook's Caution You may have to adjust your margins if you want to locate your text box like the one in this sample.

Insert the graphics lines.

7. Select Graphics. • Select Custom Line. • Line Type: Horizontal. • Line Style: Extra Thick Single (see the next figure). • Thickness: .425" • Click OK.

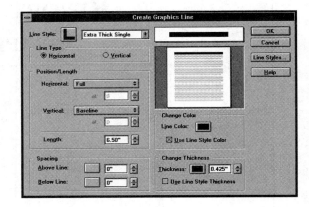

8. Drag line to bottom of page. • Resize line to fit between left margin and left border of the text box (see the next figure).

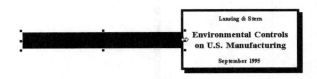

9. Select Graphics • Select Custom Line. • Line Type: Vertical. • Line Style: Thick Single. • Thickness: .150" • Click OK.

10. Drag line to left-hand margin. • Resize line to fit between top margin and horizontal graphics line (see the next figure).

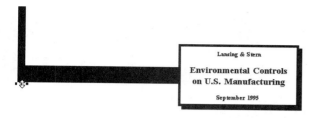

Lansing & Stern

**Environmental Controls
on U.S. Manufacturing**

September 1995

11. Save and print your cover with your report.

Chef's Tip   To start your report on the next page, press Ctrl+Enter.

VARIATIONS

A Bolder Title: *Place the title about two and a half inches from the top and about an inch and a half from the left edge, and use big, bold letters. If there's a subtitle, use smaller letters, and place it just below the main title. Now there's room in your text box for more information, such as the company address, your name, and where you can be contacted if the reader wants to offer you a terrific job.*

Gray Things Down a Bit: *Leave your text box black, but for graphics lines change the Line Color to a softer shade of gray. This makes the text box appear to stand out from the page.*

REPORT COVER
WITH TEXTART

YEARLY BUDGET

Willard, Sechrest & Sloane
Attorneys at Law

Everyone expects budgets to be "dead-on-arrival" at the Financial Division, because the CFO is going to spend what he's going to spend no matter what anyone else says. You need a budget proposal that will catch his eye and turn his head. It's not the numbers that count, but how you present them. With this recipe, you're sure to make an impression that "counts" based on the title page alone!

PREPARATION

Insert the report title.

1. Font Face: Arial. • Double-click on Font Size button. • Font Size: 50. • Click OK. • Justification: Center.

2. Select Layout. • Select Page. • Select Center. • Select Current Page. • Click OK. • Type: YEARLY BUDGET.

Use TextArt to insert the calendar year.

3. Click on TextArt button. • Font Face: Times New Roman. • Style: Bold. • Justification: Centered (see the next figure). • Type the year. • Select File. • Select Exit & Return to WordPerfect. • Click Yes.

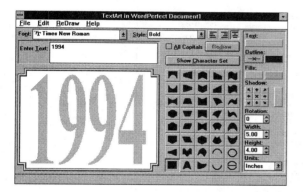

4. Click on calendar year object and drag to center of page. • Center object covering "Yearly Budget." • If necessary, resize object (see the next figure).

5. Select Graphics. • Select Edit Box. • Click on Wrap button on Graphics Box Feature Bar. • Select No Wrap. • Click OK. • Click Close.

Insert the name of your company.

6. Move cursor to next to last line of page. • Font Face: Times New Roman. • Font Size: 18. • Justification: Right. • Type your company name.

7. Move cursor to last line of page. • Font Size: 12. • Type subtitle or your division.

Insert a dividing rule.

8. Place cursor above company name. • Select Graphics. • Select Custom Line. • Line Style: Single. • Thickness: .038" (see figure below). • Position/Length: Horizontal Right. • Click OK. • If necessary, adjust size of the dividing rule.

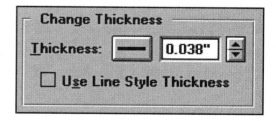

VARIATIONS

Bordering on the Fancy: *For a cover with a more classical look, click on the Border/Fill button in step 5. Place thick borders above and below the calendar year.*

What's My Logo? *A good place for your corporate logo on this page would be the lower left corner, just below the dividing rule. To create a logo, see the recipes in Part One.*

REPORT WITH TEXTART

Opening Up the Future Market

PORTABLE COMPUTING

Introduction
The class of portable computers include any computers that can be carried around from place to place. Portable computers encompass laptop and notebook computers, personal digital assistants, and palm computers. Just what are they all? Quite simply, portable computers are electronic devices that can easily be moved about via briefcase, purse, or pocket.

Types:
- Laptop
- Notebook
- Personal Digital Assistant
- Palm Computers

History
Portable computers did not start out so portable. The first portable computers made back in the 1980's weighed anywhere from 25 to 40 pounds. Needless to say, they were not very easily moved from place to place. In fact, users nicknamed the machines "luggables" because that's the type of effort that went into moving them around--lugging them to and from the office.

It wasn't until recently that the design of the computer began to reflect the necessity of portability in the truest sense, the need to get from the office to home, airport to hotel, and more. Advancements in technology have allowed the hardware to get smaller while still maintaining a great deal of power and capacity.

Specific Portables
Let's examine a few of these computers and what they are capable of doing. Laptops are small computers, about the size of a briefcase, that are ideal for the user who travels a lot and wants to work on the road or in an airplane. They are called laptops because they are small enough to fit comfortably on a person's lap. They run on an internal rechargeable battery, or can be plugged directly into an electrical outlet. Laptop

Page 1

Even if you're not a layout artist, you know a good-looking page when you see one. When you prepare a report for school or business laid out to look like a news magazine, your reader will think, "Ah, authority!" Use this recipe to create an "authoritative" report with WordPerfect's Report3 template.

PREPARATION

Revise the document template.

1. Click on Template button. • Click Options. • Select Create Template. • Under Name, type file name for your new report template (such as ALPHARPT). • Template to Base On: REPORT3. • Click OK.

2. Double-click on "Heading" in upper left of page. • Press Delete.

Add the report title.

3. Click on TextArt button. • Font Face: Arial. • Style: Bold. • Justification: Center. • Text color: light gray. • Outline: none (see the next figure). • Rotation: 90. • Width: 2". • Height: 8". • Type report title in the Enter Text Box. • Select File. • Select Exit & Return to WordPerfect. • Click Yes.

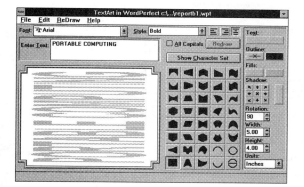

 Cook's Caution Your text will now look like it was run over by a freight train. Don't fret; it won't look that way on the page. (Confused? Well, so was I. Simply change Width and Height settings.)

4. Click on TextArt block. • Select Graphics. • Select Edit Box. • Click on Wrap button on Graphics Box Feature Bar. • Select No Wrap. • Click OK.

5. Resize TextArt object to fit left side of page (see the next figure). • Click Close.

Save the report template.

6. Using template format, type in your report text.

7. Click on Exit Template on Template Feature Bar. • Click Yes.

 Chef's Tip You can use your new template as you would any other WordPerfect template. Select Template from the File menu, choose this template from the list, and click OK. For the sample, I used Arrus 12-point for the body text.

VARIATIONS

Shadowy Characters: *A favorite TextArt option is the drop-down shadow, found at the far right of the TextArt dialog box, under a tightly-defined region marked Shadow. Click one of the pointing arrow buttons to create the shadow. Then click once on the color selector box and choose a color for the drop-down shadow.*

15 min.

Moderate

REPORT WITH WATERMARK

Portable Computing

Opening Up the Future Market

Introduction
The class of portable computers include any computers that can be carried around from place to place. Portable computers encompass laptop and notebook computers, personal digital assistants, and palm computers. Just what are they all? Quite simply, portable computers are electronic devices that can easily be moved about via briefcase, purse, or pocket.

Types:
- Laptop
- Notebook
- Personal Digital Assistant
- Palm Computers

History
Portable computers did not start out so portable. The first portable computers made back in the 1980's weighed anywhere from 25 to 40 pounds. Needless to say, they were not very easily moved from place to place. In fact, users nicknamed the machines "luggables" because that's the type of effort that went into moving them around--lugging them to and from the office.

It wasn't until recently that the design of the computer began to reflect the necessity of portability in the truest sense, the need to get from the office to home, airport to hotel, and more. Advancements in technology have allowed the hardware to get smaller while still maintaining a great deal of power and capacity.

Specific Portables
Let's examine a few of these computers and what they are capable of doing. Laptops are small computers, about the size of a briefcase, that are ideal for the user who travels a lot and wants to work on the road or in an airplane. They are called laptops because they are small enough to fit comfortably on a person's lap. They run on an internal rechargeable battery, or can be plugged directly into an electrical outlet. Laptop keyboards usually have small keys that are close together, and sometimes include a trackball (a mouse-like device attached to the keyboard). They have either monochrome LCD screens or color screens; color screens are either passive-matrix (soft color) or active-matrix (crisp, clean color) and use more battery power than monochrome screens. Laptops are almost as powerful as their desktop cousins (personal computers), being fully capable of running the same applications. Because they run off a battery, however, laptops are generally slower. In addition, laptops do not contain as large a hard drive as desktop computers do, and their screens are not as bright and clean.

There is a growing category of smaller, lighter portables called notebooks that usually weigh 6 to 8 pounds. The main difference between laptops and notebooks is weight--note

PAGE 1

R-E-S-P-E-C-T, that's what your report will get when you present it with a dramatic heading. With this recipe, you can create a report that uses subtle changes in gray tones to create a professional look. Best of all, you'll use the Report1 template to give you a head start.

PREPARATION

Create a new template.

1. Click on Template button. • Click Options. • Select Create Template. • Type your new template name (such as RPTWATER). • Base the Template On: Report1. • Click OK.

2. Select Layout. • Select Margins. • Left: 1.5". • Right: 1". • Top: 2.5". • Bottom: .5". • Click OK.

Get your feet wet with a watermark.

3. Click on Watermark button. • Select Watermark A. • Click Create.

4. Select Graphics. • Select Custom Line. • Line Type: Horizontal. • Line Style: Extra Thick Single. • Thickness: 1.35". • Line Color: very light gray. • Click OK.

5. Resize watermark bar (see the next figure). • Click Close on Watermark Feature Bar.

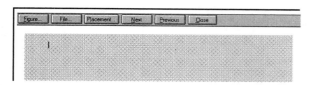

Cook's Caution You'll be working blind in the Watermark area, so you may have to jump back and forth between here and the document to get the effect you want. To edit the watermark again, click on the Watermark button, then select Edit.

6. Click on Figure button. • Select your art. • Click OK. • Resize artwork as needed (see the next figure). • Drag art into place, as shown.

7. Click on Border/Fill button on Graphics Box Feature Bar. • Fill Style: Button style. • Click OK. • Click on Wrap button. • Select No Wrap. • Click OK. • Click Close.

Finish up.

8. Click on Exit Template button on Template Feature Bar. • Click Yes. To use template later, type over title, subheading, and other text to replace with your report text.

VARIATIONS

Change the Footer: *You might want to print only the page number at the bottom of the page as in the sample.*

SCHOOL PLAY

Swim a Mile Up the Nile

a play by Sherry Willard

Plot Summary: A team of English archeologists digging around some Egyptian tombs encounter some strange adventures, with lots of action, laughs, and music.

Characters: Professor Wiggins, Professor Wiles, Miss Sally Smiles, Bruno, The Mummy, Pharoah Tutenkomedian, Porter, Pizza Delivery Guy, Chorus, Tammy Tile, Charles, Narrator.

Background Sounds: Creaks & groans, rattling chains, airplane flying, waterfall, "perils of Pauline"-style music, symphony music, large crashing noises.

Backdrop Settings: Egyptian tomb, Outdoor tomb tunnel, River scene with reeds and crocodiles, Pharoah's palace, Archeologist camp.

Scene 1: The Arrival of Tammy Tile

Offstage: Sounds of airplane overhead. (large fan can add wind effects)
Enter: Professor Wiggins and Bruno enter quickly from stage right, holding hats onto head and panting from running.

Professor Wiggins:	Quick, Bruno, Miss Tile has landed!
Offstage:	Sound of large thud. (Tammy: Ooww!)
Bruno:	Hey, Professor, aren't they going to land the plane?
Professor Wiggins:	Evidently, not, Bruno.

Enter: Tammy Tiles with parachute and suitcase.

Tammy:	Whoah, what a landing. I thought my parachute wasn't going to open.
Professor Wiggins:	Good heavens, girl, are you all right?
Tammy:	Sure, just a bumpy ride down, that's all.
Professor Wiggins:	Bruno, help her with her luggage.
Tammy:	Why thank you. I seem to have dropped a small suitcase near those reeds over there.
Professor Wiggins:	No problem, Bruno can fetch it.
Bruno:	But there are crocodiles over there!
Professor Wiggins:	Don't be a ninny, Bruno. They're more afraid of you than you are of them.

Nothing's cuter than seeing your little one dressed in a tomato costume, reciting a speech about vegetable preparation at the annual third grade production of "Vegetables Are Our Friends." What better way to rehearse the school play than with a professional-looking script? This project makes it easy, and if you also have the debatable honor of producing such a play, create a nice printed copy to "share the joy" with other parents so they can rehearse the unforgettable lines with their child.

PREPARATION

Add a colorful header.

1. Click on TextArt button. • Font Face: OzHandicraft, Stylus, or a similar font. • Justification: Center (see the next figure). • Width: 8". • Height: 1". • Select File. • Select Exit & Return to WordPerfect. • Click Yes.

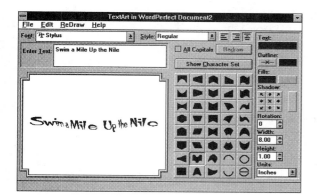

2. Click on TextArt and resize as needed (see the next figure). • Drag TextArt to top of page.

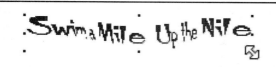

3. Click on Text Box button. • Click on Border/Fill button on Graphics Box Feature Bar. • Click Customize Style. • Line Style: Thick Single. • Border Color: orange. • Click OK.

4. Fill Style: Waves. • Click OK. • Drag box under title. • Resize box to fit margins. • Click Close.

Type your play.

5. Font Face: Arial. • Font Size: 12. • Justification: Center. • Click on Bold button. • Type: "a play" by followed by your name. • Justification: Left. • Click Bold button to deselect. • Type the summaries.

6. Select Graphics. • Select Horizontal Line. • Press Enter. • Font Size: 14. • Click on Bold. • Justification: Center. • Type name of scene.

7. Justification: Left. • Select View. • Select Ruler Bar. • On Ruler, drag paragraph margin markers to 3" mark (see the next figure). • Press Ctrl. • Drag top (first line) marker to left margin. • Drag off the two tab marks in front of 3" mark to delete them.

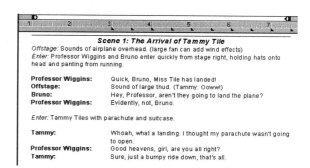

8. Type stage directions. • Type actor's lines. • Bold name of character. • Press Tab.

VARIATIONS

Indent the Stage Directions: *You can indent the stage directions to the 1 ½" mark to distinguish them more easily from actor's lines.*

STORYBOARD

You already know that WordPerfect can partition a page into square sections and divide text among these partitions; the program has to do this to make such things as mailing labels. If you're in advertising, or if your kids just want to tell a story the way commercial producers or cartoonists do it, why not use one of WordPerfect's big tables to make a framework for a storyboard? Just follow this recipe.

PREPARATION

Add a header.

1. Select Layout. • Select Margins. • Top and Bottom margins: .5". • Click OK.

2. Select Layout. • Select Header/Footer. • Select Header A. • Click Create. • Font Face: Times New Roman. • Font Size: 12. • Type name of your client and length of commercial.

Create the table framework.

3. Click on Table Create button. • Drag to select 3 columns and 4 rows.

4. Highlight entire table (see the next figure).

5. Click on Format Tbl button. • Select Column. • Width: 2.16" (see the next figure).

6. Select Row. • Row Height: Fixed 2.4" (see the next figure). • Click OK.

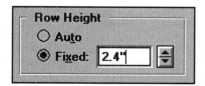

Type your story.

7. Place cursor in upper left-most frame. • Type your text. • Tab to next frame.

Finish up and fill in the storyboard.

8. Save and print your storyboard. Add hand-drawn sketches to illustrate your story.

Chef's Tip To import graphics to a frame, move the cursor inside the frame, select Figure from the Graphics menu, then select a file name from the dialog box that appears.

VARIATIONS

Adding a Bolder Outer Frame: *Change the style and thickness of the frame surrounding the table by highlighting the entire table, selecting Lines/Fill from the Table menu, and setting a new Inside frame option under the Line Styles frame.*

Get to the Bottom of Things: *Some TV stations and producers want the captions for each storyboard frame to appear at the bottom of the frame. If that's the case, select Format from the Table menu, click on the Table option button, and set Vertical Alignment option to Bottom.*

TABLE OF CONTENTS PAGE

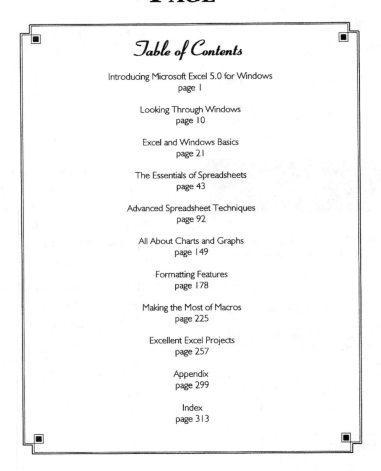

Table of Contents

The table of contents of a book or report is often dull and boring, but with this recipe, you can create one with real appeal. This example may look fancy, but it's not. The secret is the choice of font and creative use of white space—the easiest feature to enter with WordPerfect. Just insert everything else around it, and there it is.

PREPARATION

Add the border.

1. Click on GrphPgBrdr button on Design Tools Button Bar. • Select Square Corners (see the next figure). • Click OK.

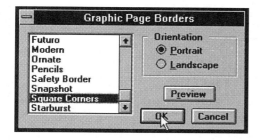

Enter the table title.

2. Font Face: Ribbon131 Bd BT. • Click on Bold button. • Double-click on Font Size button. • Font Size: 30. • Click OK. • Justification: Center. • Type: Table of Contents. • Press Enter.

Insert the table entries.

3. Font Face: Humanst521 Lt BT. • Click on Bold button to turn boldface off. • Double-click on Font Size button. • Font Size: 13. • Click OK.

4. Type each entry in table of contents: type name of item on one line, and its page number location on line below. Leave one line between entries (see the next figure).

Table of Contents

Cook's Caution   If your TOC does not fill an entire page, you may want to center the text between the top and bottom margins. Move to the top of the page, select Page from the Layout menu, then select Center.

VARIATIONS

Not Writing a Book?   *Well, we're in the book business, so when we see a format like this, we see it in a book. When you think about it, though, this looks as though it would make a fine wine list.*

A Bit Too Sweet?   *The Ribbon131 font "Table of Contents" does give this page a dramatic, suave touch. If you're looking for something a bit more demure, but you like the overall style and border, consider a bold variant of one of the Humanst fonts supplied with WordPerfect—a bolder form of the typeface used in the table entries.*

TERM PAPER

Computers On the Go
How To Carry Technology Around With You

The class of portable computers include any computers that can be carried around from place to place. Portable computers encompass laptop and notebook computers, personal digital assistants, and palm computers. Just what are they all? Quite simply, portable computers are electronic devices that can easily be moved about via briefcase, purse, or pocket.

Portable computers did not start out so portable. The first portable computers made back in the 1980's weighed anywhere from 25 to 40 pounds. Needless to say, they were not very easily moved from place to place. In fact, users nicknamed the machines "luggables" because that's the type of effort that went into moving them around--lugging them to and from the office.

It wasn't until recently that the design of the computer began to reflect the necessity of portability in the truest sense, the need to get from the office to home, airport to hotel, and more. Advancements in technology have allowed the hardware to get smaller while still maintaining a great deal of power and capacity.

Let's examine a few of these computers and what they are capable of doing. Laptops are small computers, about the size of a briefcase, that are ideal for the user who travels a lot and wants to work on the road or in an airplane. They are called

Computer Science 101   March 20, 1995   Page 1

Yech. It's that time of year again, and the term paper that's 75% of your grade is due tomorrow. Thank goodness you're almost done. When you're ready to type up your notes (providing you can still see straight and your fingers move), do it with style using this recipe.

PREPARATION

Add a graphic header.

1. Select Insert. • Select File. Select ENDER10.WPG from WordPerfect Graphics directory. • Click Insert.

2. Click Position button on Graphics Box Feature Bar. • Select Put Box on Current Page option. • Horizontal: 0" from Left Margin. • Vertical: .001" from Top Margin. • Click OK.

3. Click on Size button. • Width: 8". • Height: .5". • Click OK.

4. Click on Border/Fill button. • Border Style: None (see the next figure). • Click OK.

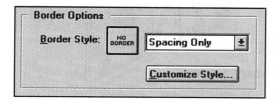

Add a footer.

 5. Select Layout. • Select Header/Footer. • Select Footer A. • Click Create. • Font Size: 10.

 6. Type the term paper's title. • Tab to the center. • Click on Date Text button. • Tab to the right-hand margin. • Type: Page. • Click Number on Header/Footer Feature Bar. • Select Page Number. • Click Close.

Type a title.

 7. Font Face: Arrus BT. • Double-click on Font Size button. • Font Size: 16. • Click OK. • Justification: Center. • Type first line of title. • Press Enter.

 8. Font Size: 12. • Click on Bold button to deselect it. • Type second line of title.

 9. Select Layout. • Select Line. • Select Spacing. • Line spacing: 1.5". • Click OK. • Justification: Left. • Type your term paper.

Finish up.

10. Save and print it.

Cook's Caution Check your spelling with WordPerfect's spell checker before you print your term paper.

VARIATIONS

Whose Paper Is This Anyway? *Add your name in the footer so it will appear on every page. That way, your teacher will know which term paper a stray sheet belongs to if it drops out.*

TICKETS

Before the turn of the last century, a ticket to a gala event was a real work of art, looking more like a stock certificate than an admission to a movie theater. Just because those days are over doesn't mean your tickets for the school carnival need to be squares of recycled newsprint. In the tradition of the ticket engravers of old, we present this recipe for an old-style admission ticket.

PREPARATION

Build the text box.

1. Select Layout. • Select Page. • Select Paper Size. • Choose Letter Landscape. • Click Select. • Select Layout. • Select Margins. • All margins: .25". • Click OK.

2. Click on Text Box button. • Click on Border/Fill button on Graphics Box Feature Bar. • Border Style: Triple. • Click OK. • Click on Wrap button. • Select No Wrap. • Click OK. • Resize text box to fit size of ticket (see the next figure).

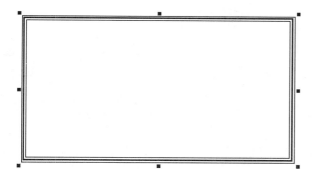

Enter the ticket information.

3. Font Face: Algerian. • Font Size: 24. • Click on Bold button. • Justification: Center. • Type admission price. • Press Enter.

4. Font Face: Arial. • Font Size: 12. • Click on Bold button to deselect it. • Type location of event. • Press Enter.

5. Font Face: Arrus Blk BT. • Font Size: 36. • Click on Italic button. • Type: Spring Fling. • Font Face: Arial • Font Size: 14. • Type dates and times for event.

6. Resize text box so all four text lines fit snugly inside (see the next figure).

$1.00

to Cherry Tree Elementary School

SPRING FLING

Friday Night, April 25, 6:00-10:00 at the school

Admit one.

7. Click on TextArt button. • Font Face: Algerian. • Text color: black. • Outline: none. • Justification: Center. • Click on archway shape (see the next figure).

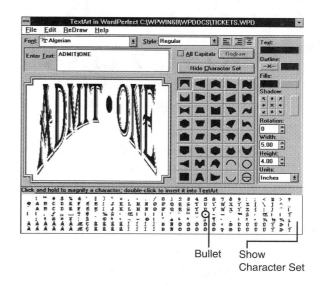

Bullet   Show Character Set

8. Type: ADMIT. • Click on Show Character Set. • Double-click on the dot character. • Type: ONE. • Select File. • Select Exit & Return to WordPerfect. • Click Yes. • Click on TextArt and resize as needed. • Drag TextArt into place.

Finishing the job.

9. Select the ticket. • Click on Copy button. • Click on Paste button. • Drag new ticket into place below the first ticket (see the next figure). • Repeat until you've filled a page.

10. Save and print your ticket. Take sample to a professional printer, or print them yourself on colored paper.

VARIATIONS

A Bit of Added Dimension: *A slight gray shadow falling to the lower right might enhance your design. From the TextArt dialog box, under Shadow, click on the lower-right pointing arrow, and change the color box setting to a light gray. This may be a bit confusing, because the box's "natural" color is already light gray (for "blank"), so make certain you pick a real color from the color box.*

Old Style Borders: *For a truly engraved look, you might import a graphic image file as a border for the text box. Try BORD04P.WPG, BORD10P.WPG, or BORD12P.WPG.*

TRAINING EVALUATION

Beginning WordPerfect for Windows

Facilitator: Kirstin Scott
Date of Class: _____
Your Name: _____

Classroom	Poor	Disliked Somewhat	Liked Somewhat	Excellent
Comfort				
Coffee and Rolls				
Computer Equipment				

Comments

Facilitator	Poor	Disliked Somewhat	Liked Somewhat	Excellent
Answered Questions Fully				
Cheerful Disposition				
Appeared Knowledgeable				
Provided Extra Attention When Necessary				

Comments

Course	Poor	Disliked Somewhat	Liked Somewhat	Excellent
Will help me do my job better				
All topics were covered				
Adequate time was spent on each topic				
Handouts, Flipchart, and Overheads				

Comments

Nowadays, it seems everyone has an opinion on something, including the effect of hair spray on the ozone layer and the number of sheets in a roll of toilet paper. So, before you tell your students it's okay to go home, find out what they thought of your presentation. With this recipe, you'll create a simple evaluation to help you locate trouble spots in your class so you can improve your effectiveness.

PREPARATION

Enter the basic information.

1. Font Face: Times New Roman. • Font Size: 24. • Click on Bold button. • Justification: Center. • Type the name of your class.

2. Font Size: 14. • Type: "Facilitator:" followed by your name. • Press Enter. • Type: Date of Class:. • Type a blank line to be filled in later. • Type: Your Name:. • Type a blank line.

Create your table.

3. Click on Tables Create button. • Columns: 5 and rows: 20. • Drag column borders to resize them as shown (see the next figure).

		Poor	Disliked Somewhat	Liked Somewhat	Excellent
		↔			

4. Font Size: 10. • Type headings for last four columns.

Chef's Tip Press Shift+Enter to type two-line headings, such as Disliked Somewhat.

Add a touch of color.

5. Select the four headings. • Click on TblLineFill button. • Fill Style: 100% Fill. • Foreground Color: medium gray (see figure below). • Click OK.

Classroom		Poor	Disliked Somewhat	Liked Somewhat	Excellent
Comfort					
Coffee and Rolls					
Computer Equipment					

6. Select remaining cells just below headings. • Click on TblLineFill button. • Fill Style: 100% Fill. • Foreground Color: lighter gray. • Click OK.

Add the questions.

7. Select first cell in table. • Font Size: 24. • Type: Classroom. • Click on TblLineFill button. • Outside: Thick/Thin 2. • Click OK.

8. Move down one cell. • Select View. • Select Ruler Bar. • Drag left margin marker to 1.5" (see the next figure). • Click on Bold button to turn bold off. • Font Size: 12. • Enter your questions beginning in cell A2.

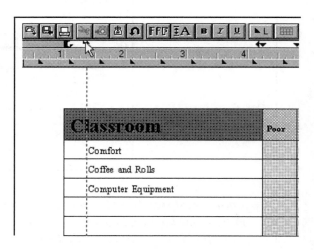

Add a comment section.

 9. Select several rows. • Right-click the mouse. • Select Join Cells. • Click on Bold button. • Type: Comments. • Click on TblLineFill button. • Inside: None. • Top: Double. • Click OK.

 10. To add a blank line after a section, select the last row. • Click on TblLineFill button. • Inside, Outside, and Fill Style: None. • Top and Bottom: Single. • Click OK.

11. Repeat steps 5 to 10 for each section.

12. Save and print your evaluations.

VARIATIONS

Conference Craziness: *You can adapt this recipe easily for a conference evaluation. You'll get good feedback plus a good head-count, both from the same document. Change the heading for each session for easy record keeping.*

Quality Survey: *Adapt this recipe for a customer-satisfaction survey, and mail it out to a random number of clients.*

TRANSPARENCY WITH
TEXT BOXES

**QUALITY IS
NUMBER 1**

"The biggest mistake a company can make is assuming that one dissatisfied customer can't do any harm...they tell everyone they know about the poor service they've received."

For some speakers, adding visuals to a presentation means gesturing grandly while speaking in a loud voice. However, you can follow a different course of action and put your message up in lights. With this recipe, you'll create a transparency proof to copy onto transparency sheets (see your local office supply) using an ordinary copier.

Preparation

Reset the paper orientation.

1. Select Layout. • Select Page. • Select Paper Size. • Choose Letter Landscape. • Click Select.

Situate the first text box.

2. Click on Text Box button. • Click on Border/Fill button on Graphics Box Feature Bar. • Border Style: Shadow.

3. Click on Customize Style. • Drop Shadow Width: 0.155". • Click OK twice.

4. Click inside text box. • Font Face: Arial. • Font Size: 24. • Justification: Left. • Type your message.

5. Resize text box to fit text (see the next figure). • Drag it to lower right of the page.

> "The biggest mistake a company can make is to assume that one dissatisfied customer can't do any harm...he will tell everyone he knows about the poor service he received."

Situate the second text box.

6. Click on Text Box button. • Click on Border/Fill button on Graphics Box Feature Bar. • Border Style: None. • Fill Style: Gradient 2. • Click OK.

7. Click inside new text box. • Select Layout. • Select Font. • Font Face: Arial. • Font Size: 40. • Select Bold. • Color: white. • Click OK.

8. Justification: Center. • Type your slogan (see the next figure). • Click Content. • Vertical Position: Top. • Click OK.

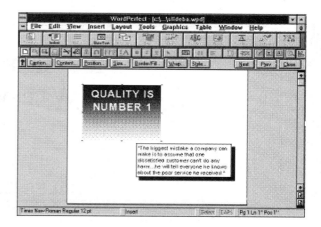

Insert the graphics line.

9. Select Graphics. • Select Custom Line. • Line Style: Extra Thick Single. • Line Color: medium gray. • Click OK. • Drag resulting line about 2 ½" below top of page.

10. Save and print your transparency proof. • Load transparency sheet into copier and copy your proof.

Variations

What's the Line For? *You may be asking yourself, why the graphic? It improves the appearance of your transparency and helps distinguish the main subject from the sub-topic. You can also use it to help identify groups or sessions by adding "Group 17" or "Day Three" above the line.*

TRANSPARENCY WITH WATERMARKS

SALES GOALS 1995

$ALES

- Increased revenues of $1.2 billion
- Expansion into new foreign markets
- International sales of $50 million
- 35 new product lines
- 75% company growth

It's easy to create an overhead transparency for that big presentation. All you need is WordPerfect, a good printer, and some transparencies suitable for use in a copier. Best of all, the subtle design of the combined watermarks used in this recipe will not overwhelm either your audience or your message.

PREPARATION

Reset the paper orientation.

1. Select Layout. • Select Page. • Select Paper Size. • Choose Letter Landscape (see the next figure). • Click Select.

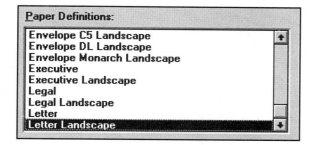

Insert the first watermark.

2. Select Layout. • Select Watermark. • Select Watermark A (see the next figure). • Click Create. • Press Enter five times.

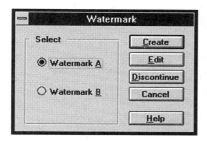

 3. Font Face: Times New Roman. • Select Bold. • Double-click Font Size button. • Font Size: 150. • Click OK.

4. Justification: Center. • Press Spacebar twice. • Type: ALES (see the next figure). • Click Close on Watermark Feature Bar.

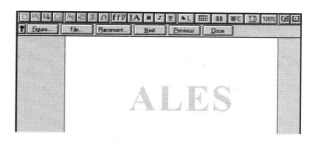

Insert the second watermark.

5. Select Layout. • Select Watermark. • Select Watermark B. • Click Create. • Press Enter five times.

6. Select Layout. • Select Font. • Font Face: Times New Roman. • Select Bold. • Under Font Size, type in 250. • Click OK.

7. Press Spacebar once. • Type: $ (see the next figure). • Click Close.

Enter the title text.

 8. Move cursor to upper left of page. • Font Face: Arial. • Font Size: 24. • Click on Bold button. • Justification: Center. • Type: SALES GOALS 1995.

9. Select Graphics. • Select Custom Line. • Line Style: Thick Single. • Click OK. • Drag resulting line below text header.

Enter the bullet items.

 10. Press Enter until the cursor appears just below the "$." • Double-click on Font Size button. • Font Size: 30. • Click OK. • Justification: Left.

 11. Click on Bullet button. • Styles: Large Circle. • Select New Bullet or Number on ENTER. • Click OK. • Type your list.

12. Save and print your transparency proof. Load transparency sheet into copier, and copy your proof.

VARIATIONS

Chart Your Success: *Add a chart to emphasize your point. To create one, click on the Chart button.*

Biting the Bullet: *You can choose an effective alternate bullet called Triangle from the Bullets & Numbers Styles list. It points to the right, so it helps point out the text line.*

Biting Your Tongue: *Feel free to use these figures in your sales presentation. I use them all the time. If your company's growing at an annual rate of 75%, congratulations. If it isn't, juggle the numbers so it looks as though it is.*

PART THREE

FRUITS: ADVERTISING AND PUBLICITY

P.T. Barnum said, "There's a sucker born every minute." Well, you won't need a sucker to sell your wares with the great brochures, flyers, catalogs, coupons, and response cards you'll find in this section.

Even if you're not in the sales or advertising field, you'll find plenty of recipes you can use, such as eye-catching garage sale signs, professional-looking newsletters, and bookmarks.

And if you're the "sucker" who got stuck planning this year's company picnic or other major event, help is on the way with fun invitations, name tags, bulletin board notices, and maps.

5 min.

Easy

ADVERTISING FLYER

An advertising flyer is handy in all kinds of situations, whether it's a business flyer, a school event flyer, or even a flyer for a yard sale—there's no end to its use. With WordPerfect's TextArt and Draw features, you can make flyers with flair in a few simple steps. Advertising flyers are a great way to show off your creativity!

PREPARATION

Insert a graphic.

1. Click on Figure button. • Select PIANO.WPG. • Click OK.

2. Click on Border/Fill button on Graphics Box Feature Bar. • Border Style: None. • Click OK.

3. Click on Wrap button. • Select Contour. • Click OK.

4. Resize figure. • Drag it into place.

Insert text box.

5. Click on text box button.

6. Font Face: ShelleyVolante BT. • Font Size: 48. • Type: The Sound of Music...

7. Resize text box if necessary; drag it into place next to piano graphic. (See the next figure.)

Type in the ad text.

8. Click the cursor outside of the text box. • Press Enter key until cursor is below the text box you inserted in steps 5–7. • Font Face: Arrus Blk BT, Souvenir, or similar font. • Font Size: 18. • Click on Bold button. • Type in ad text to wrap around right side of piano graphic.

9. To type in last three lines of text, press Enter to move cursor below piano graphic. • 1st line, Font Size: 24. • 2nd line, Font Size: 18. • Press cursor twice to move 3rd line down, Font Size: 12. • Justification: Center. (See the next figure.)

Wilkin's piano sale - a once a year event.
Two days only....Saturday and Sunday....April 9th and 10th.

Wilkin's Music ◆ 15 West Washington Boulevard ◆ Indianapolis, Indiana

Chef's Tip To insert a bullet (round dot), as shown in the last line of this project, select Insert Character and Typographic Symbols. Choose the bullet/circle (see the next figure). Click on Insert and Close to exit the box.

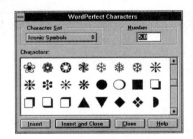

10. Save and print your flyer.

VARIATIONS

Get the News Out: *You can also turn an advertising flyer into a newspaper ad. To create a newspaper display ad, first set the document page to the dimensions used in your local paper. Then, build your ad within those dimensions. Print out your ad on a quality laser printer and presto chango!*

BOOKMARK WITH LOGO

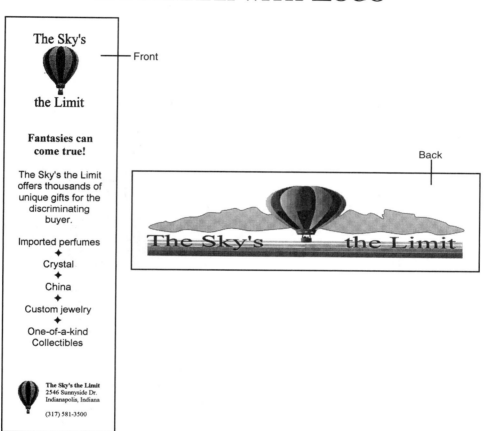

While bookmarks are certainly useful for marking your place in the latest John Grisham or Danielle Steele novel, you might not have thought of using them to promote something. You can design a bookmark to advertise your business, promote an upcoming event, or help spread the word about an important school fund-raiser. Granted, you can't fit a lot of text onto a bookmark, but you can get your message across—and at a fairly low cost at that. Here's a relatively simple idea for a bookmark advertising a gift shop.

PREPARATION

Create a bookmark size.

1. Select Layout. • Select Page. • Select Paper Size. • Click on Create button. • Paper Name: bookmark. • Paper Size options: 2" by 8". • Click OK. • Click Select.

2. Select Layout. • Select Margins. • All margins: .25". • Click OK.

Insert a graphic or logo.

 3. Click on Figure button. • From list of graphics, select your logo, or another clip art graphic. • Click OK.

4. Resize inserted graphic; drag to fit in top portion of your bookmark. (See the next figure.)

5. Click on Border/Fill button on the Graphics Box Feature Bar. • Border Style: None. • Click OK. • Click Close.

Type in text.

   6. Move cursor below graphic and type in bookmark text (see the next figure). • Font Face: Arial. • Font Size: 12. • Justification: Center.

Chef's Tip To get the diamond symbols shown in this project's text, select Insert Character and Typographic Symbols. Click on the diamond shape. Click on Insert and Close to exit the box.

Create a bookmark backside.

 7. To create a backside for your bookmark, move to next page of your document by pressing Ctrl+Enter. • Click on Figure button. • Select your logo or graphic from list. • Click OK.

8. Click the right mouse button. • Select Image Tools. • Click on Rotate button. • Rotate image. (See the next figure.) • Resize graphic as necessary.

Rotate tool

Two-page view

9. Save and print your bookmark.

VARIATIONS

Bookmarks with Bite: *Use WordPerfect's TextArt tool to insert interesting text shapes into your bookmark, then rotate them with the Rotate tool to fill the space. Or use scissors to cut out interesting shapes, such as scallops, along the edges of the paper. Don't forget to add yarn or braided string through a hole cut out of the top of the bookmark to give it visual appeal. To keep your bookmarks sturdy, take them to a professional printing shop to have them copied onto heavier-weight paper, or laminate them with plastic.*

BROCHURE WITH LOGO

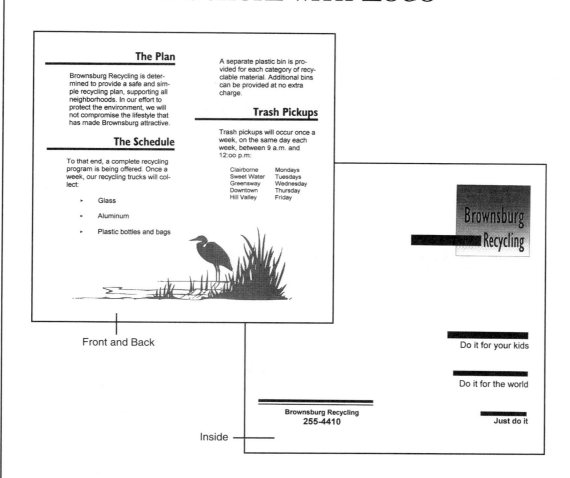

Front and Back

Inside

A brochure is the perfect tool for presenting more information about a company, organization, or educational curriculum. As with any other visual material, design is the heart of the message. A good brochure design makes its information attractive, easy to read, and even easier to follow. This project recipe presents a folded two-column design that's simple and appealing to the eye. You'll find steps for creating both the inside and outside of this brochure.

PREPARATION

Create paper size and column format.

1. Select Layout. • Select Page. • Select Paper Size. • Click on Create button. • Paper Name: Brochure 2-fold. • Paper Size: 8 1/2" by 8 1/2". • Click OK. • Click Select.

2. Select Layout. • Select Margins. • All margins: .5". • Click OK.

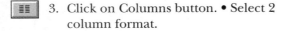 3. Click on Columns button. • Select 2 column format.

Create outside page of brochure.

4. Press Enter several times to move to bottom of 1st column. • Select Graphics. • Select Custom Line. • Line style: Thick/Thin 1. • Line thickness: .153". • Click OK. (See the next figure.)

Custom line

Brownsburg Recycling
255-4410

5. Type in text below line. • Font Face: Arial. • Font Size: 18. • Click on Bold button. • Justification: Center. • Type company name. • Font Size: 24. • Type telephone number.

Create logo.

6. Click on Draw button. • Select File. • Select Page Layout. • Page width: 2". • Height: 1.5". • Click OK.

7. Select Attributes. • Select Fill. • Fill Type: Gradient. • Center Color: gray. • Outer Color: white. • Click OK.

 8. Select Rectangle tool. • Draw a rectangle in drawing area (see the next figure).

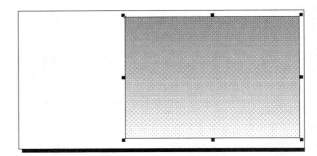

9. Select Text. • Select Font. • Font Face: Humanst 521 Cn BT. • Font Size: 36. • Click OK. • Select Text tool; click in drawing area. • Type: Brownsburg. • Click on Select tool; drag text into place. • Select Text • Select Font. • Font Face: Humanst 521 Cn BT. • Font Size: 36. • Select Text tool; click in drawing area. • Type: Recycling. • Click on Select tool; drag text into place.

10. Select Attributes. • Select Fill. • Fill Type: Pattern. • Foreground Color: black. • Click OK.

11. Click on Rectangle tool. • Draw a rectangle shaped like a bar. • Click on Select tool; drag the bar into place (see the next figure).

12. Select File. • Select Exit and Return to Document. • Select Yes.

13. Right-click and select Wrap. • Select No Wrap. • Click OK.

Add text to brochure cover page.

14. To add cover text, press Enter 25 times. • Font Face: Arial. • Font Size: 18. • Justification: Right. • Click on Bold button. • Type 1st line, "Do it for your kids." • Press Enter four times. • Type 2nd line, "Do it for the world." • Press Enter four times. • Type 3rd line, "Just do it."

Add graphic lines.

15. Select Graphics. • Select Custom Line. • Line style: Single. • Thickness: .198". • Click OK. • Drag line above "Do it for your kids."

16. Repeat step 15 to set next two graphic lines, changing line thickness each time to .159" and .123".

17. Click cursor below 3rd line of text. • Press Ctrl+Enter to move to page 2 of brochure.

Create inside page.

18. Select Layout. • Select Watermark. • Select Watermark A. • Click on Create button. • Click on Placement button on Feature Bar. • Select Even Pages. • Click OK. • Click on Figure button. • Select MARSH.WPG. • Click OK. • Click on Position button. • Vertical placement: .002" from bottom margin. • Click OK. • Click Close.

19. Font Face: Humanst 521 Cn BT. • Font Size: 24. • Justification: Right. • Type first headline.

20. Select Graphics. • Select Custom Line. • Line thickness: .063". • Click OK.

21. Press Enter twice; type in text. • Select View. • Select Ruler. • Drag left paragraph margin markers in 1/2" from margin (see the next figure). • Font Face: Arial. • Font Size: 14. • Justification: Left.

Drag the paragraph margin markers to indent the paragraph.

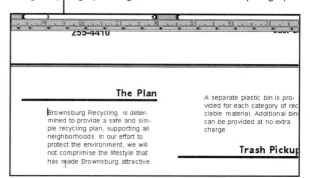

22. Repeat steps 19–21 for rest of headings, graphics lines, and text in brochure. • Before adding each new heading and graphics line, drag the margin back to its original position.

23. Save and print your brochure.

VARIATIONS

Could You Use Some Shading? *Another way to add more emphasis to the headers in this brochure is to add shaded, or screened, text boxes behind the header text and ruled lines. Simply add a text box, click on the Border/Fill button on the Feature Bar, and change the Fill Options pattern to a 10% screen fill. Make sure the Border Style is set to None. Also, click on the Wrap button, and change the option to No Wrap. Then, resize the text box to encompass the header text and the ruled line.*

BROCHURE WITH THREE COLUMNS

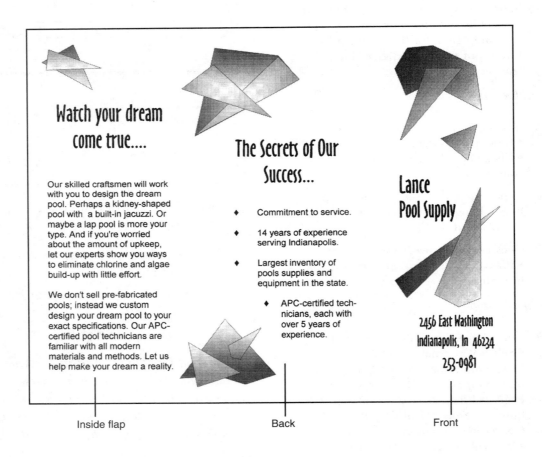

Watch your dream come true....

Our skilled craftsmen will work with you to design the dream pool. Perhaps a kidney-shaped pool with a built-in jacuzzi. Or maybe a lap pool is more your type. And if you're worried about the amount of upkeep, let our experts show you ways to eliminate chlorine and algae build-up with little effort.

We don't sell pre-fabricated pools; instead we custom design your dream pool to your exact specifications. Our APC-certified pool technicians are familiar with all modern materials and methods. Let us help make your dream a reality.

The Secrets of Our Success...

♦ Commitment to service.

♦ 14 years of experience serving Indianapolis.

♦ Largest inventory of pools supplies and equipment in the state.

   ♦ APC-certified tech-nicians, each with over 5 years of experience.

Lance Pool Supply

2456 East Washington
Indianapolis, In 46234
253-0981

Inside flap   Back   Front

A tri-fold brochure is another type of design you can create using WordPerfect for Windows. In this project idea, many shapes are used to add interest to the design. They are softly patterned with a gradient screen or shading. Look complicated? They are, slightly. But they sure add to the design of the brochure.

PREPARATION

Change paper size and columns.

1. Select Layout. • Select Page. • Paper Size: Letter Landscape. • Click Select.

2. Click on Columns button on Power Bar. • Select 3 columns from the list.

Create the inner fold page.

3. Font Face: OzHandicraft BT. • Font Size: 36. • Justification: Center. • Type header. • Press Enter two times.

4. Font Face: Arial. • Font Size: 14. • Justification: Left. • Type text (see the next figure). • Press Ctrl+Enter to move to the next column.

Watch your dream come true....

Our skilled craftsmen will work with you to design the dream pool. Perhaps a kidney-shaped

Create the back fold page.

5. Font Face: OzHandicraft BT. • Font Size: 36. • Justification: Center. • Type header. • Press Enter two times.

6. Type in body text. • Font Face: Arial. • Font Size: 14. • Justification: Left. • Click on Bullet button. • Select Diamond. • Click OK. • Type text. • Repeat to enter more bullets for new text lines. • Press Ctrl+Enter to move to cover page column (the last column on the right).

Create the tri-fold cover.

7. Click on Draw button. • Select File. • Select Page Layout. • Width: 3". • Height: 8". • Click OK.

8. Select Text. • Select Font. • Font Face: OzHandicraft BT. • Font Size: 46. • Click OK.

9. Click on Text tool. • Click in place where type should appear. • Type in company name. • Press Enter. • Select Text. • Select Font. • Font Size: 42. • Click OK. • Click on Text tool again. • Click in place; type remaining company name. • Press Enter. • You may have to select text line and move into place.

10. Select Text. • Select Font. • Font Size: 28. • Click OK. • Click on Text tool. • Click in place; type address and phone number lines. • When finished, select text lines and drag into place. (See the next figure.)

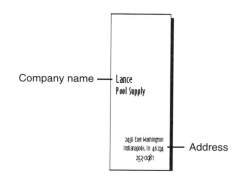

11. Select Attributes. • Select Fill. • Select Gradient. • Center Color: gray. • Outer Color: white. • Angle: 55. • Click OK.

12. Click on Polygon tool. • Draw shapes (see the next figure). • When drawing each shape, change the Angle and Color options. • When finished, select File. • Select Exit and Return to Document. • Click Yes.

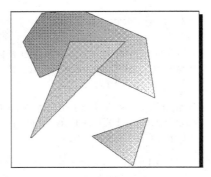

Add the finishing touches.

 13. Click on Draw button to add additional graphic objects, and repeat steps 11 and 12. • Change Page Layout settings each time to reflect the size of the finished graphic.

14. When finished with last column, press Ctrl+Enter to create a new page for the flip side of brochure. • Here you can add more text and shapes as needed (see the next figure.)

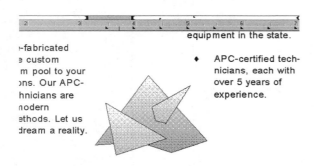

equipment in the state.

-fabricated
e custom
m pool to your
ns. Our APC-
hnicians are
nodern
ethods. Let us
dream a reality.

♦ APC-certified tech-
nicians, each with
over 5 years of
experience.

15. After both sides of the tri-fold brochure are complete, save and print brochure. • Copy brochure with a copier using both pages to create a front and back for the brochure.

VARIATIONS

Shape Up! *Try placing some object shapes between the columns so they bend over the fold. That will really add some interest to the pages. Or, instead of random shapes, try multiple watermarks that are shaded and off to the sides in the background of the design. These can be especially effective going across the folds and columns of the brochure.*

 Cook's Caution   Careful—Don't get carried away with too many floating shapes in your brochure. They can cause your design to look busy, making text hard to read and drawing the reader's attention away from important information.

BULLETIN BOARD NOTICE

What's the matter? Can't get enough people to sign up for your office exercise class? Need a sign that catches attention in a hallway or on a wall? You need a bulletin board notice with visual impact. WordPerfect's powerful Draw program lets you combine text and graphics to get your message across. Best of all, you don't have to go to a lot of trouble to do it. Here's an easy workout for a simple, yet striking bulletin board notice design.

PREPARATION

Design your message.

 1. Click on Draw button. • Select File. • Select Page Layout. • Width: 10". • Height: 7.5". • Click OK.

 2. Click on Fill Color tool. • Color: black. • Click on Rectangle tool. • Draw horizontal rectangle across drawing area.

 3. Click on Fill Color tool. • Color: gray. • Click on Rectangle tool. • Draw square-like shape on top of bar shape (see the next figure). • You may have to reposition or resize the box to fit.

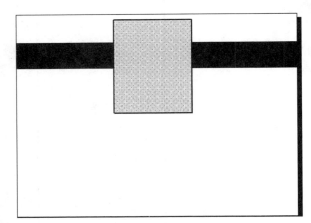

 4. Select Text. • Select Font. • Font Face: Impact, Futura Md BT, Swiss721 BlkEx BT, or a similar style. • Font Size: 72. • Click OK. • Click on Text tool. • Click on Text tool on the drawing screen where you want to type text. • Type: DO. • Press Enter. • Type: IT. • Press Enter. • Resize to fit text into box (see the next figure).

 5. Click on Fill Color tool. • Color: black. • Click on Ellipse tool. • Draw the two parts of an exclamation point. (See the next figure.)

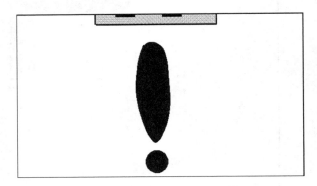

Place art in document.

6. Select File. • Select Exit and Return to Document. • Click Yes.

7. Select Layout. • Select Margins. • Margins: .25" on all sides. • Click OK.

8. Click on art and resize to fit page, leaving room at the bottom for a line of text.

Add text line.

 9. Font Face: Arial. • Font Size: 24. • Click on Bold button. • Justification: Center. • At the bottom of document page, type rest of notice.

Chef's Tip   To set the bullets in the text line, as shown in this project, select Insert Character. Select Typographic Symbols. Scroll through, and click on the circle shape. Then click on Insert and Close to exit the box (see the next figure).

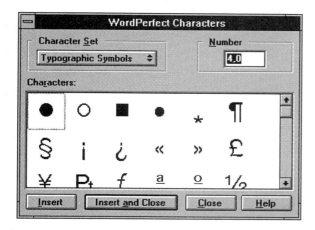

VARIATIONS

Frame It!   *Add custom borders to your notices using the WordPerfect clip art files. You'll find a selection of borders by clicking on the Figure button and scrolling through the list. Take a preview look by highlighting the graphic file name and clicking on the View button. Click on Select when you've found one you want. You can also use the Layout, Page, Border/Fill command to add a ruled line border to your document.*

BUTTONS

Another form of advertising and publicity is the simple pin-it-on-and-wear-it button that is popular for campaigning, fund-raising, and more. Mind you, you won't be able to fit an entire essay on a button; however, you can fit a few choice words to get your point across. This is an easy project that is limited only by your imagination.

PREPARATION

Start with some TextArt

 1. Click on TextArt button. • Font Face: Times New Roman, Amerigo BT, or similar font. • Select Bold style. • Type in text (all capital letters). • Select bottom right TextArt shape. • Width: 3". • Height: 3" (see the next figure). • Select File. • Select Exit & Return to WordPerfect. • Click Yes. • Resize object as needed.

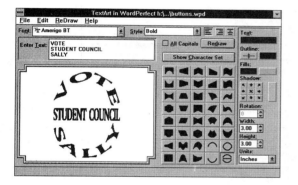

 Chef's Tip If you have a color printer, you can pick a color for your text while you're in the TextArt dialog box.

Add a nifty background pattern.

2. Click the right mouse button. • Select Border/Fill. • Fill Style: Waves. • Click OK (see the next figure).

3. Save and print your button. • When printed, use scissors to trim around edges. • Apply to button pin.

VARIATIONS

Button Up: *Take your button project to a professional printer or advertising materials rep to make plastic buttons. Some schools have their own "button making machines." See if yours does. Or if you've got absolutely no budget to do that, mass produce your buttons, printing several on a page, and use tape to adhere them to lapels.*

Politics As Usual: *Use the Draw feature to turn your buttons into a patriotic work of art. In the example shown here, stars and stripes were created using the drawing tools. Try your own campaign button variation on this.*

BUSINESS   ORGANIZATION   HOME   SCHOOL

Moderate

CALENDAR OF MONTHLY EVENTS

Time flies when you're having fun, and even when you're not. Use WordPerfect to make monthly calendars detailing events, appointments, holidays, and more. This design uses a watermark with a theme relating to the month. Obviously, you will want to substitute appropriate graphics for your own calendar.

PREPARATION

Set up the template.

1. Click on Template button. • Select CAL_SIDE.WPT. • Click OK. • Specify month and year. • Click OK.

Insert a watermark.

2. Click on Watermark button. • Select Watermark A. • Select Create.

3. Click on Figure button. • Select OCTBFEST.WPG or another graphic. • Click OK. • Click Close (see the next figure). • Click Close again.

Cook's Caution You may want to move your watermark before you click on the Close button. For a better overall view, click on Zoom button on the Power Bar and select Full Page view.

Apply the finishing touches.

4. Type monthly calendar events in appropriate date boxes (see the next figure). (I used Humanst Cn BT 18 pt.) • To move from day to day, press arrow keys or click in next box.

5. Save and print your calendar.

VARIATIONS

Not Enough Art? *If you can't find enough WordPerfect graphics to use in your calendars, try creating your own with the Draw feature.*

Shrink It: *Another idea is to miniaturize the graphic objects to fit inside a calendar day box. For example, if you have a birthday cake graphic, you can place it inside the box on the day of someone's birthday.*

CATALOG

Joe's Computer Store

Word Processing

WordPerfect 6.0 for Windows

➥ Button Bars for quick command access.

➥ WP Draw - create your own art!

➥ TextArt - create stunning text effects

Item number: 10-24589
Price: $310 **Upgrade:** $89

Word 6.0 for Windows

➥ Quick Menus speed access to often used commands.

➥ Graphing and charting

➥ Microsoft Draw - create your own art!

Item number: 10-24589
Price: $299 **Upgrade:** $119

1

Here's a great idea for businesses, clubs, and schools—make a catalog of products or classes for your clients or members. Why pay a printing shop oodles of money for something you can do with your own computer? If you create your own catalog, you can write detailed product information, add product photos or illustrations, and even tag on an order sheet at the end of the catalog. This particular project shows one catalog page set up to sell computer products.

PREPARATION

Set up your catalog.

1. Select Layout. • Select Page. • Select Binding/Duplex. • Binding Width: Right. • Amount: .5". • Click OK.

Add a header to the top of each page.

2. Select Layout. • Select Header/Footer. • Select Header A. • Click on Create. • Font Face: Arrus Blk BT, Times New Roman, GeoSlab 703 Md Cn BT, or similar font. • Font Size: 24. • Click on Bold button. • Type company name (see the next figure).

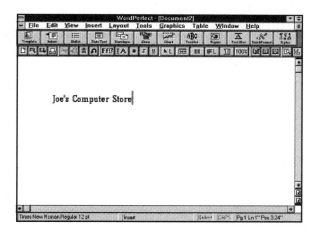

3. Click on Placement button. • Select Odd pages. • Click OK.

4. Click on Draw button. • Select File. • Select Page Layout. • Size: 1" by 1". • Click OK. • Click on Closed Curve tool. • Select Fill Color tool. • Color: light gray. • Draw shape pointing to the left (see the next figure). • Select File. • Select Exit and Return to Document. • Click Yes.

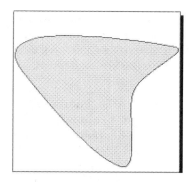

5. While shape is highlighted, click the right mouse button. • Choose Wrap. • Select No Wrap. • Click OK. • Move shape over company name (see the next figure). • Click on the Copy button. Click on the Close button.

6. Press Ctrl + Enter to move to page two. • Repeat Step 2. • Justification: Right. • Click on Placement button. • Select Even pages. • Click OK.

7. Click inside header. • Click on the Paste button. • Place mouse pointer over shape. • Click right mouse button. • Choose Select Box. • Click on Tools button on the Graphics Box Feature Bar. • Click on Mirror Vertical tool. • Drag shape into place. • Click Close button twice. • Return to page one.

Create catalog text.

8. Click on Text Box button. • Click on Border/Fill button on Graphics Box Feature Bar. • Border Style: Thin Top/ Bottom. • Fill Style: Gradient 2. • Foreground Color: medium gray. • Click OK.

9. Type in heading text. • Font Face: Arial, Futura Md BT, or a similar font. • Font Size: 18. • Click on Close button. • Resize the box as needed.

10. Type in body text. • For product name, Font Face: Arial, Futura Md BT, or a similar font. • Font Size: 18. • For product bullet points, Font Face: Arial. • Font Size: 12. • Click on Bullet button. • Select Triangle. • Click OK. • Type in selling information, repeating bullet step when needed. • For item number text, change font back and forth between Bold and Normal for easy reading.

Add catalog boxes for illustrations or photos.

11. Select Graphics. • Select Custom Box. • Select Figure. • Click OK. • Resize box to fit beside catalog description. • Unselect box and press Enter twice.

12. Select Graphics. • Select Horizontal Line.

13. Repeat steps 10–12 to add items.

Finish up with a footer.

14. Select Layout. • Select Header/Footer. • Select Footer A. • Click Create. • Click on Number button. • Select Page Number. • Click Paste button to copy header graphic into footer.

15. Right-click and select Wrap. • Select No Wrap. • Click OK. • Move shape over page number. • Click on Placement button. • Select Odd Pages. • Click OK. • Click on Close button to exit the footer.

16. Repeat steps 14–15 for even page footers. • Select Even Pages in step 15. • Using Mirror Vertical tool, flip graphic so it points to the right.

17. Save and print your catalog.

VARIATIONS

Best-Sellers: *To draw attention to special products, such as best-sellers or award winners, use an appropriate graphic element scaled down in size. For example, the WordPerfect graphic CREST.WPG has a blue ribbon look with a space for text, such as "Voted #1." Once it's created, you can place this graphic over a photo, illustration, or scanned image.*

CONFERENCE ANNOUNCEMENT FLYER

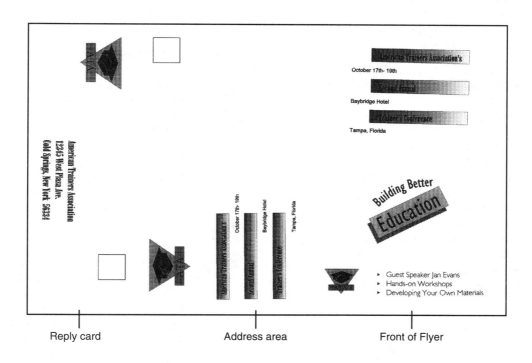

Reply card   Address area   Front of Flyer

One of the best and most effective ways of announcing an upcoming conference, seminar, family gathering, or event is by sending out a professional-looking flyer or brochure detailing important information. This project shows you the steps for creating a tri-fold, design-oriented brochure/flyer combination on legal-sized paper. Use one tri-fold page to contain all of the pertinent information, just like a regular flyer. Use the other tri-fold page (shown in this project) to make a cover, mailing label address, and reply card. The reply card is flap-fold for a registration card that is meant to be mailed back.

PREPARATION

Set up the mailer.

1. Select Layout. • Select Page. • Select Paper Size. • Select Legal Landscape. • Click Select.

2. Select Layout. • Select Margins. • Set all to .25". • Click OK.

 3. Click on Columns button. • Select 3 column format. • Using the ruler, reset the column margins to 3.75 and 8.75 (see the next figure).

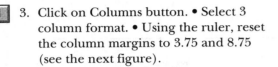

Create the reply card.

 4. Click on Figure button. • Select your logo. • Click OK. • Click on figure. • Click on Border/Fill button on Graphics Box Feature Bar. • Border Style: None. • Click OK. • Click the right mouse button. • Click on Image Tools button. • Click on Rotate tool. • Rotate logo (see the next figure). • Resize logo to fit. • Click Close on the Feature Bar.

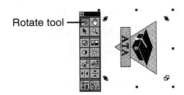
Rotate tool

5. Click on Draw button. • Select File. • Select Page Layout. • Page size: 5" by 3". • Click OK. • Select Text. • Select Font. • Font Face: Onyx BT. • Font Size: 36. • Click OK. • Click on Text tool. • Click in drawing area and type address text. • Press Enter.

6. Select Edit. • Choose Select. • Select All. • Select Edit. • Select Rotate. • Rotate text to face left. • Select File. • Select Exit and Return to Document. • Click Yes.

 Chef's Tip Add a small text box for a postage stamp outline. Just position where needed on page. (You may have to change the Wrap to No Wrap if text is near the box.) Change the Border/Fill to a thin line style.

Set up the address area.

 7. Select the logo inserted in step 4. • Click on Copy button. • Press Ctrl+Enter to move to 2nd column (address area) of tri-fold design. • Click the cursor on the page. • Click on Paste button. • Drag logo to lower left corner. • Click the right mouse button. • Select Image Tools. • Click on Rotate tool. • Rotate logo to face right.

 8. Click on Draw button. • Select File. • Select Page Layout. • Page size: 6" by 6". • Click OK. • Select Attributes. • Select Fill. • Fill Type: Gradient. • Center Color: medium gray. • Outer Color: white. • Angle: 90. • Click OK. • Click on Rectangle tool. • Click in drawing area; draw a rectangle shape.

9. After drawing first shape, select it. • Select Edit. • Select Duplicate. • Drag new shape next to the first (see the next figure). • Repeat sequence again to create third rectangle, dragging it into place (see the next figure).

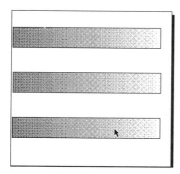

 10. Select Text. • Select Font. • Font Face: Onyx BT. • Font Size: 36. • Click OK. • Click on Text tool. • In each rectangular box, type in conference titles.

11. Select Text. • Select Font. • Font Face: Arial. • Font Size: 20. • Click OK. • Click on Text tool. • Between rectangular boxes, type in date and place information, as shown.

12. Select Edit. • Choose Select. • Choose Select All. • Select Edit menu again. • Select Rotate. • Rotate to face right.

13. Select File. • Select Exit and Return to Document. • Click Yes. • Click on figure and drag block to lower right corner, below logo. • Click on Copy button.

Set up the cover fold page.

14. Press Ctrl+Enter to move to 3rd column. • Click pointer in 3rd column. • Click on Paste button. • Double-click the selected copy to open the Draw feature.

15. In Draw, select Edit. • Choose Select. • Choose Select All. • Select Edit. • Select Rotate. • Rotate block back to horizontal position. • Drag each text line and box and move to opposite side of where it was originally positioned, as shown in this figure.

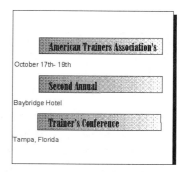

16. Select File. • Select Exit and Return to Document. • Click Yes to save changes in document.

17. Select logo from one of other tri-fold areas. • Click on Copy button. • Move pointer to cover fold page. • Click pointer anywhere on page. • Click on Paste button. • Click the right mouse button. • Select Image Tools. • Click the Rotate tool. • Rotate logo to horizontal position. • Resize logo as needed. • Move to the bottom left corner of cover page.

18. For rest of brochure, create your own slogan; add any additional text.

Chef's Tip You can easily design a catchy logo, such as the "Building Better Education" one shown here, using Draw.

19. Press Ctrl+Shift+Enter to open another document page. • Reverse column margin settings for back page of flyer; set at 6" and 11". • Type conference details or highlights, or add a map in any of the first two columns. • In the last column, design a mail-in reply card that fits with fold page you built with steps 4–6.

20. When finished, save and print your flyer.

VARIATIONS

Add More Stuff! *With this design, you can be very creative. Try adding shaded watermarks that extend across folds. Or make a dotted graphic line and place where your recipient should cut out the reply card. You're limited only by your imagination!*

COUPONS

Bargains, bargains, bargains! Nothing pulls in business like money-saving coupons. Not only do they bring in new customers, they are also a good way to show seasoned customers that you care about their patronage. The following coupon project incorporates your logo. Depending upon your type of business or sale, you may want to emphasize the coupon price, amount saved, or a particular product.

PREPARATION

Begin with a border.

1. Click on Figure button. • Select BORD05L.WPG. • Click OK. • Click on figure. • Right-click and choose Border/Fill. • Border Style: None. • Click OK.

2. Double-click selected border figure. • Click on Text tool. • Click Font button. • Font Face: Brush 738 BT. • Font Size: 72. • Click OK. • Click inside the border. • Type: Sale! • When finished, resize text block to make it bigger.

3. Select Edit. • Select Rotate. • Rotate text at an angle (see the next figure).

4. Click on Insert Figure tool. • Drag to create area for logo. • Select logo from list of graphic files. • Click Retrieve. • Move logo into place.

5. Click on Text tool. • Click Font button. • Font Face: Humanst 521 Cn BT, CopprplGoth Hv BT, AvantGarde Bk BT, or similar font. • Font Size: 48. • Click OK. • Click tool in drawing area; type in text. • Add additional lines for coupon limitations and expiration date. • Move text to desired place in coupon (see the next figure).

6. Select File. • Select Exit and Return to Document. • Click Yes to save changes.

7. Save and print your coupon.

VARIATIONS

Copy, Copy! *Repeat these project steps to place several coupons on one document page if you're going to copy and distribute the coupons yourself. Or just take your single coupon to a professional printing shop, and have it copied onto colored paper for added emphasis.*

Front and Back: *Don't forget to design a back to your coupon. Try a giant dollar sign design, or use a fancy border. You might also add a map to the back of the coupon, showing your store's location.*

CUSTOMER RESPONSE CARD

Return
Postage
Guaranteed

Alphabet Soup
201 West 103rd Street
Indianapolis, Indiana 46290

We care about what you think!

❏ Single
❏ Married

❏ Under 25
❏ 25-35
❏ 36-45
❏ Over 45

Visits last 6 months:
❏ 0 times
❏ 1-2 times
❏ 3 or more times

I was asked if I needed help.
❏ Yes   ❏ No

I found what I wanted without trouble.
❏ Yes   ❏ No

Items I would like to see you carry:
❏ Braun Kitchenware
❏ Voegle Knives
❏ Watkins Spices
❏ Paper products such as napkins, plates
   Other _____

This project is a clever idea for gauging customer response. It's a mailable customer response card. One side contains mailing information, and the flip side can contain store service feedback, buyer information, or even a grading scale.

PREPARATION

Set up your page and add a border.

1. Select Layout. • Select Page. • Select Paper Size. • Click on Create button. • Paper Name: Index Cards. • Paper Size: 3" by 5". • Select Wide Form. • Click OK. • Click Select.

2. Select Layout. • Select Margins. • Margins: .02" on all four sides. • Click OK.

3. Select Layout. • Select Page. • Select Border/Fill. • Select Hairline Border Style. • Click OK.

Add your logo and address.

4. Press Enter to move cursor to middle of card. • Click on Figure button. • Select your logo. • Click OK. • Click on Border/Fill button. • Border Style: None. • Click OK. • Click on Close button. • Move logo to middle of card. • Use ruler to adjust left margin to middle of card.

5. Font Face: Times New Roman. • Font Size: 12. • Justification: Left. • Type company name beside logo. • Type address beneath logo (see the next figure).

6. Click on Text Box button. • Click on Border/Fill button on Feature Bar. • Border Style: Hairline. • Click OK. • Font Face: Times New Roman. • Font Size: 10. • Justification: Center. • Type in postal information, such as permit number. • Resize and move to top-right corner (see the next figure).

7. Press Ctrl+Shift+Enter to start back of response card. • Select Layout. • Select Page. • Select Border/Fill. • Border Style: Hairline. • Click OK.

8. Font Face: Brush 738 BT. • Font Size: 18. • Type the headline.

9. Font Face: Arial. • Font Size: 10. • Select Insert. • Select Character. • Select Iconic Symbols. • Select check box symbol (see the next figure). • Click Insert. • Click in document; type first question.

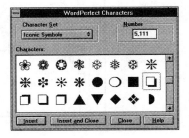

10. Click Insert to add next check box.
    • Click in document to type question.
    • Repeat, adding the rest of the questions (see the next figure). • Click Close to close the dialog box.

11. Save and print your project.

 Chef's Tip If you need a blank line for writing on as part of your question text, use the Custom Line feature to add a line. Simply select Graphics Custom Line. Set the length to 1" or 1.5". When finished, click OK, and use pointer to move line wherever you want it to go.

VARIATIONS

More Responses: *Take both sides of your response card to a professional printer and have them copied onto a post card for easy mailing. If you're going to mail them in bulk, be sure to put your permit number on the card. Another idea is to use preprinted labels, such as those created from a customer database, to know exactly which customer the card is from. See Part One for help creating custom labels.*

INFORMATIONAL SIGN—GARAGE SALE

GARAGE SALE
FRI/SAT   9-5
2019 E. Willow

One man's junk is another man's treasure, so they say. One way to make your junk stand out from the rest is with some spiffy signs made with your WordPerfect program. Here's a simple garage sale sign you can post in and around your neighborhood. (This will look a lot better than those hand-drawn signs written in crayon!) There's only one rule to follow: keep it simple.

PREPARATION

Set up the paper size.

1. Select Layout. • Select Page. • Select Paper Size. • Select Letter Landscape. • Click Select.

2. Select Layout. • Select Margins. • Margins: .5" on all four sides. • Click OK.

Add a border and TextArt.

3. Select Layout. • Select Page. • Select Border/Fill. • Border Style: Thick/Thin 2. • Click OK.

4. Click on TextArt button. • Font Face: Swis721 Blk Ex BT, Boulder, or a similar font. • Justification: Center. • Type: Garage Sale. (See the next figure.) • Select File. • Select Exit & Return to WordPerfect. • Click Yes.

5. Click on TextArt and place at top of document; resize to fill entire space (see the next figure).

Add a text box.

6. Click on Text Box button. • Click on Border/Fill button on Feature Bar. • Border Style: None. • Click OK.

7. Move text box below TextArt object. • Resize text box to fit in lower half of document (see the next figure).

8. Type in text lines. • Font Face: Arial, Univers, or a similar font. • Double-click on Font Size button. • Font Size: 72. • Bold the 2nd line. • Justification: Center.

VARIATIONS

More Flash: *To really get your signs to stand out, copy or print them onto colored paper. Be sure to select a color that lets the text or art stand out clearly. It's also a good idea to laminate the signs if posting outdoors.*

INFORMATIONAL SIGN—LOST PET

Making signs to use in and around your neighborhood is another good way to put WordPerfect to work. Signs are easy to create and can help you get the word out about a lost pet, a car for sale, a lemonade stand, and more. The best approach for creating signs is to keep them simple. Try not to cram too many words or images onto a sign that is meant to be read from a distance. The following project is an easy way to create a lost pet sign that catches the eye.

PREPARATION

Set up the paper size.

1. Select Layout. • Select Page. • Select Paper Size. • Select Letter Landscape. • Click Select.

Add a graphic.

2. Click on Figure button. • Select graphic. • Click OK.

Chef's Tip   I wanted a cat silhouette, so I used a clip art file of a cat from another program. If you can't locate a graphic of a lost pet, use WordPerfect Draw to create a simple silhouette, or use the graphic tools to reset the brightness level of a graphic to turn it into a silhouette.

3. Resize graphic using the mouse (see the next figure). • Click on Wrap button on Feature Bar. • Select No Wrap option. • Click OK.

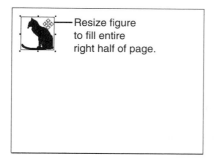

Resize figure to fill entire right half of page.

4. Click on TextArt button. • Font Face: Arrus Blk BT, CooperBlack WP, or a similar font. • Type: LOST. • Select File. • Select Exit & Return to WordPerfect. • Click Yes. • Click on figure and resize. • Place in upper left corner of document page.

5. Click on Text Box button. • Click on the Border/Fill button on Feature Bar. • Border Style: None. • Click OK.

6. Font Face: Arial, Univers, or similar font. • Font Size: 36. • Click on Bold button. • Justification: Center. • Type in details about lost pet (four lines are maximum at this point size).
   • Move box below TextArt object; resize to fit space (see the next figure).

7. Click on Text Box button again. • Click on Border/Fill button on Feature Bar. • Border Style: None. • Click OK.

8. Font Face: Arial. • Double-click on Font Size button. • Font Size: 55. • Click on Bold button. • Justification: Center. • Type in phone number. • Move box below first text box.

9. Save and print your sign.

VARIATIONS

Photo Finish: *Rather than insert a graphic image of the pet, why not use a real photograph? Take a recent picture of the pet to a photo shop and have enlargements made for your sign. Just attach a photo to each sign you make. Be sure to wrap or seal the sign in case of rain or heavy winds.*

INVITATION—OPEN HOUSE

Sun Realty, Inc. cordially invites you to a neighborhood open house on Sunday, May 29 at Westwick Farms subdivision in Sunblest.

There are four distinct and beautiful model homes to view, all are perfect for families and professional couples. Styles include 4-bedroom, 2-car garage, fireplace, and vaulted ceilings throughout.

Drop in anytime from 1:00 p.m. to 4:00 p.m. for refreshments, and detailed information about each home. Plus, a walk-thru tour of each model. Come on out and see how your community is growing!

Sun Realty, Inc.   3902 Magnolia Drive, Sunblest, AL 09490
Phone: (838) 000-0000   Fax: (838) 000-0000

If your company or organization ever holds an open house for clients or members, you may want to try this idea. Make a simple invitation flyer using WordPerfect's many formal font styles. In this project, I incorporated a company logo at the top of the invitation, and a company phone and address at the bottom. This makes an excellent mailer to clients or customers. This particular idea is tailored to a real estate office, but it would work equally well for a retail store. And, of course, you can use this idea to create an invitation to a gathering, reunion, or party.

PREPARATION

Insert a graphic.

 1. Click on Figure button. • Select SUN_DSG.WPG graphic file, or your own company logo. • Click OK.

2. Move graphic to top of page, leaving room for the company name above it (see the next figure). • Click on Border/Fill button on Feature Bar. • Border Style: None. • Click OK. • Click on the Size button. • Width: 2.71". • Height: 2.49". • Click OK.

Add a TextArt object.

 3. Click on TextArt button. • Font Face: Onyx BT, Broadway Engraved, or a similar font. • Justification: Center. • Select the arch shape. • Type your company name. • Select File. • Select Exit & Return to WordPerfect. • Click Yes.

4. Click on TextArt. • Resize to fit above graphic object placed in steps 1 and 2 (see the next figure).

Add body text and ruled lines.

   5. Type in body text. • Font: ShelleyVolante BT. • Font Size: 18. • Justification: Center.

 Cook's Caution When working with script fonts (fonts that look like they're written in cursive), avoid using all capital letters. These font styles were never intended to be used without lowercase letters. With all caps, they are difficult to read and rather sloppy looking.

 6. Click the Text Box button. • Click on Border/Fill button on Feature Bar. • Click on Customize Style. • Select sides to modify: Top. • Line Style: Gray Mat. • Click OK twice.

7. Type in company name, address, phone number. • Set company name in Font Face: Onyx BT, Broadway, or a similar font. • Font Size: 24. • Set address in Font Face: Arial. • Font Size: 12. • Click on Bold button. • Move address over to right margin by clicking the cursor in front of address and pressing Spacebar. • Set phone numbers on second line in Font Face: Arial. • Font Size: 14.

Add a horizontal rule beside the phone number.

8. Click the cursor on end of text line. • Select Graphics. • Select Custom Line. • Line: .25" thick. • Line Color: dark gray. • Click OK. • Resize to fit as needed.

Add a watermark.

9. Select Layout. • Select Watermark. • Click on Create button. • Click on Draw button.

10. Select Attributes. • Select Fill. • Fill Type: Gradient. • Center Color: orange. • Outer Color: white. • Click Line. • Select No Line. • Click OK twice.

11. Click on Ellipse tool; draw large circle in drawing area.

12. Click on Fill Color tool. • Fill Color: white. • Click on Line style tool; change to no line. • Click on Rectangle tool. • Draw empty box that covers bottom half of circle created in step 11 (see the next figure).

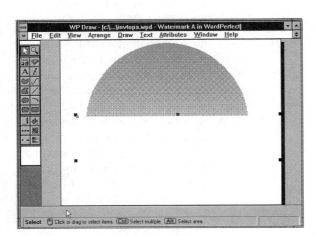

13. Select File. • Select Exit and Return to Document. • Click Yes to place graphic into document. • Back in Watermark window, select graphic. • Resize graphic background (see the next figure) to fit under logo you created in beginning of this project. • Click Close.

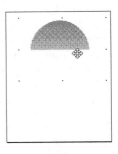

 Cook's Caution You'll probably have to go back and forth between the Watermark screen and the document to place the background under the logo the way you want it. This is a little tricky, but persevere! To edit this watermark, select Layout, Watermark, and click on the Edit button. This returns you to the Watermark window to make changes.

14. Save the flyer and print.

VARIATIONS

Run for the Borders: *Don't forget about WordPerfect's nifty border selection. You can use them to really set off a project like this one. Try to match a border to your invitation design, without distracting from the overall appearance. You can access and preview the borders using the GrphPgBrdr button on the Design Button Bar.*

BUSINESS   ORGANIZATION   HOME   SCHOOL

20 min.

Moderate

MAP TO AN EVENT

3rd Annual Telemarketing Conference
May 19-22
at Spearwick Springs

Join us for four days of market updates, techniques, and training at the beautiful Merrimack Conference Center. Package includes food, hotel, and recreational activities. Registration is absolutely necessary, so call now 1-800-000-0000.

LAKE SPEARWATER

I-465

HOLIDAY INN RESORT HOTEL

GROVE STREET

SPEARWATER GOLF COURSE

MERRIMACK CONFERENCE CENTER

MERRIMACK DRIVE

Would you believe you can use your word processing program to make maps? Yes, it's true, with the ever-so-resourceful Draw feature, you can create maps of all kinds. The ability to add a map to a flyer, invitation, or conference brochure will really come in handy. Maps will give your printed materials a professional look and communicate important information: directions. The following project idea incorporates a map onto a conference flyer.

PREPARATION

Build your map.

1. Click on Draw button. • Using Draw tools, create your map piece by piece. • Use the Line tool to draw simple straight-line streets. • Use the Curved Line tool to add any curved streets or highways. • Use Rectangle tool to add buildings. • Use Closed Curve tool to add waterways and golf courses; fill them in with patterns (see the next figure).

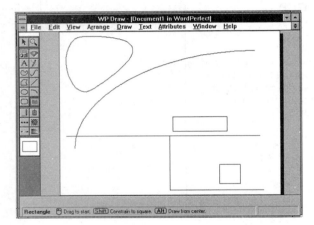

2. When map is completed, select File. • Select Exit and Return to Document. • Click Yes. • Select graphic and resize as needed to fill lower half of page (see the next figure).

Add map text with text boxes.

3. Click on Text Box button. • Click on Border/Fill button on Feature Bar. • Border Style: None. • Click OK.

4. Font Face: Arial. • Font Size: 12. • Click on Bold button. • Justification: Center. • Type in text. • Resize box as necessary; place in appropriate position on map (see the next figure).

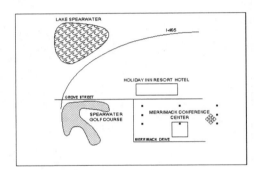

5. Repeat steps 3 and 4 for each text box needed.

Set rest of flyer.

6. Font Face: Arrus Blk BT or ChelmsfordBook WP. • Font Size: Heading=36, Date=24, and Body Text=20. • Justification: Center. • Type in event text at top of document page.

VARIATIONS

Map Mania: *Now that you know how easy it is to make maps, you'll be able to whip them up for party invitations, business brochures, and even buried treasure games for the kids. Use the Draw feature to create small artwork, such as trees, hills, rivers, and a compass.*

Advanced

MENU

If you own a restaurant or food service organization, use WordPerfect to create menus for breakfast, lunch, or dinner. As with all printed materials, visual appeal is the key to success. This project uses a variety of WordPerfect features to create a stylish art deco menu that captures a certain '50s flair. With the many shapes and fonts available, you can create menus ranging from formal to fun.

PREPARATION

Start with the menu text.

1. Select Layout. • Select Margins. • Set all sides at .5". • Click OK.

2. Type the menu body text, such as menu categories, items, and prices. • Set category headers in Font Face: Onyx BT or Broadway; Set body text in Font Face: Humanst 521 Lt BT or Moderne. • Category headers Font Size: 18; Body text Font Size: 12. • Be sure to use ruler to set tabs and leader tabs as needed. • Design shown will fit approximately 30 text lines (see the next figure).

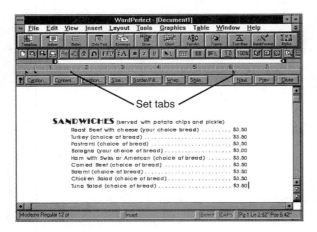

Position menu body text in the lower section of the page.

3. Click cursor at beginning of first text line. • Press Enter to move entire block down until it reaches just before the last line breaks to a new page.

Add a border and TextArt.

4. Select the Design Tools Button Bar. • Click on GrphPgBrdr button. • Page Border: Safety Border. • Click OK.

5. Click on TextArt button. • Font Face: Onyx BT or Broadway WP. • Justification: Center. • Select rounded top arch shape. • Type in restaurant name (see figure below). • Select File. • Select Exit & Return to WordPerfect. • Click Yes.

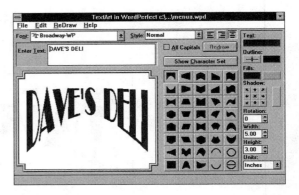

6. Select TextArt and resize to fit at top of document page.

Add text box tag line.

7. Click on Text Box button. • Click on Border/Fill button on Feature Bar. • Border Style: None. • Click OK.

8. Resize text box to fit below TextArt object. • Font Face: ShelleyVolante BT. • Font Size: 24. • Justification: Center. • Type in text, a restaurant tag line, for example.

Add text boxes to create sections in your menu.

9. Click on Text Box button. • Click on Border/Fill button on Feature Bar. • Border/Style: None. • Select Fill: 10%. • Click OK. • Click on Wrap button. • Select No Wrap. • Click OK. • Resize filled text box to fit over menu header (see the next figure). • Repeat this sequence for each menu header.

```
Pastrami (choice of bread).....................$3.50
Bologna (your choice of bread)....................$3.00
Ham with Swiss or American (choice of bread) ........$3.50
Corned Beef (choice of bread) ....................$3.50
Salami (choice of bread) ......................$3.50
Chicken Salad (choice of bread) ..................$3.50
Tuna Salad (choice of bread).....................$3.50

FROM THE GRILL (served with french fries)
Hamburger ...................................$4.50
Cheeseburger.................................$4.50
Reuben ......................................$4.50
Spinach Melt.................................$3.50
Tuna Melt....................................$3.50
Grilled Three Cheeses ........................$3.00
BBQ Chicken ................................$4.50
```

10. Save and print your menu.

 Cook's Caution   For best readability, stick with larger font sizes, especially if your clientele includes senior citizens. Nobody likes squinting at menu lists and prices, so make sure you use 12-point text or larger.

VARIATIONS

Folded Menus: *Use the instructions in the brochure recipes to create menus that fold. If you plan to use the menus for a long period of time, laminate them for durability.*

NAME TAG

Use WordPerfect for Windows to create name tags for conferences, seminars, social events, and competitions. (A conference just isn't a conference without everyone wearing a "Hello, my name is ?" badge.) You can tailor-make a name tag for everyone, or mass produce a bunch of blank ones that can be filled in later. This is a simple project that can help you look organized and professional, and all it takes is a few short project steps.

PREPARATION

Set up the margins and add a border.

1. Select Layout. • Select Margins. • Set all margins at .5". • Click OK.

2. Click on Text Box button. • Select Size button on Feature Bar. • Set width at 3.68" and height at 2.66". • Click OK.

3. Click on Border/Fill button. • Border Style: Thick/Thin 2. • Click OK. • Click on Wrap button. • Set to No Wrap. • Click OK. • Move box to upper left corner of page.

Add a graphic.

4. Click on Figure button. • Select SUN_DSG.WPG. • Click OK. • Click on figure. • Click on Size button on Feature Bar. • Width: .963". • Height: .825". • Click OK. • Click on Border/Fill button. • Border Style: None. • Click OK. • Move graphic into box set in step 2; place in upper left corner.

Create a TextArt logo.

5. Click on TextArt button. • Font Face: Onyx BT or Broadway Engraved. • Justification: Center. • Type in text. • Select the text arch shape. • Width: 5". • Height: 2". • Select File. • Select Exit & Return to WordPerfect. • Click Yes.

6. Select graphic and resize in upper left corner (see the next figure).

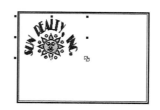

Add more text boxes for name tag text.

7. Click on Text Box button. • Click on Border/Fill button on Feature Bar. • Border Style: None. • Click OK. • Font Face: Onyx BT or Broadway. • Font Size: 24. • Justification: Center. • Type in text. • Resize and move block as necessary to fit inside of box border next to logo art (see the next figure).

8. Click on Text Box button. • Click on Border/Fill button on Feature Bar. • Border Style: None. • Click OK. • Font Face: Brush 738 BT. • Double-click on Font Size button. • Font Size: 60. • Justification: Center. • Resize and move block as necessary to fit in remaining space of name tag.

9. Print and save the name tag.

VARIATIONS

Lots of Labels: *Use this same recipe to create labels for luggage, filing drawers, food canning, and more. Just tailor-make your label size using the Layout Page menu.*

Newsletter with Screened Masthead

COMPUTER KIDS

Spring 1994   TeleElectronics Publishing Company, San Diego, California   Issue 2

COMPUTERS ON THE GO
They Just Get Smaller and Smaller

Computers are changing so fast, it's hard to keep up with them. Did you know that computers are getting smaller? That's right, they're getting small enough to carry around anywhere. If you've ever taken a plane trip or visited an airport, you've probably noticed business people using laptop computers. Laptop computers are smaller than regular computers. They usually look like a briefcase. They open up just like a briefcase to reveal a small keyboard and a monitor screen. Laptop computers, like Apple's PowerBook, weigh 6-8 pounds and run off of batteries instead of electricity.

Another kind of portable computer is called a palmtop, or hand-held computer. It's small enough to fit into the palm of your hand. Palmtop computers are useful for recording information, such as names and addresses, with the help of a pen instead of a keyboard. There's just not

enough room for a keyboard in the palm of your hand, you know! To enter data, you use the pen to "write" on the monitor screen. The computer then translates your handwriting into computer type. Pretty neat, eh? The Newton MessagePad by Apple is a palmtop computer that does this. Other palmtop computers can act like electronic dictionaries or translate foreign languages.

Although these tiny computers can't do as many things as larger computers, they're still very handy. Who knows how small the computers of tomorrow will be!

Article by Debbie Stewart, Jefferson Elementary School, grade 5

COMPUTER TRIVIA
Did You Know?

If you read the article "Computers On The Go" you learned a little about portable computers, computers that you can carry around. The very first portable computers released in the early 1980's weren't so portable at all! In fact, they usually weighed anywhere from 25 to 35 pounds. Even though the people who made them said the computers were easy to carry, the people who used them nicknamed them "luggables." Why? Because, it was very difficult to take them from place to place, and most users felt like they were just lugging the computers around.

Can you imagine carrying around a 35-pound computer? Thank goodness we don't lug our computer's anymore!

INSIDE

Software Reviews 2
Book Reviews 2
Fun and Games 3
Letters and Art 4

Want to indulge your unspoken journalistic fantasies? Thinking of becoming editor of a famous worldwide news conglomerate? Want to run around your neighborhood hollering, "Extra, extra, read all about it!"? Then creating a newsletter is a project just for you. Newsletters are one of the most common ways to communicate information, news, and upcoming events. Today's communication age is ripe with newsletters for business, school, and even home. Here's a great idea to start your newsletter right: make a masthead (newsletter title) with a screened-background look.

PREPARATION

Select a template to use.

 1. Click on Template button. • Click on Options button. • Select Create Template. • Type in name of new template you're designing, such as NEWS1. • Select WordPerfect template NEWSLTR1.WPT to base your design on. • Click OK.

Add your own masthead text.

 2. Replace template masthead text with your own (see the next figure). • Highlight text line; press delete. • Set your own newsletter font, such as Algerian, and size. (I used Font Face: Scribble. Font Size: 60.) • Justification: Center.

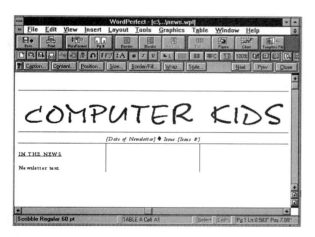

Add a text box with a screened background.

 3. Click on Text Box button. • Click on Border/Fill button on Feature Bar. • Border Style: None. • Fill Style: 10% Fill. • Click OK. • Click on Wrap button. • Select No Wrap. • Click OK.

4. Resize text box to fit around masthead title, as shown below.

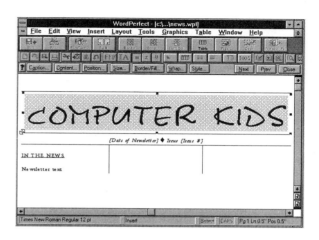

Add the finishing touches.

 5. The rest of this 3-column newsletter follows template design. I added graphics for illustrating, and used different fonts for articles. • For article headlines, I used Font Face: Times New Roman, Bold; Font Size 24; Justification: Center. • For the subheads, I used Font Face: Arial; Font Size: 14; Justification: Center. • For body text, I used Font Face: Arial; Font Size: 12; Justification: Full. • Horizontal rules were inserted to end articles.

6. Click on Exit Template button. • Click yes.

VARIATIONS

More Shading: *The screened text box (or you might call it "shaded") used in the masthead can also be repeated in the article headlines to add a consistent look throughout your newsletter pages. Another variation would be to use a shaded watermark instead of text boxes.*

Part Four

Vegetables: Forms

If anything can make my mind feel like a vegetable, it's filling out a form. Credit applications, employment applications, invoices, and questionnaires—they all make my head spin. Worse than filling out a form is trying to design one. If you're stuck with this thankless task, these recipes may be the carrot you've been digging for. Whether your form is a simple permission slip, or a complex sales proposal, you'll find the perfect recipe in this section.

CREDIT APPLICATION

Westlake Music

Credit Application

Application No.

Westlake Music
1334 West Virginia Ave.
San Diego CA 86290
(780) 581-8180
Fax:(780) 581-8181

Name:	
Address:	
Telephone:	

Type of Credit Desired: ☐ Monthly Plan ☐ Revolving Charge ☐ Gold Plan

Credit Card References

Name of Card	Account Number	Current Balance

Bank References

Bank Name & Address	Account Number(s)	Contact Name & Phone

I certify that the above information is true. This information is to be used only for opening an account.

Sign & Date

Why spend the money to purchase costly preprinted credit applications when you can generate your own with WordPerfect for Windows? If your company logo is saved as a graphic file or scanned in, you can easily add it to the WordPerfect template. This particular project shows you how to do just that, along with a few other tune-ups to the existing template. If you don't have a company logo, you can design one with the recipes you'll find in Part One.

PREPARATION

Set up the template.

1. Click on Open button. • Select CREDITAP.WPT. • Click OK.

Cook's Caution   This project changes the default credit application to a credit card application. If you want to keep the original template intact, select File Save As, and save this project template under another name, such as CRCARD.WPT.

Add a logo.

2. Select Insert. • Select Figure. • Select your logo from the list of graphic files. • Click OK.

3. Resize logo; move to fit in upper left corner of form. • Click on Border/Fill button on Feature Bar. • Border Style: None. • Click OK (see the next figure).

Change description headings.

4. Switch to Tables Button Bar. • Click on Format Tbl button. • Select Table option button. • Select Disable Cell Locks. • Click OK.

5. Change personal fields as shown. • Modify name and address information to include a "Type of Credit Desired" line with check boxes for options (see the next figure).

Name:	
Address:	
Telephone:	
Type of Credit Desired:	❑ Monthly Plan ❑ Revolving Charge ❑ Gold Plan

6. Modify "Partners or Corporate Officers" section to be "Credit Card References," with additional rows (see the next figure).

Credit Card References		
Name of Card	Account Number	Current Balance

Add and delete rows.

7. Click pointer where a new row is to be inserted. • Click on Tbl Insert button on Table Button Bar. • Select number of rows to be added.• Click OK. • To delete rows not needed, click pointer on row to be deleted. • Click on Delete Tbl button. • Specify table option to delete. • Click OK.

Chef's Tip   To add check boxes, select the Insert Character command. Scroll through Typographic Symbols to find the check box symbol. Click Insert and Close to exit.

8. Click on Exit Template button. • Click Yes to save template.

VARIATIONS

Mobile Logo: *To make your application look different from the one shown, place your graphic logo in another area, or use it as a watermark. If you do not have a logo to use, try creating one using WordPerfect Draw and the recipes in Part One.*

EMPLOYMENT APPLICATION

Application For Employment

Mike's Photography
1334 West Virginia Ave.
Newark, New Jersey 78690
(614) 587-9000
Fax: (614) 587-9101

Personal Information	
Name:	Date:
Social Security Number:	
Home Address:	
City, State Zip:	
Home Phone:	Business Phone:
US Citizen?	If Not Give Visa No. & expiration:

Position Applying For	
Title:	Salary Desired:
Referred By:	Date Available:

Education	
High School (Name, City, State):	
Graduation Date:	
Business or Technical School :	
Dates Attended:	Degree, Major:
Undergraduate College :	
Dates Attended:	Degree, Major:
Graduate School:	
Dates Attended:	Degree, Major:

Prior Employment	
From/To:	Job Title
Salary Received:	Supervisor/Phone Number:
From/To:	Job Title:
Salary Received:	Supervisor/Phone Number:
From/To:	Job Title:
Salary Received:	Supervisor/Phone Number:
From/To:	Job Title:
Salary Received:	Supervisor/Phone Number:

References

Here's an idea for a two-page employment application that is based on a WordPerfect template. I added information areas on the template to include previous employment. Of course, you can tailor this to include any special applicant information your company may need.

PREPARATION

Set up the template.

1. Click on Open button. • Select JOBAPP.WPT from list of template files. • Click OK.

Cook's Caution This project makes changes to the employment application template. If you don't want to do that, save the project template under another name (such as JOBAPP2.WPT) with the File Save As command.

2. Switch to Tables Button Bar. • Click on Format Tbl button. • Select Table option. • Select Disable Cell Locks. • Click OK.

Add a logo and spiff up the headings.

3. Select Graphics. • Select Figure. • Select your logo from list of graphic files. • Click OK. • Resize logo; place in upper left corner of form (see the next figure). • Click on Border/Fill button on Feature Bar. • Border Style: None. • Click OK.

Application For Employment

Mike's Photography
1314 West Virginia Ave.
Newark, New Jersey 78490
(616) 587-9000
Fax: (616) 587-9101

4. Click on "Personal Information" cell. • Click on TblLineFill button. • Fill Style: Honeycomb. • Foreground Color: light gray . • Click OK.

5. Repeat step 4 for each title field in the form.

6. Select the three rows in "Position Applying For" section. • Click on Copy button. • Click Row. • Click OK. • Move pointer to just before "References" section. • Click on Paste button.

7. Change the second "Position Applied For" section to "Prior Employment." • Change "Title" to "From/To:." • Change "Salary Desired" to "Job Title." • Change "Referred By" to "Salary Received." • Change "Date Available" to "Supervisor/Phone Number (see the next figure).

From/To	Job Title
Salary Received	Supervisor/Phone Numbers

8. Select "From/To:" cell. • Click the right mouse button. • Select Split Cell. • Columns: 3. • Click OK. • Repeat sequence for "Salary Received" cell (see the next figure).

From/To		Job Title	
Salary Received		Supervisor/Phone Numbers	

9. Select the two cells shown. • Click the right mouse button. • Select Join Cells. • Repeat this sequence for lower two cells.

10. Select "From/To:" and "Job Title" cells. • Click on TblLineFill button. • Top: Double line. • Click OK.

11. Select both rows. • Click on Copy button. • Click on Paste button three times to add additional employment information areas.

12. Click on Exit Template button. • Click Yes to save template.

EXPENSE REPORT

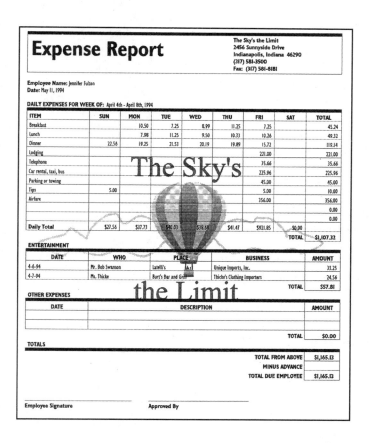

Expense Report

The Sky's the Limit
2456 Sunnyside Drive
Indianapolis, Indiana 46290
(317) 581-3500
Fax: (317) 581-8181

Employee Name: Jennifer Fulton
Date: May 11, 1994

DAILY EXPENSES FOR WEEK OF: April 4th - April 8th, 1994

ITEM	SUN	MON	TUE	WED	THU	FRI	SAT	TOTAL
Breakfast		10.50	7.25	8.99	11.25	7.25		45.24
Lunch		7.98	11.25	9.50	10.33	10.26		49.32
Dinner	22.56	19.25	21.53	20.19	19.89	15.72		119.14
Lodging						221.00		221.00
Telephone						35.66		35.66
Car rental, taxi, bus						225.96		225.96
Parking or towing						45.00		45.00
Tips	5.00					5.00		10.00
Airfare						356.00		356.00
								0.00
								0.00
Daily Total	$27.56	$37.73	$40.03	$38.68	$41.47	$921.85	$0.00	
						TOTAL		$1,107.32

ENTERTAINMENT

DATE	WHO	PLACE	BUSINESS	AMOUNT
4-6-94	Mr. Bob Swanson	Latelli's	Unique Imports, Inc.	33.25
4-7-94	Ms. Thicke	Burt's Bar and Grill	Thicke's Clothing Importers	24.56
			TOTAL	$57.81

OTHER EXPENSES

DATE	DESCRIPTION	AMOUNT
	TOTAL	$0.00

TOTALS

TOTAL FROM ABOVE	$1,165.13
MINUS ADVANCE	
TOTAL DUE EMPLOYEE	$1,165.13

_____   _____
Employee Signature   Approved By

This is one of the simplest projects you can do. Use the WordPerfect Expense Report template, but spruce it up with an interesting graphic watermark, or a watermark of your company logo. Since the WordPerfect watermarks appear as shaded text or art in the background of your document, they are perfect for adding interest to an otherwise boring form.

PREPARATION

Set up the template.

1. Click on Open button. • Select EXPENSE.WPT. • Click OK.

Cook's Caution This project makes changes to the original expense template. If you don't want to do that, save the project template under another name (such as EXPENSE2.WPT) with the File Save As command.

2. Select Layout. • Select Watermark. • Select Watermark A. • Click on Create button (see the next figure).

4. Click on Format Tbl button. • Select Table option. • Select Disable Cell Locks (see the next figure). • Click OK. • Type in changes you want to make to the basic expense template.

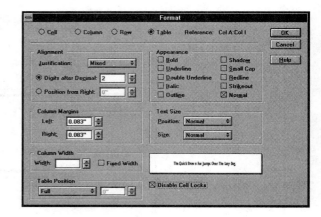

5. Click on Exit Template button. • Click Yes to save template.

Cook's Caution You may have to edit the watermark's placement in your form. Just select Layout Watermark Edit. Reposition or resize the graphic as needed.

VARIATIONS

No Logo? *If you don't have a graphic logo to use as a watermark, try using WordPerfect's TextArt feature instead. Create a "word graphic" using your company's name. In the TextArt dialog box, select a shape for your company name, and experiment with the various colors and outlines.*

3. Click on Figure button. • Select your logo file. • Click OK. • Click on Close button on Feature Bar. • Click on Close button again (see the next figure).

GRADE BOOK

Student Name	Test Scores									Avg.	Grade
Jennifer Fulton	97	88	89	91						91.25	
Bob Wilson	70	67	79	81						74.25	
Joe Schuller	90	78	84	87						84.75	
Sally Stocks	70	67	55	70						65.5	
Billy Budd	76	92	67	80						78.75	
Patty Whitler	63	89	74	81						76.75	
Scott Flynn	96	92	100	89						94.25	
Beth Lynn Wills	89	78	87	79						83.25	
Meghan Ryan	90	92	87	92						90.25	
Ryan Adams	67	72	67	75						70.25	
Peggy Matley	66	74	87	76						75.75	
Jim Babbett	92	91	83	79						86.25	
Bob Tasker	68	75	77	81						75.25	
Sherry Cooper	96	82	85	90						88.25	
Tim Booth	93	89	76	81						84.75	
										0	
										0	
										0	
										0	

You can create all kinds of tables, ranging from simple to sophisticated, using WordPerfect. This project idea features a table created specifically for teachers. It's a grade book sheet for keeping track of test scores in the classroom. Although WordPerfect provides a Grade Book template, the shaded fills for alternating rows in our project make it easy to read and even easier to record on. In addition, averages are calculated automatically.

PREPARATION

Set up the paper size and table.

1. Select Layout. • Select Page. • Select Paper Size. • Select Letter Landscape. • Click Select.

2. Click on Table Create button. • Column settings: 13. • Rows: 10. • Switch to Tables Button Bar.

Format the column headings.

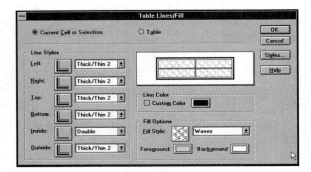
3. Select top row of table. • Click on TblLineFill button. • Outside setting: Thick/Thin 2 border. • Inside setting: Double border. • Fill Style: Waves. • Foreground: light gray (see the next figure). • Click OK.

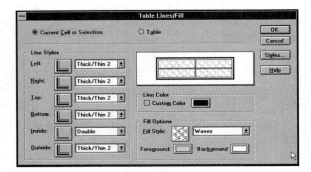

4. Select cells B1 to K1. • Click the right mouse button. • Select Join Cells. • Select cells B2 to K2. • Click on Format Tbl button. • Select Column. • Width: .470". • Click OK.

Chef's Tip   Table cells have addresses based on their position in the table: what row and column they occupy. The address for a cell appears in the Title Bar and the Status Bar when you select that cell. (See the Basic Skills section of the book for more information about tables and cell addressing.)

5. Click in cell A1. • Click on Format Tbl button. • Select Column. • Width: 3". • Click OK.

6. Font Face: Arial. • Font Size: 12. • Click on Bold button. • Type in column headings (see the next figure).

Format the rest of the table.

7. Select cells A2 to A10. • Click on TblLineFill button. • Left: Double. • Bottom: Double. • Click OK. • Repeat this sequence for cells B2–K10 and L2–L10.

8. Select cells M2 to M10. • Click on TblLineFill button. • Left, Bottom, and Right sides: Double border style (see the next figure). • Click OK.

9. Select row 2. • Click on TblLineFill button. • Fill Style: 80% Fill. • Foreground Color: light gray. • Click OK. • Click on Copy button. • Choose Selection. • Click OK. • Click on row 4. • Click on Paste button. • Continue pasting for every other row.

Add a formula to calculate the grade average.

10. Move pointer to cell L2, and click. • Click on TblFormBar button. • Click on Functions button. • Select AVE (List). • Click Insert. • Drag over cells B2 to K2. • Press Enter (see the next figure).

11. Click on Copy Formula button. • Down:
    8. • Click OK. • Click on Close button.

Enlarge your table as needed.

12. Select Rows 7 and 8. • Click on Copy
    button. • Select Row. • Click OK.
    • Click on Paste button. • Repeat for
    additional rows.

13. Save and print your grade book sheet.

Chef's Tip As you add student names and
grades, recalculate the averages by
selecting the Table Calculate command.
Click on Calc Table button.

VARIATIONS

Adding Extras: *If your class grading system
requires you to grade on a curve, you can add
extra columns that reflect those grades. You can
also add rows that give specifics about each test
given, dates given, and so on.*

INVOICE

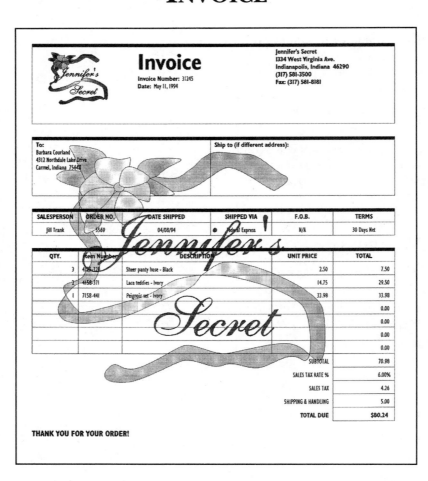

Creating a custom invoice for your company or organization using WordPerfect is painless and fun (especially when the money starts rolling in). If you're interested in making an invoice that really reflects your company or organization, add a watermark. These lightly shaded graphics fade into the background of your WordPerfect form. Based on an existing template, you'll find the company invoice to be an easy project to whip up.

PREPARATION

Set up the template and logo.

1. Click on Open button. • Select INVOICE.WPT. • Click OK.

2. Click on Figure button. • Select your company logo from list of graphics files. • Click OK. • Click on logo. • Click on Border/Fill button on Feature Bar. • Border Style: None. • Click OK. • Resize logo to fit in top table box (see the next figure). • Click Close.

Invoice

Add a watermark.

3. Select Layout. • Select Watermark. • Click Watermark A. • Click on Create.

4. Click on Figure button on Feature Bar. • Select your logo again. • Click OK.

Edit your logo to softer patterns and colors.

5. Select Graphics. • Select Edit Box.

6. Click on Tools button on Feature Bar. • Click on Brightness tool (see the next figure). • Select a lighter brightness level. • Click Close. • Click Close again.

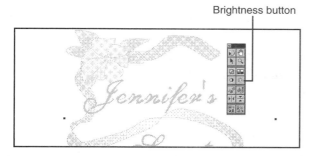

Brightness button

Insert an item number column.

7. Select cells B8 to B15. • Select Table. • Select Split. • Select Cell. • Select 2. • Click OK. • Select "Description" and drag to cell C8.

Chef's Tip Table cells have names based on their position in the table: what row and column they occupy. The address for a cell appears in the Title Bar and the Status Bar when you select that cell. (See Part 7: Basic Kitchen Skills for more information about tables and cell addressing.)

8. Type "Item Number" in cell B8. • Drag column borders to readjust size of columns A and B (see the next figure).

SALESPERSON	ORDER NO.	DATE SHIPPED	SHIPPED VIA	F.O.B.	TERMS
[Salesperson]	[Purchase Order Number]	[Date Shipped]	[Shipped Via]	[F.O.B.]	[Terms]

QTY.	Item Number	DESCRIPTION	UNIT PRICE	TOTAL
				0.00
				0.00
				0.00
				0.00
				0.00
				0.00
				0.00
			SUBTOTAL	0.00

9. Click on Exit Template button. • Click Yes to save template.

VARIATIONS

Make It Official: *Take your newly created invoice to a professional printer to have a triplicate form made. They can use your laser printer output as camera-ready art for making a form. But be careful. Make sure you've double-checked all the spelling!*

MEMBERSHIP APPLICATION

Application For Membership

LawnBridge Country Club
12 Golf Lane Road
Westerville, Illinois 60690

(606) 456-7878

Personal Information	
Name:	Date:
Social Security Number:	Date of Birth:
Home Address:	
City, State Zip:	
Home Phone:	Business Phone:
Number of Years at Current Residence?	State reason for wanting to become a member:

Type of Membership Desired			
❑ Golden Lifetime	❑ Full Annual (Golf, Tennis, Pool)	❑ Pool, Tennis Only	❑ Dining, Events Only

References			
Name:	Phone:	❑ Member	❑ Non-Member
Name:	Phone:	❑ Member	❑ Non-Member
Name:	Phone:	❑ Member	❑ Non-Member
Name:	Phone:	❑ Member	❑ Non-Member
Name:	Phone:	❑ Member	❑ Non-Member

Another popular form you can make with WordPerfect for Windows is a membership application sheet. Similar to employment applications and credit applications, a membership application can be used in clubs and organizations to track membership enrollment. The following design includes a logo created with WordPerfect Draw.

PREPARATION

Set up the template and logo.

1. Click on Open button. • Select JOBAPP.WPT. • Click OK.

2. Select File. • Select Save As. • Save file as MEMBER.WPT. • Click OK.

3. Click on Format Tbl button. • Select Table option. • Select Disable Cell Locks. • Click OK.

4. Click on Figure button. • Select your logo. • Click OK. • Click on logo. • Click Border/Fill button on Graphics Box Feature Bar. • Border Style: None. • Click OK. • Resize logo to fit at top of form as shown (see the next figure).

5. Change form's title from "Employment" to "Membership."

Change the personal information section.

6. Click inside cell G5. • Click the right mouse button. • Select Split Cells. • Select 2. • Click OK.

Chef's Tip Table cells have names based on their position in the table: what row and column they occupy. The address for a cell appears in the Title Bar and the Status Bar when you select that cell. (See the Basic Skills section of the book for more information about tables and cell addressing.)

7. Click in cell J5. • Click on TblLineFill button. • Left: Hairline border. • Click OK. • Type: Date of Birth.

8. In the remaining cells, change the text as shown (see the next figure).

Personal Information		
Name:		Date:
Social Security Number:		Date of Birth:
Home Address:		
City, State Zip:		
Home Phone:	Business Phone:	
Number of Years at Current Residence!	State reason for wanting to become a member:	

Change the membership section.

9. Change heading "Type of Position Applying For" to "Type of Membership Desired."

10. Select all four cells beneath heading. • Click the right mouse button. • Select Join Cells.

11. Add check boxes and text. • To add check box symbols, select Insert. • Select Character. • Select Typographic Symbols, and choose the check box. • Click Insert and Close. • Repeat this sequence for each check box needed.

Remove the Education section.

12. Select all rows in Education section. • Click on Delete Tbl button. • Select Rows. • Click OK.

Adjust the References section.

13. Select first row in the References section, beneath the heading cell. • Click the right mouse button. • Select Split Cell. • Select Column. • Setting: 3. • Click OK. • Move table lines to make cells the size needed for filling in information.

14. Click on Bold button. • Type "Name:" in first cell of section beneath heading cell. • Type "Phone:" in next cell.

15. For last column of in formation, use Insert Character command to add check boxes before text categories.

16. Select the row. •Click on Copy button. • Select Row. • Click OK. • Click on Paste button. • Repeat to add more reference rows to the section.

17. Click on Exit Template button. • Click Yes, and save your template.

VARIATIONS

Bigger Logo: *Want a bigger logo on your application? Instead of setting it up as a graphic figure, make it into a watermark instead. Follow the instructions listed in steps 3–6 in the previous project for inserting a watermark logo.*

BUSINESS   ORGANIZATION   HOME   SCHOOL

Moderate

ORDER FORM

Order Form

Order 24 hours a day, seven days a week. Operators are always standing by!

**1092 Westwind Dr.
San Diego, CA 00000**

1-800-000-0000
Fax: (423) 000-0000

To:	Ship to (if different address):

QTY.	DESCRIPTION	UNIT PRICE	TOTAL
			0.00
			0.00
			0.00
			0.00
			0.00
			0.00
			0.00
	SUBTOTAL		0.00
	SALES TAX RATE %		
	SALES TAX		0.00
	SHIPPING & HANDLING		
	TOTAL DUE		$0.00

THANK YOU FOR YOUR ORDER!

Take your weary old order form and add some pizzazz. Here's a project idea for adding a logo and TextArt to create a sensational order form that will impress any customer. Your company name and logo is displayed grandly in the upper right corner for all to see.

PREPARATION

Set up the template.

1. Click on Template button. • Click on Options. • Select Create Template. • Type in a new name for your template, such as ORDERFRM. • Select INVOICE.WPT template in Template to Base On. • Click OK.

Replace existing text.

2. Change the word "Invoice" to "Order Form." • Replace existing template text in this section with your company's ordering information, such as address, toll-free number and fax number (see the next figure).

Order Form

Order 24 hours a day, seven days a week. Operators are always standing by!

1092 Westwind Dr.
San Diego, CA 00000

1-800-000-0000
Fax: (423) 000-0000|

 Cook's Caution Changing the sizes in this area of the template may affect font sizes in the rest of the template. Be sure to reset them to your desired sizes and fonts.

Build a logo.

3. Click on Draw button. • Click on Insert Figure tool. • Drag dotted line to full-screen size and release. • From the list of graphics, select WORLD.WPG. • Click Retrieve.

4. Select the figure. • Select Attributes. • Select Fill. • Foreground Color: light gray. • Click on Line Style button. • Click No Line. • Click OK (see the next figure).

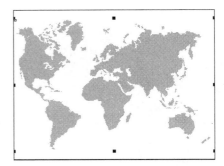

5. Select Attributes. • Select Fill. • Foreground Color: light blue. • Click on Line Style button. • Line style: thin. • Click OK. • Click on Ellipse tool. • Draw large oval encompassing the drawing area. • Select oval shape. • Select Arrange. • Select Back (see the next figure).

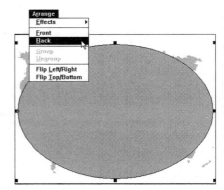

6. Resize world map to fit inside ellipse, as shown below. • Select File. • Select Exit and Return to Document. • Click Yes to save changes.

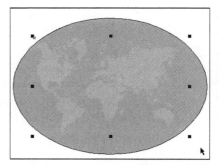

Insert the logo and add TextArt.

7. Right-click and select Feature Bar.
   • Click on Position box on Graphics Box Feature Bar. • Select Put Box on Current Page. • Click OK. • Click on Border/Fill button. • Border Style: None. • Click OK. • Resize the art as needed to fit. • Click on Close button.

 8. Click on TextArt button. • Font Face: Arrus Blk BT, Sherwood, or a similar style. • Pick a shape. • Type your text. • Select File. • Select Exit & Return to WordPerfect. • Click Yes to embed. • Right-click and select Position. • Select Put Box on Current Page. • Click OK. • Reposition TextArt over world map graphic (see the next figure).

9. Change the rest of the form as needed to suit your company's ordering process.
   • Click on Exit Template button.
   • Click Yes.

VARIATIONS

Add It: *Add your order form to a company catalog—another great project you can create with WordPerfect for Windows. See Part Three for instructions for making a catalog.*

PACKING LIST

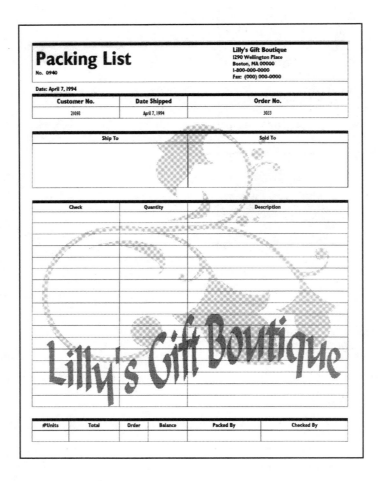

Adding graphics to an ordinary packing list can help you present a professional, polished image to customers and clients. This project idea incorporates both a watermark and TextArt to create an attractive graphic logo.

PREPARATION

Set up the template.

1. Click on Template button. • Click on Options button. • Select Create Template. • Type in a new name for your template, such as PACKLST1. • Select PACKING.WPT template to base this project on (see the next figure). • Click OK.

Add a watermark.

2. Select Layout. • Select Watermark. • Select Watermark A. • Click on Create button.

3. Click on Figure button. • Select your company logo, or to copy this project exactly, choose ENDER05.WPG. • Click OK.

4. Select Graphics. • Select Edit Box. • Double-click on graphic to open WordPerfect Draw. • Select Edit. • Select All. • Select Attributes. • Select Fill. • Foreground Color: lightest gray. • Click on Line Style button. • Line setting: No Line. • Click OK (see the next figure).

5. Select File. • Select Exit and Return to Document. • Click Yes.

6. Select graphic. • Move graphic and resize to fit in lower portion of page.

Add TextArt to Watermark.

7. Select Graphics. • Select TextArt. • Font Face: Algerian, Calligrapher, or another font. • Text Color: light gray. • Outline: None. • Select a wavy shape (see the next figure). • Width: 5". • Height: 2". • Type company name. • Select File. • Select Exit & Return to WordPerfect. • Click Yes.

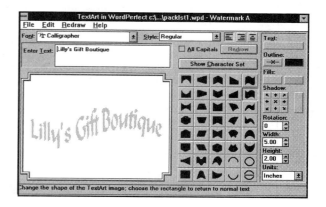

8. Position TextArt appropriately over graphic, resizing as needed.

9. Change any additional text on the template. • Click Exit Template. • Click Yes to save your new template.

VARIATIONS

Smaller Stuff: *Your packing list doesn't have to fill a whole page. Retool the template to a smaller size, or create your own table from scratch. Another project to spin off this idea is to create inspection slips, "Inspected by Number 12" to include in the package sent.*

5 min.

Easy

BUSINESS   ORGANIZATION   HOME   **SCHOOL**

PERMISSION SLIP

Washington Elementary School
Mrs. Williams 1st grade class ● PERMISSION SLIP

Dear Parents,
We have scheduled a class field trip on Friday, October 22 to the Whitfield Museum of Natural History. This all day trip will require a packed lunch and beverage for each child. We will be leaving the school by bus at 9:00, arriving at the museum at 9:30. We will return from the museum at 1:30, arriving back at the school at 2:00. Permission slips must be filled out and returned by Wednesday, October 20. Thank you for your attention to this matter.

October 1, 1995

Washington Elementary School,

_____
(your child's name)
has my/our permission to participate in the Museum field trip on October 22.

Sincerely, _____
(parent's signature)

If your school or classroom participates in field trips, designing a permission slip is a perfect idea for you. The following idea will help you build a simple take-home slip. Use your own creative ideas to add a school logo, a border, or other features.

PREPARATION

Create the heading.

1. Type in title of permission slip and additional information. • Font Face: Bookman Old Style, Cooper Black WP, or a similar font. • Font Size: 24. • Second line of information; Font Size: 16. • Justification: Center.

Add a horizontal line.

2. Select Graphics. • Select Custom Line. • Line Style: thick shape. • Click OK (see the next figure).

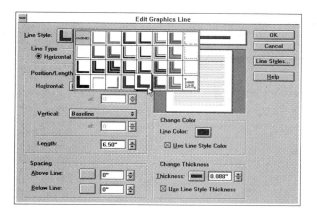

3. Place the graphic line below the title.

4. Type the rest of permission slip information as shown. • Font Face: Times New Roman. • Font Size: 14.

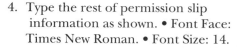

Washington Elementary School
Mrs. Williams 1st grade class • PERMISSION SLIP

Dear Parents,
We have scheduled a class field trip on Friday, October 22 to the Whitfield Museum of Natural History. This all day trip will require a packed lunch and beverage for each child. We will be leaving the school by bus at 9:00, arriving at the museum at 9:30. We will return from the museum at 1:30, arriving back at the school at 2:00. Permission slips must be filled out and returned by Wednesday, October 20. Thank you for your attention to this matter.

October 1, 1995

Add a text box.

5. Click on Text Box button. • Click on Border/Fill button on Feature Bar. • Border Style: Dashed. • Fill Style: 10% Fill. • Click OK.

6. Enlarge text box and place below permission slip information created in step 4. • Double-click and type in text. • Font Face: Times New Roman. • Font Size: 14. • Change text margins to 2" and 6.5" (see figure below).

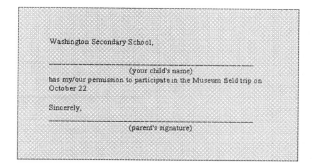

7. Save and print your project.

VARIATIONS

Smaller Slips: *You may want to experiment with smaller permission slips. Use the Paper Size dialog box to try different paper sizes appropriate to the size you would like to create. You may also try copying your permission slip so that two are printed on one document page.*

Startling Slips: *Print your slips on colored paper to really make them stand out. How about those fluorescent colors, like hot pink? Drawing attention to the paper will help parents notice it and respond.*

PURCHASE ORDER

Purchase Order

P.O. Number: [Purchase Order Number]
Date: April 8, 1994

<Organization>
<Address>
<City, State Zip>
<Telephone>
Fax: <Fax>

To:	Ship to (if different address):

PLACED BY	DATE EXPECTED	SHIP VIA	F.O.B.	TERMS
[Placed By]	[Date Expected]	[Ship Via]	[F.O.B.]	[Terms]

QTY.	DESCRIPTION	UNIT PRICE	TOTAL
			0.00
			0.00
			0.00
			0.00
			0.00
			0.00
			0.00
			0.00
		SHIPPING	
		SUBTOTAL	0.00
		TAX RATE %	
		TAX	0.00
		TOTAL	$0.00

Authorized Signature

Here are a few interesting adjustments you can make to perk up the look of a regular purchase order form: add a fill and a gradient box to bring the design alive. With WordPerfect's templates and their preset tables, you can easily fill cells that need emphasis with a pattern or give the appearance of a distinctive design.

PREPARATION

Create the top of the form.

1. Click on Template button. • Select Options. • Select Create Template. • Type in a new name for your template, such as PURCHAS1. • Select PURCHASE.WPT template to base this project on. • Click OK (see the next figure).

Fill a cell.

2. Select the first row of the table. • Click on TblLineFill button on Table Button Bar. • Fill Style: 10% Fill. • Click OK (see the next figure).

Add a text box with a gradient fill.

3. Move to bottom of document to add a text box. • Click on Text Box button. • Click on Border/Fill button on Feature Bar. • Border Style: None. • Fill Style: Gradient 1. • Click OK.

4. Resize text box to fill lower portion of form. • Click Exit Template button. • Click Yes to save template.

VARIATIONS

Go to the Pros: *Take your newly created purchase order to a professional printer to have a triplicate form made. They can use your laser printer output as camera-ready art for making a form. But be careful. Make sure you've double-checked all the spelling!*

QUESTIONNAIRE

ABS Conference
QUESTIONNAIRE

DIRECTIONS: Please fill out the following questionnaire rating our recent 1994 ABS Conference in Chicago, Illinois. Your feedback will help us evaluate and improve future ABS conferences. Return this form in the enclosed postage-paid envelope. Thank you for your time, we look forward to seeing you at next year's ABS Conference in San Francisco, California!

1. Did you find the conference informative, on the cutting edge, and valuable to your business?
   ❑ Very informative   ❑ Somewhat informative   ❑ Not informative

2. Were the panel discussions and topics covered of interest to you and your company?
   ❑ Very interesting   ❑ Somewhat interesting   ❑ Not interesting

3. What topics would you like to see covered at our next ABS conference? _____
   _____
   _____

4. How would you rate the accomodations at the conference site?
   ❑ Very comfortable   ❑ Adequate   ❑ Rather poor   ❑ Unacceptable

5. Rate the hotel facilities in terms of service, cleanliness, quality, and staff courtesy.
   ❑ Very good   ❑ Good   ❑ Fair   ❑ Rather poor   ❑ Very poor

6. What was your level of satisfaction with the conference's booth and exhibit area and displays?
   ❑ Very good   ❑ Somewhat good   ❑ Need more booths and demonstrations

7. Did you find the registration process satisfactory?
   ❑ Very satisfactory   ❑ Satisfactory   ❑ Unsatisfactory

8. What suggestions would you like to make concerning any aspect of the conference? _____
   _____
   _____
   _____
   _____
   _____

An important part of any business or organization is feedback. What better way to solicit feedback than with a custom-designed questionnaire created with your own WordPerfect for Windows program? Using typographic symbols, text boxes, and graphic lines, you can create a questionnaire for any occasion.

PREPARATION

Start at the top.

1. Select Layout. • Select Margins.
   • Margins: All sides .5". • Click OK.

 2. Click on Text Box button. • Click
   Border/Fill on Feature Bar. • Border
   Style: None. • Fill Style: Gradient 2.
   • Click OK.

Add body text.

3. Select Layout. • Select Font. • Font
   Face: Brush 738 or BrushScript-WP.
   • Font Size: 48. • Select Bold. • Color:
   white. • Click OK. • Justification:
   Center. • Type in your questionnaire
   title.

4. Press Enter to start second line of text.
   • Double-click on Font Face button.
   • Font Face: Arrus Blk BT. • Font Size:
   40. • Color: black. • Click OK. • Type:
   QUESTIONNAIRE.

5. Resize text box as needed to fill top of
   form (see the next figure).

ABS Conference
QUESTIONNAIRE

6. Click outside of text box. • Press Enter
   to move the cursor below text box.
   • Type in a paragraph of directions
   for filling out and returning the
   questionnaire. • Font Face: Arial.
   • Font Size: 10.

Add a graphic line beneath directions.

7. Select Graphics. • Select Custom Line.
   • Set line thickness. • Click OK.
   • Reposition line if needed (see the
   next figure).

DIRECTIONS: Please fill out the following questionnaire rating our recent 1994 ABS Conference in Chicago, Illinois. Your feedback will help us evaluate and improve future ABS conferences. Return this form in the enclosed postage-paid envelope. Thank you for your time, we look forward to seeing you at next year's ABS Conference in San Francisco, California.

Type out the questionnaire.

8. Font Face: Humanst 521 Lt BT. • Font
   Size: 14. • To set check boxes, select
   Insert. • Select Character. • Select
   Typographic Symbols; choose a check
   box (see the next figure). • Click Insert
   and Close. • Repeat this sequence for
   each check box needed. • To type lines
   for answers, press Shift+Hyphen until
   you reach the right margin. • Use tabs
   to align answer boxes.

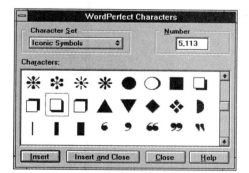

Chef's Tip   To continue to add check box
symbols, press Ctrl+W to open the
WordPerfect characters box rather than
using the menu bar. Scroll through the
typographic symbols to find the check box
symbol. Click Insert and Close to exit.

9. Save and print your questionnaire.

VARIATIONS

What Else?   *There are a variety of ways you can
create a questionnaire. You can even incorporate
the brochure ideas found in Section 3 into a folded
questionnaire. The best tools for building any kind
of brochure are tabs and WordPerfect typographic
characters.*

5 min.

BUSINESS ORGANIZATION HOME SCHOOL

Moderate

SALES PROPOSAL

SALESPROPOSAL

Greg Loving Designs • 34003 Westwind Boulevard, Suite 900 • San Francisco, CA 00000 • 1-800-000-0000 • Fax: (000) 000-0000

Client:: Farmington Estates/BL Kinkoph & Assoc.
Date: 9/23-94
Proposal: Development of Farmington Estates, homes and clubhouse

If you haven't figured this out yet, there are many things you can do with the WordPerfect for Windows templates. You can add graphics, company logos, watermarks, and special text effects. Each element adds a new design. As a WordPerfect chef, don't be afraid to experiment with lines and boxes, too. Here's a simple addition of a vertical graphic line to an existing template that creates a snazzy sales proposal for your business.

PREPARATION

Set up the template and text.

 1. Click on Open button. • Select PRESS2.WPT. • Click OK.

 2. Change the existing template text. • Change "PRESS RELEASE" to "SALES PROPOSAL." • Add your company name, address, and phone number. • Justification: Left (see the next figure).

SALESPROPOSAL

Greg Loving Designs • 34003 Westwind Boulevard • San Francisco, CA 00000 • (000) 000-0000 • fax (000) 000-0000

 3. Select the remaining template text. • Press Delete. • Type in your sales proposal information (see the next figure). • Font Face: Humanst 521 Lt BT. • Font Size: 12. • Justification: Left.

SALESPROPOSAL

Greg Loving Designs • 34003 Westwind Boulevard • San Francisco, CA 00000 • (000) 000-0000 • fax (000) 000-0000

Add the vertical line.

4. Select Graphics. • Select Custom Line. • Setting: Vertical. • Set thickness desired. • Click OK (see the next figure).

5. Select the line. • Reposition and resize as necessary, aligning top of vertical line with existing horizontal line (see the next figure).

Join the two lines

6. Click on Exit Template button. • Click Yes to save template.

VARIATIONS

Other Ways: *Of course, there are other ways of improving an ordinary sales proposal, such as adding company logos, bold font styles, and fancy borders. But don't underestimate the power of simplicity; a simple line, a shaded fill over the title, or a watermark in the background can make an attractive proposal that gets noticed.*

TIME SHEET

Employee Bi-Weekly Time Sheet

Employee: _____
Employee Number: _____
Department Number: _____
Weeks ending: _____
_____

Employee Signature & Date: _____
Supervisor Signature & Date: _____

	Reg. Hrs.	Vacation	Personal	Sick	Holiday	Other	Total Hrs
Monday							
Tuesday							
Wednesday							
Thursday							
Friday							
Saturday							
Sunday							
Totals							

	Reg. Hrs.	Vacation	Personal	Sick	Holiday	Other	Total Hrs
Monday							
Tuesday							
Wednesday							
Thursday							
Friday							
Saturday							
Sunday							
Totals							

Is time slipping away from you and your employees? Want to improve your company's time sheet? How about this project idea: incorporate a sleek time-piece graphic that you can easily make with WordPerfect Draw (I'll show you how). Then add a table for tracking daily hours, and you can create a professional time sheet that's easy to fill out and looks good as well.

PREPARATION

Start with creating a graphic.

 1. Click on Draw button. • Select Attributes. • Select Fill. • Fill Type: Gradient. • Outer Color: gray. • Center Color: white. • Click on Line button. • Click No Line. • Click OK.

 2. Click on Ellipse tool. • Draw a large circle that fills drawing area.

 3. Click on Ellipse tool. • Draw circle denoting 12 o'clock. • Select Edit. • Select Duplicate. • Move duplicate circle to 3 o'clock. • Repeat for 6 and 9 o'clock.

 4. To set the clock hands, click on Line tool. • Select Attributes. • Select Line. • Line Color: gray. • Line Width: .25". • Select Arrowhead Ending. • Click OK.

5. Starting at the center of the large ellipse, draw the hour hand as shown (see the next figure).

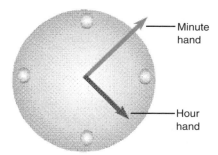

Minute hand

Hour hand

6. To set the smaller hand, select Attributes. • Select Line. • Color: light gray. • Click OK.

 7. Click on Line tool. • Starting at the center of the large ellipse again, draw the minute hand as shown.

8. Select File. • Select Exit and Return to Document. • Click Yes to save changes. • Select graphic and move to upper left corner. • To remove border, click on Border/Fill button on Feature Bar. • Select Border Style None. • Click OK.

Add text.

 9. Font Face: Humanst 521 Lt BT. • Font Size: 18. • Type: Employee Bi-Weekly Time Sheet. • Font Size: 12. • Add pertinent time sheet information. • Press Shift+Hyphen to create lines for filling in information later (see the next figure).

Employee Bi-Weekly Time Sheet

Employee
Employee Number
Department Number
Weeks ending

Employee Signature & Date
Supervisor Signature & Date

Set the table.

10. Click on the Table Create button. • Columns: 8; Rows: 20. • Click OK.

11. Select the first cell (see the next figure). • Click on TblLineFill button. • Left Line Style: None. • Top Line Style: None. • Click OK.

12. Add text to rest of table, including days of the week and categories. • Select row 10. • Click on TblLineFill button. • Fill Style: 10% Fill. • Click OK. • Repeat step 11 to make cell A11 look like cell A1 (see the next figure).

Thursday							
Friday							
Saturday							
Sunday							
Totals							
	Reg. Hrs.	Vacation	Personal	Sick	Holiday	Other	Total Hrs
Monday							
Tuesday							
Wednesday							
Thursday							
Friday							
Saturday							

13. Save and print your new time sheet.

VARIATIONS

More Fills? With WordPerfect's Table commands you can fill any cell, row, or column you desire. Create interesting designs by filling in every other row or column. Or add emphasis to columns, such as "Total Hours," by shading them.

PART FIVE

BREAD: PLANNERS AND ORGANIZERS

I have a great way of organizing: throw everything on the floor. That way, when I need to find something, it's right where I can step on it. If you prefer a more conventional way of organizing addresses, homework assignments, recipes, sales contacts, or your things-to-do list, check out the recipes in this section. They're even *organized* alphabetically for your convenience.

ADDRESS BOOK

Firstname	Lastname	Address	Address2	City	State	Zip	BPhone	HPhone
Scott	Adams	23 Westbury	#A	Chicago	IL	60690	(606) 788-9090	(606) 789-9334
Beth	Adams	3456 South Street		New York	NY	41334	(415) 789-9000 x1123	(415) 743-8922
Kathy	Johnson	2134 Western Ave.	#B	Chilton	OK	56780	(408) 755-6000 x3145	(408) 789-9823
Jennifer	Wilson	2434 116th		Indianapolis	IN	46244	(317) 788-9091	(317) 789-7376

I have a perfect memory: it perfectly disregards any information involving numbers—and usually at the worst times (like when my car broke down in the middle of nowhereland, and I couldn't remember what my secret decoder number was, so I couldn't get any money out of the cash machine to pay the nice haven't-taken-a-bath-in-weeks-because-I've-been-on-the-lam gentleman who had just towed me to civilization). Don't let this happen to you! With this recipe, you'll create a nice address book with important numbers you need to use (that is, if you ever want to see your loved ones again).

PREPARATION

Create a data file.

1. Select Tools. • Select Merge. • Select Place Records in a Table. • Click on Data.

2. Type each field name pressing Enter after each one: Firstname, Lastname, Address, Address2, City, State, Zip, BPhone, and HPhone. • Click OK.

Enter address information.

3. Type data into each field, pressing Enter to move from field to field (see the next figure). • Press Enter to begin a new record. • Click on Close when done. • Click Yes and enter a file name, such as ADDRESS.WPD. • Click OK.

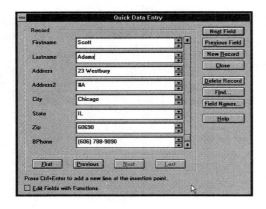

Chef's Tip To enter more addresses later on, open the file and click on Quick Entry.

4. Select Layout. • Select Page. • Select Paper Size. • Select Letter Landscape. • Click on Select.

Make the database easier to use.

5. Click on Options button. • Select Sort. • Cell: 2. • Click OK.

Cook's Caution After adding new data later on, repeat step 5 to alphabetize your address book.

6. Drag the right-hand edge of columns to adjust for the size of your data (see the next figure). For example, make State and Zip columns smaller; enlarge Lastname column.

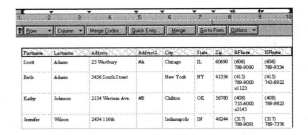

7. Select the first row. • Click on TblLineFill button on Tables Button Bar. • Outside: Double. • Fill Style: Waves. • Foreground Color: light gray. Do not close the dialog box yet.

8. Click on Table. • Custom Color: medium gray. • Click OK.

9. Save and print your address book.

VARIATIONS

Vital Data: *Don't get caught without the numbers you need! Add a different table at the beginning of the file for other data, such as your PIN number, credit card numbers, and important birthdays.*

But It Won't Fit! *If you have a day planner, create a page layout size to fit it in step 4. You can even print it on the day planner paper by adjusting line spacing and running a few tests.*

ATTENDANCE RECORD

Attendance Record

For the month of: _____

Names	Week 1	Week 2	Week 3	Week 4	Week 5
Gwen DeLaJuen					
Dennis Shale					
Ben Butler					
Scott Wilson					
Meghan Ryan					
Jim Brown					
Maria Artiste					
Beth Whitmer					
Pat Flynn					
Larry Brown					

I've always wanted a twin for those times when I had to be somewhere and I didn't want to go (like a funeral, a surprise birthday party for me, or a trip to the dentist). Keeping track of people like me (who don't always want to be where they're supposed to be) is even more boring. But whether it's for the meeting minutes, the classroom, or even your own employees' vacation and sick days, you'll be able to tell who was where and when with this simple attendance record.

PREPARATION

Create your table.

1. Select Layout. • Select Page. • Select Paper Size. • Select Letter Landscape. • Click on Select.

2. Click on Table Create button. • Select 31 x 12.

3. Click on Format Tbl button on Tables Button Bar. • Select Table. • Column Width: .190". • Click OK.

Create a heading.

4. Click in cell A1 (see the next figure). • Click on Format Tbl button. • Select Column. • Column Width: 3". • Click OK.

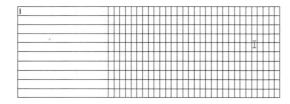

Chef's Tip *Table cells* have names based on their position in the table: what row and column they occupy. The address for a cell appears in the Title Bar and the Status Bar when you select that cell. (See the Basic Kitchen Skills section of the book for more information about tables and cell addressing.)

5. Select the first row. • Right-click; select Join Cells. • Font Face: Humanst521 Cn BT. • Font Size: 36. • Type: Attendance Record. • Press Enter.

6. Font Size: 24. • Type: For the month of:. • Press Shift+Hyphen to add blank line. • Press Enter.

7. Click on TblLineFill button. • Outside: None. • Bottom: Double. • Click OK.

Format the table headings.

8. Select cells C2 through G2. • Click the right mouse button. • Select Join Cells. • Repeat for cells I2 through M2, O2 through S2, U2 through Y2, and AA2 through AE2 (see the next figure).

Attendance Record
For the month of:_____

9. In cell A2, type: Names. • In cell C2, type: Week 1. • In cell I2, type: Week 2. • In cell O2, type: Week 3. • In cell U2, type: Week 4. • In cell AA2, type: Week 5.

10. Select column B. • Click on TblLineFill button. • Inside: None. • Outside: None. • Left and Right: Hairline. • Click OK. • Repeat for columns H, N, T, and Z.

11. Click in cell A2. • Click on TblLineFill button. • Bottom: Double. • Fill Style: 100% Fill. • Foreground Color: medium gray. • Click OK. • Repeat for cells C2, I2, O2, U2, and AA2 (see the next figure).

Attendance Record
For the month of:_____

| Names | Week 1 | Week 2 | Week 3 | Week 4 | Week 5 |

Format the rest of the table.

12. Select the five columns under "Week 1." • Click on TblLineFill button. • Fill Style: Fish Scale. • Foreground Color: very light gray. • Click OK. • Repeat for other weeks (see the next figure).

13. Select all rows in table except row 1. • Click on TblLineFill button. • Outside: Double. • Click OK.

Complete the table.

14. Click in cell A3. • Font Size: 18. • Type names of your attendees in column A.

15. Save and print your attendance record.

VARIATIONS

Sick of Vacation? *Keep track of your employees' sick, vacation, and personal days by marking a small "s," "v," or "p" in the appropriate column.*

Get Personal: *Add your department name and number or your company name and logo to the attendance record to dress it up.*

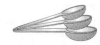

AUTO MAINTENANCE LOG

Time to Take the Car In!

Make: Plate Expires:

Model: Serial ID#:

License #:

		7,500 ● 22,500 ● 37,500 52,000
		15,000 ● 45,000 75,000
		30,000 ● 60,000 90,000

| Date of Service | | | | | | | |
| Odometer | | | | | | | |

What to Do	When to do it						
Oil/Oil Filter Change							
Lubricate Chassis							
Inspect Cooling System							
Flush Cooling System							
Inpect Antifreeze							
Flush Antifreeze							
Rotate Tires							
Inspect Alignment							
Replace Tire(s)							

Adjust Brakes							
Reline Brakes							
Change Brake Fluid							
Replace Plugs & Points							
Adjust Idle							
Engine Tune-up							
Change Transmission Fluid							
Change Clutch Fluid							
Adjust Clutch							
Change Air Filter							
Adjust Steering							
Inspect Exhaust System							
Lubricate Doors and Locks							
Check Headlights							
Inspect Belts and Hoses							
Inspect Battery							
Inspect Wipers							
Replace Fuel Filter							

I love cars—when they run. Don't get me wrong; I don't exactly hate car maintenance. Like many women of the '90s, I can change the oil, the spark plugs, and even the anti-freeze—trouble is, I still have to remember to do it. With this recipe, you'll create a nice log sheet to remind you about all those things you'd rather forget that you learned how to do growing up in a family with six boys.

PREPARATION

Create your table.

1. Select Layout. • Select Page. • Select Paper Size. • Select Letter Landscape. • Click on Select.

2. Click on Table Create button. • Select 11 x 36.

Add a title.

3. Select the first row. • Click the right mouse button. • Select Join Cells.

4. Font Face: Humanst521 Cn BT. • Font Size: 24. • Click on Bold button. • Type: Time to Take the Car In!

5. Select columns B, C, and D. • Click on Format Tbl button. • Click on Column. • Column Width: .480". • Repeat, setting columns E–K to .830". • Repeat, setting column A to 1.75".

> **Chef's Tip**   Table cells have names based on their position in the table: what row and column they occupy. The address for a cell appears in the Title Bar and the Status Bar when you select that cell. (See the Basic Kitchen Skills section of the book for more information about tables and cell addressing.)

6. Click in cell A2. • Justification: Right. • Font Size: 14. • Click on Bold button. • Type: Make: (see the next figure). • Repeat in cell A3, type: Model:. • Repeat in cell A4, type: License:. • Repeat in cell E2, type: Plate Expires:. • Repeat in cell E3, type: Serial ID#.

Time to Take the Car In!						
Make:			Plate Expires:			
Model:			Serial ID#:			
License:						

7. Select cells A1–K9. • Click on TblLineFill button. • Outside: None. • Inside: None. • Click OK.

8. Select cells B2–D2. • Click the right mouse button. • Select Join Cells. • Repeat for rows 3–7, selecting the three cells in columns B, C and D.

9. Select cells E2 and F2. • Click the right mouse button. • Select Join Cells. • Repeat for cells E3 and F3.

Add a legend.

10. Click in cell I2. • Click on TblLineFill button. • Fill Style: Diagonal Lines 1. • Repeat for cell I3. Fill Style: Diagonal Lines 2. • Repeat for cell I4. Fill Style: Diagonal Crosshatch.

11. Select cells J2–J4. • Font Size: 10. • Click on Bold button.

12. Click in cell J2. • Type: 7,500 22,500 37,500 52,000 (see the next figure). • Click between the first two numbers. • Select Insert. • Select Character. • Select Typographic Symbols. • Select the black circle. • Click Insert. • Click between next two numbers. • Click Insert. • Repeat for last two numbers.

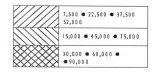

13. Click in cell J3. • Type: 15,000 45,000 75,000 (see preceding figure). • Insert black circles between numbers. • Click in cell J4. • Type: 30,000 60,000 90,000 (see preceding figure). • Insert black circles between numbers. • Click Close.

14. Select cells J2 and K2. • Click the right mouse button. • Select Join Cells. • Repeat with cells J3–K3, and J4–K4.

15. Select cells I2–I4. • Click on TblLineFill button. • Outside: Single. • Inside: Single.

Add the maintenance tasks.

16. Select cells B6 and B7. • Click on Bold button. • Font Size: 14. • Justification: Right.

17. Click in cell B6. • Type: Date of Service: (see the next figure). • Click in cell B7. • Type: Odometer:. • Select cells B6 and B7. • Click on TblLineFill button. • Fill Style: 100%. • Foreground Color: light gray. • Click OK. • Select cells B6–K7. • Click on TblLineFill button. • Outside: Double. • Inside: Single.

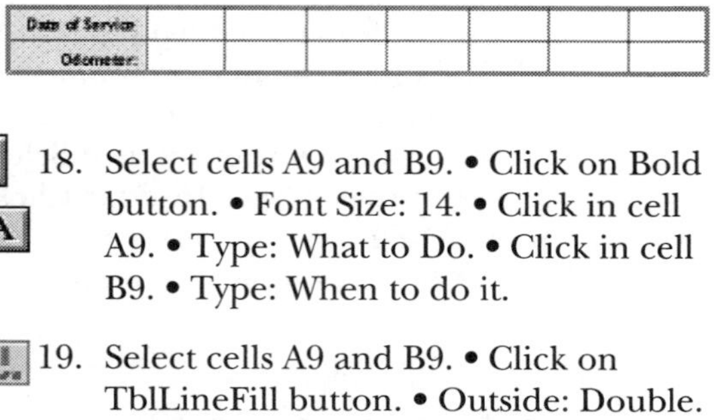

18. Select cells A9 and B9. • Click on Bold button. • Font Size: 14. • Click in cell A9. • Type: What to Do. • Click in cell B9. • Type: When to do it.

19. Select cells A9 and B9. • Click on TblLineFill button. • Outside: Double. • Fill Style: 100%. • Foreground Color: light gray (see the next figure). • Click OK.

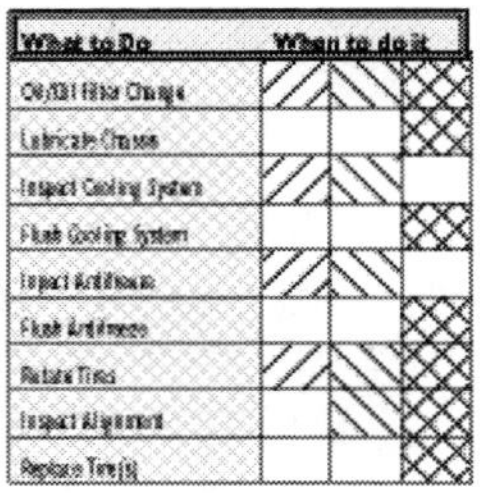

20. Type the maintenance tasks in cells A10–A36 (see preceding and following figures). • Select cells A10–A36. • Click on TblLineFill button. • Fill Style: 100%. • Foreground Color: lightest gray.

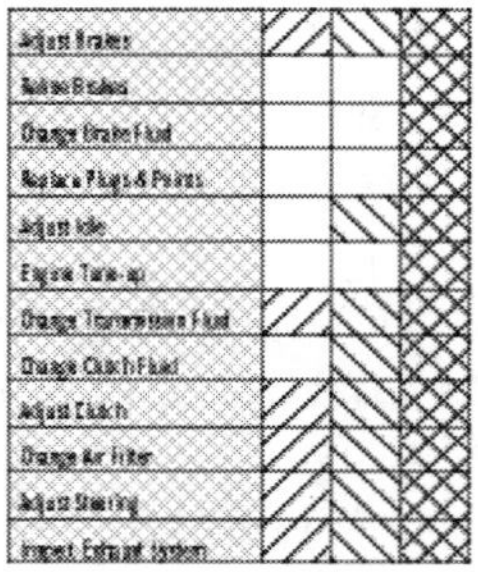

21. Select the appropriate cells in column B. • Click on TblLineFill button. • Fill Style: Diagonal 1. • Click OK. • Repeat with appropriate cells in column C. Fill Style: Diagonal 2. • Repeat with appropriate cells in column D. Fill Style: Diagonal Crosshatch.

22. Save and print your auto maintenance log.

Variations

Spring Cleaning: *Adapt this maintenance log to other chores, such as home maintenance (cleaning the windows, cleaning out the gutters, and so on) or yard work (trimming trees, mulching roses, fertilizing, and so on).*

BASEBALL LINEUP

Braves Line-Up
Blue Rivers Junior League
July 16th, 1994

Pitcher: Joey Bloome
First Base: Ryan Wilson
Second Base: George Allison
Third Base: Tim Ryan
Short Stop: Jack Kemper
Left Field: Steve Stocks
Center Field: Jack Anderson
Right Field: Andy Hendricks
Catcher: Bobby Whitmer

Ah, spring. Time for America's favorite pastime: shouting at the little league coach. If you're one of these beleaguered few wearing the coach's cap, put an end to face-to-face "discussions" with parents by posting your line-up as far away from the playing field as possible (like, say, China). With this recipe, you can create a simple line-up chart that's guaranteed parent-proof. Create a scoring sheet, too, using the recipe that follows this one.

PREPARATION

Create a watermark.

1. Select Layout. • Select Watermark.
   • Select Watermark A. • Click on Create.

Draw your watermark design.

2. Click on Draw button on WordPerfect Button Bar. • Select Attributes.
   • Select Fill. • Select Gradient. • Center Color: light tan. • Outer Color: brown.
   • Type: Circular. • Click OK.

3. Click on Line Style tool. • Select None.
   • Click on Closed Curve tool. • Draw the bat body (see the next figure).

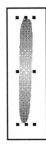

4. Draw the bat handle. • Select the bat handle. • Select Arrange. • Select Back.

5. Click on Ellipse tool. • Draw the bat end (see the next figure).

6. Select Edit. • Choose Select. • Select All. • Select Edit. • Select Rotate.
   • Rotate bat to the left.

7. Select Text. • Select Font. • Font Face: Times New Roman. • Font Size: 20.
   • Click on Attributes button. • Foreground Color: brown. • Click OK.
   • Click OK.

8. Click on Text tool. • Click in drawing area and type: Louisville Slugger.
   • Select the text box. • Select Edit.
   • Select Rotate. • Rotate text to match the bat (see the next figure). • Drag text box onto the bat.

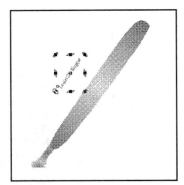

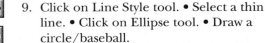

9. Click on Line Style tool. • Select a thin line. • Click on Ellipse tool. • Draw a circle/baseball.

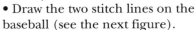

10. Click on Line Style tool. • Select the Dots style. • Click on Curved Line tool.
    • Draw the two stitch lines on the baseball (see the next figure).

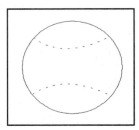

11. Select File. • Select Exit and Return to Document. • Select Yes.

 Cook's Caution If you want to save and reuse your baseball logo in other projects, such as a baseball scoring sheet, select Save As from the File menu before you do step 11. Enter a file name, such as BASEBALL.WPG.

12. Click on the bat. • Click the right mouse button. • Select Size. • Select Full. • Click OK. • Click Close. • Click Close again.

Add your players.

 13. Font Face: Brush738 BT. • Font Size: 48. • Justification: Center. • Type: Braves Line-Up.

14. Font Face: Swis721 Blk Ex BT. • Font Size: 18. • Justification: Center. • Type: Blue Rivers Junior League. • Press Enter; type the date.

15. Press Enter six times. • Justification: Left. • Font Size: 14.

16. Select View. • Select Ruler. • Drag left margin marker to the 2" mark. • Type: Pitcher:. • Press Tab three times. • Type the name of your player. • Continue with other players and positions.

17. Save and print your line-up sheet.

VARIATIONS

Let's Go Bowling: *Use this same format to create a bowling league tournament line-up, but draw a bowling ball for the watermark.*

BASEBALL SCORING SHEET

 Score Sheet

Date: April 12, 1994

Location: Brightstown Park

Team	1	2	3	4	5	6	7	8	9		R	H	E
Brightstown Braves	2	0	0	1	0	2	1	0	1		7	12	7
Cathedral Fighting Irish	1	3	0	0	2	1	2	2	1		12	18	6

Whether you're a little league coach, in charge of the company softball team, or an armchair warrior, you can use this recipe to track the team that's closest to your heart. You can even add a logo (created using the Baseball Line-Up recipe earlier in this section) to brighten things up when your team is falling behind.

PREPARATION

Start with your title.

1. Select Layout. • Select Page. • Select Paper Size. • Select Letter Landscape. • Click Select.

2. Font Face: Brush738 BT. • Double-click on Font Size button. • Font Size: 58. • Justification: Center. • Type: Score Sheet.

3. Font Face: Swis721 Blk Ex BT. • Font Size: 18. • Justification: Left. • Press Enter twice. • Type Date:. • Change Font Size to 14. • Type the date (see the next figure).

Score Sheet

Date: April 12, 1994

Location: Brightstown Park

4. Change Font Size back to 18. • Type: Locations:. • Change Font Size to 14. • Type the location (see preceding figure). • Press Enter.

Insert the baseball logo.

5. Click on Figure button. • Select your logo file. • Click OK. • Drag to resize.

6. Click on Border/Fill button. • Border Style: None. • Click OK. • Click on Wrap button. • Select No Wrap. • Drag the figure to the left-hand side of the title (see the next figure).

7. Click on the logo. • Click on Copy button. • Click in document. • Click on Paste button. • Drag the copy to right-hand side of the title. • Click on Tools button. • Click on Flip Vertically button (see the next figure). • Click Close.

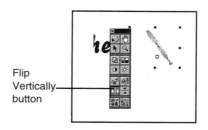

Flip Vertically button

Create a scoring table.

8. Click on Table Create button. • Select 15 x 3.

9. Click in cell A1. • Click on Format Tbl button on Tables Button Bar. • Select Column. • Width: 2". • Click OK. • Select cells B1 through O1. • Repeat, setting width to .5".

10. Click in cell A1. • Font Face: Arial. • Font Size: 18. • Type: Team. • Type: 1–9 in cells B1–J1. • Type: R, H, and E in cells M1–O1.

11. Click in cell A1. • Click on TblLineFill button. • Fill Style: 100%. • Foreground Color: medium gray. • Click OK.

12. Select cells A1 to A3. • Click on TblLineFill button again. • Outside: Double. • Click OK.

13. Select cells B1 to L1. • Click on TblLineFill button. • Outside: Thick/Thin 1. • Fill Style: 100%. • Foreground Color: light gray. • Click OK (see the next figure).

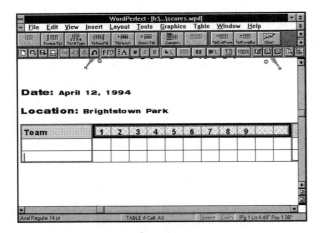

17. Save your scoring sheet. • Print a blank sheet; use it to keep score at the game. • Enter your data. • Click Calculate to compute the total number of runs.

VARIATIONS

Bowling, Anyone? *Adapt this scoring sheet for keeping track of your team's progress in your league. For that matter, you can change this form for any sporting event, such as volleyball, football, basketball, and so on.*

 14. Select cells M1 to O1. • Click on TblLineFill button. • Fill Style: 100% • Foreground Color: medium gray. • Click OK. • Select cells M1 to O3. • Click on TblLineFill button. • Outside: Double. • Click OK.

Add a few formulas.

15. Click on TblFormBar button. • Click in cell M2. • Click in the formula bar. • Click on Functions. • Select Sum (List). • Click Insert. • Select cells B2 through L2 (see the next figure). • Press Enter.

16. Click on Copy Formula. • Select Down and 1. • Click OK. • Click Close.

5 min.

Easy

CLASS SCHEDULE

Class Schedule

	MON.	TUES.	WED.	THURS.	FRI.
8:00 am	Homeroom	Homeroom	Homeroom	Homeroom	Homeroom
8:30 am	English	History	English	History	English
9:00 am					
9:30 am		Study		Study	
10:00 am	Geometry	Gym	Geometry	Gym	Geometry
10:30 am					
11:00 am	Health Science	Art	Health Science	Art	Art
11:30 am					
12:00 pm	Lunch	Lunch	Lunch	Lunch	Lunch
12:30 pm					
1:00 pm	Biology	Typing	Biology	Typing	Biology
1:30 pm					
2:00 pm	Lab	Study	Lab	Study	Lab
2:30 pm	French	French	French		French
3:00 pm					

Recurring nightmares of showing up late for Professor Blaigh's class? Banish them with an organized class schedule created with this recipe. If you have the same nightmares about forgetting an important assignment, check out the "Homework Assignments" recipe later in this section. If you have nightmares about summer trips to Aunt Hildegard's, I can't help you there—sorry.

PREPARATION

Start with a nice title.

1. Font Face: OzHandicraft BT. • Font Size: 36. • Justification: Center. • Type: Class Schedule. • Press Enter.

2. Click on Table Create button. • Select 6 x 16.

Format your table.

3. Click in cell A1. • Click on Format Tbl button on Tables Button Bar. • Select Column. • Width: .75". • Click OK. • Select cells B1 to F1. • Repeat. •Width: 1.13".

4. Click in cell A1. • Click on TblLineFill button. • Left: None. • Top: None. • Click OK (see the next figure).

5. Select cells B1 to F1. • Click on TblLineFill button. • Outside: Double. • Fill Style: 100%. • Foreground Color: light gray. • Click OK.

6. Select cells B1 to F1. • Font Face: EngraversGothic BT. Double-click on Font Size button. • Font Size: 16. • Justification: Center. • Starting in cell B1, type the days of the week (see the next figure).

7. In cell A2, type: 8:00. • In cell A3, type: 8:30. • Select cells A2 through A16. • Click on TblDataFill button.

8. With the cells still selected, click on TblLineFill button. • Outside: Button Bottom. • Fill Style: 100%. • Foreground Color: medium gray. • Click OK.

9. Beginning in cell B2, type your class schedule. • Join cells where necessary (see the next figure).

	MON.	TUES.	WED.	THURS.	FRI.
8:00 am		Homeroom	Homeroom	Homeroom	Homeroom
8:30 am		History	English	History	English
9:00 am					
9:30 am		Study		Study	
10:00 am		Gym	Geometry	Gym	Geometry
10:30 am					
11:00 am		Art	Health Science	Art	Art
11:30 am					
12:00 pm		Lunch	Lunch	Lunch	Lunch
12:30 pm					
1:00 pm		Typing	Biology	Typing	Biology

10. Save and print your class schedule.

VARIATIONS

I'm Late, I'm Late! *Add room numbers to your class schedule so you can quickly find your way.*

Where's Charlie? *Adapt this recipe to keep track of all your kids and their after-school activities.*

DAILY CALENDAR

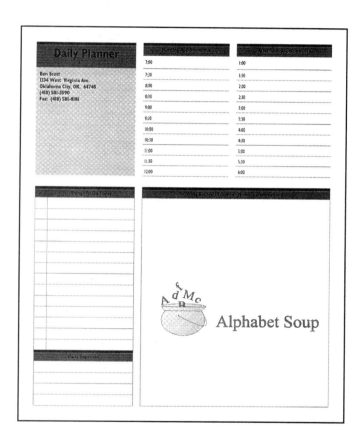

They say morning is the best time to organize your thoughts and plan your day. For me, morning is the best time to drink a pot of coffee and pry open my eyelids. I plan my mornings around noon. For this recipe, all you'll need is a WordPerfect template and your logo (if you don't have a logo, you can create one with the recipes you'll find in the Appetizer section of this book). With a little help from the PLANDAY template, you can practically do this project with your eyes closed, which, if you're anything like me, is a good thing if you attempt to complete it before noon.

PREPARATION

Start with the template.

1. Click on Open button. • Change to Template Directory if necessary. • Select PLANDAY.WPT template. • Click OK.

2. Click on View button. • Select Full Page.

Add your logo.

3. Click on Watermark button on Default Button Bar. • Select Watermark A. • Click on Create. • Click on Figure button. • Select your logo. • Click OK.

4. Place cursor over the watermark logo. • Click the right mouse button. • Choose Select Box. • Drag the watermark to lower right-hand corner of page (see the next figure). • Resize the watermark to fit the notes section. • Click Close. • Click Close again.

5. Click on Exit Template button. • Click Yes. For help using your template later on, see Part 7: Basic Kitchen Skills.

VARIATIONS

What's Your Name? *You can add your name (instead of a logo) as a watermark. At step 3, click on the Text Box button instead of the Figure button. Type your name (you may want to enlarge the font size to 36) and remove the box border. Because the text will appear somewhat dark, you may also want to change the font shading to 15%.*

BUSINESS   ORGANIZATION   **HOME**   **SCHOOL**

Moderate

EXERCISE CHART

Exercise Chart

Week Number	Leg Curls		Arm Curls		Sit-Ups	Push-Ups	Leg Lifts	
	Lbs.	Reps	Lbs.	Reps	Reps	Reps	Lbs.	Reps
1								
2								
3								
4								
5								
6								
7								
8								
9								
10								

No one really loves to exercise—it's boring. (Donuts, on the other hand, are not boring at all.) You exercise hard and never really see any progress when you need it the most. With this recipe, you'll create a chart for tracking your weekly improvements, or for covering up those donuts that are just begging to be eaten.

EXERCISE CHART

PREPARATION

Create a table.

1. Select Layout. • Select Page. • Select Paper Size. • Select Letter Landscape. • Click Select.

2. Font Face: Humanst521 Cn BT. • Font Size: 36. • Type: Exercise Chart. • Press Enter twice.

3. Click on Table Create button. • Select 9 x 12.

Add column headings.

4. Click in cell A1. • Justification: Center. • Font Size: 18. • Type: Week Number.

> **Chef's Tip** • Table cells have names based on their position in the table: what row and column they occupy. The address for a cell appears in the Title Bar and the Status Bar when you select that cell. (See the Basic Kitchen Skills section of the book for more information about tables and cell addressing.)

5. Click in cell B1. • Type: Leg Curls. • Click in cell D1. • Type: Arm Curls. • Click in cell F1. • Type: Sit-Ups. • Click in cell G1. • Type: Push-Ups. • Click in cell H1. • Type: Leg Lifts (see the next figure).

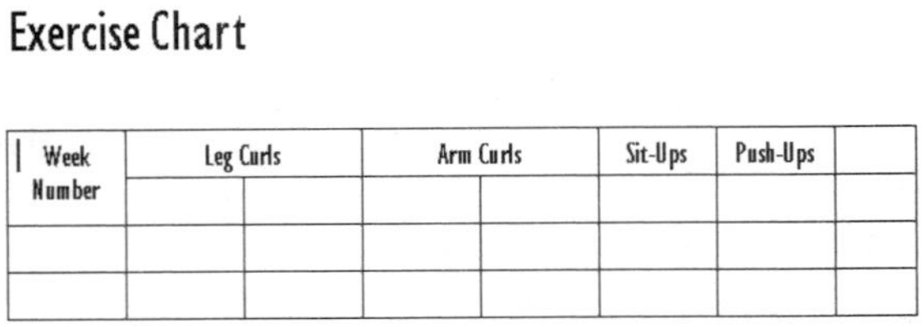

Exercise Chart

	Week Number	Leg Curls		Arm Curls		Sit-Ups	Push-Ups	

6. Select cells B1 and C1. • Click the right mouse button. • Select Join Cells. • Repeat with cells D1 and E1, H1 and I1, and A1 and A2 (see preceding figure).

7. Click in cell B2. • Type: Lbs. • Repeat in cells D2 and H2. • Click in cell C2. • Type: Reps. • Repeat in cells E2, F2, G2, and I2.

Add the week numbers.

8. Click in cell A3. • Type: 1. • Click in cell A4. • Type: 2. • Select cells A3–A12. • Click on TblDataFill button. • Justification: Center (see the next figure).

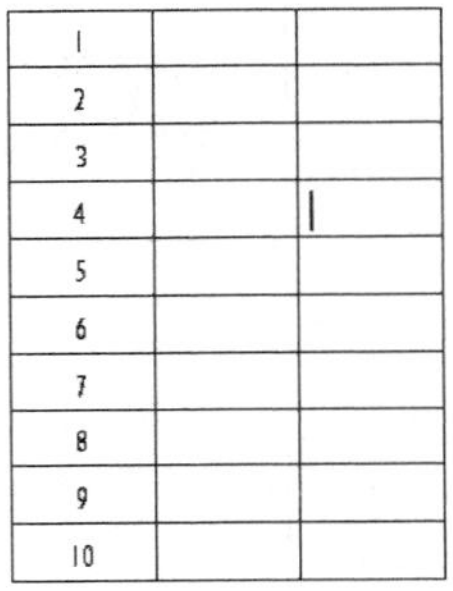

1		
2		
3		
4		
5		
6		
7		
8		
9		
10		

9. With the cells still selected, click on TblLineFill button. • Left and Top: Button Top. • Right and Bottom: Button Bottom. • Fill Style: 10%. • Click OK.

10. Click in cell A1. • Click on TblLineFill button. • Fill Style: 20%. • Click OK (see the next figure).

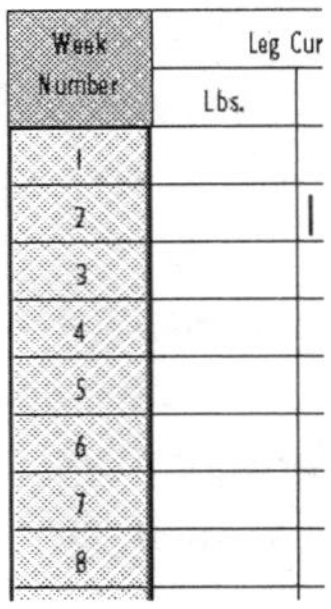

Week Number	Leg Cur
	Lbs.
1	
2	
3	
4	
5	
6	
7	
8	

Format the rest of the table.

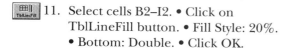 11. Select cells B2–I2. • Click on TblLineFill button. • Fill Style: 20%. • Bottom: Double. • Click OK.

12. Click in cell B1. • Click on TblLineFill button. • Left and Top: Button Top. • Right and Bottom: Button Bottom. • Fill Style: 10%. • Click OK. • Repeat for cells D1, E1, F1, and G1.

13. Select cells H2–I12. • Click on TblLineFill button. • Left, Right, and Bottom: Double. • Click OK.

14. Select cells G2–G12. • Click on TblLineFill button. • Left and Bottom: Double. • Click OK. • Repeat for cells F2–F12 and D2–E12.

15. Select cells B2–C12. • Click on TblLineFill button. • Bottom: Double. • Click OK. • Click in cell B2. • Click on TblLineFill button. • Left: Double. • Click OK (see the next figure).

16. Save and print your exercise chart. Take it to the gym with you.

VARIATIONS

It Figures: *Track your measurements instead of the number of exercises by setting up columns for chest, waist, thighs, and upper arms. Add a column for weight as well, but keep in mind that muscle weighs more than fat, so, for awhile, you may actually weigh more than you did when you began your fitness program. Bummer.*

GROCERY LIST

Grocery List

How many times have you stood in the checkout line at the grocery store wondering if you've remembered everything you were supposed to buy? Here's an idea to thwart such occurrences and reduce your checkout-line anxiety. Instead of wondering what you forgot, you can now peruse the tabloids for the latest news about the royal family, Burt and Loni, Tonya and Nancy, and others—all because you've brought along your handy-dandy WordPerfect for Windows Grocery List. Bon appetite!

PREPARATION

Select the Notepad paper size.

1. Select Layout. • Select Page.
   • Select Paper Size. • Select Notepad. • If not present, click Create. • Type: Notepad. • Enter the size 5 x 8.
   • Click OK. • Click Select.

2. Select Layout. • Select Margins. • All margins: .25". • Click OK.

Draw a heading.

3. Click on Draw button on WordPerfect Button Bar. • Select File. • Select Page Layout. • Dimensions: 5 x 2.5.
   • Click OK.

4. Select Text. • Select Font. • Font Face: Arial. • Font Size: 36. • Click OK.

5. Click on Text tool. • Click in the document. • Type: Grocery List.

6. Click on Freehand tool. • Draw a curving line.

7. Press Shift. • With Select tool, click on the line and the text (see the next figure).
   • Select Arrange. • Select Effects. • Select Contour Text. • Position: Top, Centered.
   • Click OK.

8. Click on Line Style tool. • Select the third width size. • Click on Freehand tool. • Draw a curving line under the title.

Add some carrots.

9. Select Attributes. • Select Fill.
   • Select Gradient. • Center Color: white. • Outer Color: orange.
   • Type: Rectangular. • Click OK.

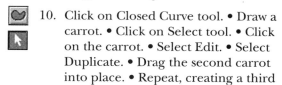

10. Click on Closed Curve tool. • Draw a carrot. • Click on Select tool. • Click on the carrot. • Select Edit. • Select Duplicate. • Drag the second carrot into place. • Repeat, creating a third carrot. • Drag third carrot into place.

11. Click on the third carrot. • Select Edit.
    • Select Rotate. • Rotate the carrot to the right (see the next figure).

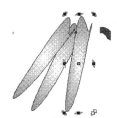

12. Select Attributes. • Select Fill. • Outer Color: green. • Click OK.

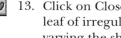

13. Click on Closed Curve tool. • Draw a leaf of irregular shape. • Repeat, varying the shape and size of each leaf so they fan out from the carrot bunch (see the next figure).

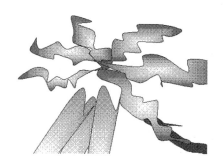

14. Drag across the completed carrot bunch to select it. • Drag into place at the left end of the line. • Select Edit. • Select Duplicate. • Place the copy at the right end of the line.

15. Select the bunch of carrots on the right. • Select Arrange. • Select Flip Left/Right.

16. Select File. • Select Exit and Return to Document. • Click Yes.

Add finishing touches.

17. Click on Wrap button on Graphics Box Feature Bar. • Select No Wrap. • Click Close.

18. Drag the heading to the top of the notepad.

19. Press Enter to move cursor beyond heading. • Click on Table Create button. • Select 1 x 17.

20. Select entire table. • Click on TblLineFill button. • Left and Right: None. • Click OK (see the next figure).

21. Save and print your notepad. • Take to a copier to have bound into pads.

VARIATIONS

Line Up! *You can add lines to any of the notepad designs in the Appetizer section of this book.*

Check It Out: *Create a two- or three-column table, and use borders to create specific sections, such as "Produce" or "Meats/Fish/Chicken." To save more time, arrange these sections as you find them in your local supermarket.*

HOMEWORK ASSIGNMENTS

Homework Assignments

Date Due	Class	Assignment
3-31-94	Math	Pg. 91, problems 2-10.
4-12-94	Math	Pg. 97, problems 10-21
4-14-94	Art	Still life due
4-15-94	Science	Read pages 108-123
4-21-94	French	Test

There's nothing worse than the feeling that you've forgotten to do something—especially when you remember just as class is starting that today's the day a report is due. Don't be caught off-guard. Keep track of those important assignments with this homework assignment recipe. Keeping track of assignments will be so much fun, you might actually want to do them. (Just kidding!)

PREPARATION

Create a table.

 1. Click on Table Create button. • Select 3 x 25.

2. Select View. • Select Ruler Bar. • Drag the borders of the table columns to adjust to the size shown (see the next figure).

	I	

Add a heading.

3. Select cells A1–C1. • Click the right mouse button. • Select Join Cells.

 4. Click in cell A1. • Font Face: Times New Roman, BerhnhardMod BT, Souvenir Lt BT, or similar font. • Font Size: 36. • Justification: Right. • Type: Homework Assignments.

Make it look like a notebook page.

 5. Click on TblLineFill button. • Select Table. • Custom Color: blue. • Click OK.

6. Select Graphics. • Select Custom Line. • Select Vertical. • Line Color: red. • Line Style: Dashed. • Click OK. • Drag line into place (see the next figure).

Homework Assi

Date Due	Class	Assignment
3-31-94	Math	Pg. 91, problems
4-12-94	Math	Pg. 97, problems
4-14-94	Art	Still life due
4-15-94	Science	Read pages 108-
4-21-94	French	Test

7. Select Graphics. • Select Custom Box. • Select User. • Click OK.

 8. Double-click inside the user box. • Select Insert. • Select Character. • Select Typographic Symbols. • Select the hole symbol. • Click Insert and Close. • Select hole. • Font Size: 48.

9. Resize the user box as shown. • Click on Wrap button. • Select No Wrap. • Click OK. • Drag into place (see the next figure).

Date Due	Class	Assign
3-31-94	Math	Pg. 91
4-12-94	Math	Pg. 97
4-14-94	Art	Still lif
4-15-94	Science	Read
4-21-94	French	Test

10. Click on Position button. • Select Put Box on Current Page (Page Anchor). • Click OK. • Click Close.

11. Click on Copy button. • Click in the document. • Click on Paste button.
    • Drag second hole into place.
    • Repeat for a total of five holes.

Add column headings.

12. Click in cell A2. • Font Face: Ribbon131 Bd BT, Script, or similar font.
    • Font Size: 24. • Justification: Right.
    • Type: Date Due.

13. Click in cell B2. • Justification: Center.
    • Type: Class.

14. Click in cell C2. • Justification: Left.
    • Type: Assignment.

Finish up.

15. Click in cell A3. • Font Face: Arial.
    • Font Size: 14. • Justification: Right.
    • Type your assignments.

16. Save your homework assignment sheet.

17. Select the records (lines in your table that have data in them) to sort. • Select Tools. • Select Sort. • Click OK (see the next figure). • Save and print your assignment sheet again.

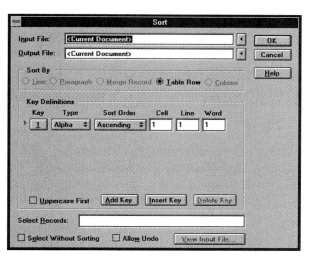

Cook's Caution   As you add new assignments, repeat step 17 to sort them by due date. Be sure to save your file before and after sorting.

VARIATIONS

Gotta Get It Done!   *Change a few titles, and you could easily create a nice to-do list with this recipe. Print out several copies and share your new project with your co-workers. That way, you won't break out into a sweat when your boss asks you how that project is coming along—it'll be done, 'cause it was on someone else's to-do list.*

Total Look: *Print your assignment sheet on yellow paper for the total "notebook" look.*

HOME INVENTORY

Our Home Inventory
Last Updated: 11/12/94

Living Room

Description	Type	Purchase Date	Purchase Price	Notes
Stereo - Toshiba	Electronics	4/10/90	$1,500	
CD Player - Sony	Electronics	5/15/93	$300	
VCR - Mitzubishi	Electronics	3/10/90	$350	
Painting - "Mexican Chilies"	Art	10/12/93	$400	
Crystal bowl - Waterford	Collectible	10/16/93	$225	Wedding gift
TV - Mitzubishi	Electronics	3/10/90	$750	

Master Bedroom

Description	Type	Purchase Date	Purchase Price	Notes
TV - RCA 20"	Electronics	8/15/93	$1,700	
Diamond earrings	Jewelry	12/20/93	$540	Christmas gift
Topaz ring	Jewelry	10/20/93	$350	
Topaz bracelet	Jewelry	10/16/94	$450	Anniversary gift

Everyone says you should have one, but who wants to create a complete inventory of household goods? Well, if disaster strikes (such as your mother-in-law coming to visit for a week and staying a month), you'll be prepared. Okay, maybe you won't exactly be prepared for her visit, but if floods or famine follow . . . with this recipe, you'll be able to provide the insurance company with the information it needs to deny your claim in the shortest time possible.

PREPARATION

Start with a heading.

1. Select Layout. • Select Page. • Select Paper Size. • Select Letter Landscape. • Click Select.

2. Font Face: Humanst521 BT. • Font Size: 24. • Type: Our Home Inventory. • Press Enter.

3. Font Size: 14. • Type: Last Updated:. • Select Insert. • Select Date. • Select Date Code. • Press Enter twice.

Create a table.

4. Click on Table Create button. • Select 5 x 8.

5. Select cells A1–E1. • Click the right mouse button. • Select Join Cells. • Click on TblLineFill button. • Outside: Single. • Fill Style: 100%. • Foreground Color: medium gray. • Click OK.

6. Click in cell A1. • Font Face: Arial. • Font Size: 18. • Type: Living Room (see the next figure).

Our Home Inventory
Last Updated: 11/12/94

Living Room				

Add column headings.

7. Click in cell A2. • Font Size: 12. • Click on Bold button. • Type: Description. • Repeat with cells B2–E2, adding column headings as shown. • Click in cell D2. • Justification: Right.

8. Select View. • Select Ruler Bar. • Adjust column widths as shown.

9. Select cells A2–E2. • Click on Format Tbl button. • Select Row. • Height: .520". • Click OK. • Click on TblLineFill button. • Outside and Inside: None. • Click OK (see the next figure).

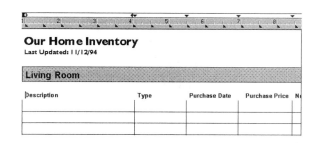

Our Home Inventory
Last Updated: 11/12/94

Living Room				
Description	Type	Purchase Date	Purchase Price	N

10. Click in cell A3. • Font Size: 10.

11. Select cells A3–E7. • Click on TblLineFill button. • Outside: None. • Inside: Hairline. • Top: Thick/Thin 2. • Click OK (see the next figure).

Living Room				
Description	Type	Purchase Date	Purchase Price	N

12. Select cells B3–B7. • Click on TblLineFill button. • Left and Right: None. • Click OK. • Repeat for cells C3–C7, D3–D7, and E3–E7.

13. Select cells A8–E8. • Click on TblLineFill button. • Outside: None. • Inside: None. • Click OK. • Click on Format Tbl button. • Select Row. • Height: .800". • Click OK.

Add final touches.

14. Enter inventory data. • Delete or insert rows as necessary.

15. Select the table. • Click on Copy button. • Click under the existing table. • Click on Paste button. • Change "Living Room" to "Master Bedroom." • Delete or insert rows as necessary. • Add inventory data.

16. Repeat step 15 to add additional sections as necessary.

17. Save and print your home inventory. • Store in your safety deposit box.

VARIATIONS

Well, It Looks Like My TV: *Add a serial number column to your inventory for easy identification of stolen items.*

Taking Stock: *Adapt this recipe to track business inventory, such as computers, printers, adding machines, and copiers. Include identifying numbers where applicable.*

School Time: *Adapt this recipe to track classroom inventory, such as projectors, screens, and overheads. You could also use this recipe to track equipment assigned to an organization, such as the band, the scouts, or the school festival committee.*

RECIPE CARDS

AUNT JEAN'S POTATO CASSEROLE

Ingredients:

1 lb. hash brown potatoes	1 stick of melted butter
8 oz. shredded cheddar cheese	8 oz. sour cream
1 can cream of chicken soup	1 tsp. salt and pepper
1 can cream of mushroom soup	1/4 cup dried onion flakes
garlic salt to taste	crushed corn flakes

Directions:
Mix all ingredients, except cornflakes and butter. Spread into large casserole dish. Top with melted butter and crushed corn flakes. Bake at 350 for
1-1 1/2 hour. Serves 8.

It's time to organize your kitchen. Really get cooking with WordPerfect, and create your own recipe cards for filing and giving. Use the TextArt feature to make attractive titles for the cards, and add a simple graphic to illustrate them. With their small size, you can fit several cards onto an 8 ½-by-11-inch page. If necessary, you can make a front and back of a card and print them on the same page. (This recipe can be frozen and used again at a later time.)

PREPARATION

Set up the card size and border.

1. Select Layout. • Select Page. • Select Paper Size. • Click on Create button. • Type in the name for your card size. • Paper Size: 5" by 3". • Click on Wide Form check box. • Click OK. • Click Select.

 Cook's Caution A message may appear telling you that your print driver won't support the paper size you've created. That's okay. You'll accept it on a regular 8½-by-11-inch page, so click OK.

2. Select Layout. • Select Margins. • Margin settings: .25" all around. • Click OK.

3. Select Layout. • Select Page. • Select Border/Fill. • Border Style: Thick/ Thin 2. • Click OK.

Add a TextArt title and type your recipe.

 4. Click on TextArt button on WordPerfect Button Bar. • Font Face: Bookman Old Style, Jester, or similar style. • Select the wavy shape. • Width: 5". • Height: 1". • Enter your text. • Select File. • Select Exit & Return to WordPerfect. • Click Yes to embed object.

5. Resize the TextArt to fit inside the border.

 6. Move the cursor down and type the recipe. • Font Face: Times New Roman. • Double-click on Font Size button. • Font Size: 9. • Use the ruler to set text margins inside border. • Set recipe ingredients in italics. • Use tabs to set ingredients into two columns (see the next figure).

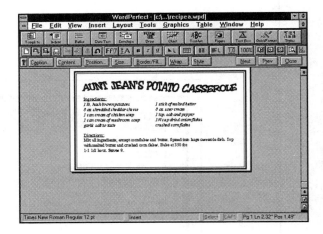

Create a graphic to place on the card.

 7. Click on Draw button. • Select Attributes. • Select Fill. • Select Gradient. • Center Color: black. • Outer Color: gray. • Change the Center Color Position Y Offset to 100%. • Click OK.

 8. Click on Ellipse tool. • Draw an oval to form the base of a bowl. • Make sure the oval is not highlighted. • Select Attributes. • Select Fill. • Setting: Pattern. • Colors: white. • Click on Line Style button. • Select the No Line check box. • Click OK.

 9. Click on Ellipse tool. • Draw another oval over the first oval, leaving the shape of a bowl on the first oval you drew (see the next figure).

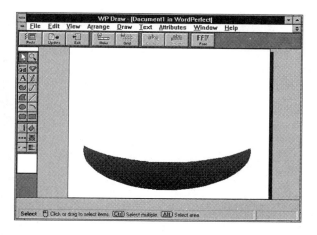

 Chef's Tip Can't see what you're drawing? Good. You're not supposed to because you changed the tool to solid white. What you're doing is blocking out part of the first oval you drew in step 8. Turning the image into a bowl isn't easy, so be patient, and expect this to take a few tries.

 10. Click on Elliptical Arc tool. • Use the tool to add two curves to complete the top of the bowl, making sure they connect (see the next figure).

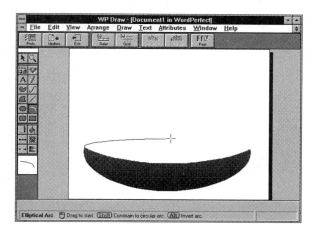

 11. Click on Closed Curve tool. • Select Attributes. • Select Fill. • Style: Gradient. • Type: Circular. • Click on Line Style button. • Make sure the No Line check box is not checked. • Click OK.

12. Above the bowl shape, draw the shape of a spoon.

 13. Click on Polygon tool. • Select Attributes. • Select Fill. • Style: Gradient. • Type: Circular. • Click on Line Style button. • Make sure the No Line check box is not checked. • Click OK.

14. Draw a handle for the spoon, making sure the lines touch the spoon shape drawn in step 12.

 15. When finished drawing the spoon, click on spoon shape with the Select tool. • Press Ctrl. • Then click the handle shape. • Select Edit. • Select Rotate. • Rotate spoon as desired, then move shape to fit on top of the bowl shape (see the next figure).

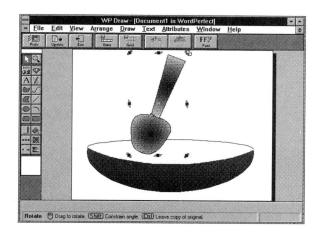

16. Select File. • Select Exit and Return to Document. • Click Yes.

17. Resize the graphic as needed to fit in lower right portion of the card.

18. Save and print your card.

VARIATIONS

Make Them Sturdy: *After printing your recipe cards, you can trim them and attach them to index cards to make them sturdier. Did you like the bowl and spoon graphic used in this project? For another creative touch, use WordPerfect Draw to design a "kitchen logo" that applies to you and your cooking style. Some possible ideas: a crumpled chef's hat, a stained apron, a boiling pot, a small grease fire, an oven exploding—use the Draw feature to come up with your own distinctive look!*

10 min.

Moderate

MILEAGE RECORD

Mileage Record

NAME:

ADDRESS:

CAR MAKE/MODEL:

TYPE OF OIL & FILTERS USED:

Date	Start	Stop	Total Miles	Gas	Oil Change/Date	Misc.
		Grand Totals				

Signed:

Is your mileage report going nowhere fast? Here's a great idea for making an attractive form to record your car's mileage. Use this for your family car or your company car. Keep track of oil changes, miles traveled, gas used, and more. This recipe is based on an existing WordPerfect for Windows template, so all you have to do is add a graphic and change the text to make a form suited to your needs. (For those of you who are really going fast, add a column for speeding tickets accumulated.)

PREPARATION

Set up the template.

 1. Click on Open button. • Select Mileage template. • Click OK.

2. Select Layout. • Select Margins. • Margins: .5" all around. • Click OK.

 3. Select Table. • Select Format. • Click on Table option button. • Select Disable Cell Locks. • Click OK. • Make any changes to the existing template text, such as new column titles, and so on. • Font Size: 10.

Create the top of the form.

 4. Select the top row of the table. • Click on TblLineFill button on Tables Button Bar. • Line Style: all sides Thick/Single. • Click OK.

 5. Select the title text. • Font Face: Arial.
 • Click on Bold button. • Click on Italics button (see the next figure). • Delete the rest of the existing template text in the row.

![Mileage Record form top with template fields]

6. Select Graphics. • Select Custom Line. • Select the Large Dashed style. • Line: .4" thick. • Click OK.

7. Move line into place, resizing as necessary, creating the look of a divided highway (see the next figure).

![Mileage Record with dashed divided highway line]

 Cook's Caution   You may have to add more space to the row to fit your graphic line. Just click the cursor after the words "Mileage Record," and press Enter to add more depth to the table box.

Build a car graphic.

 8. Click on Draw button on WordPerfect Button Bar. • Click on Polygon tool.
 • Select Attributes. • Select Fill. • Change the colors as desired (candy apple red, maybe). • Click OK.

 9. Click on Polygon tool. • Draw the car's body. • Fill Color: white. • Draw car windows on top of the car body shape.

 10. Select Attributes. • Select Fill. • Change the colors as desired; try light gray. • Click OK.

11. Click on the Ellipse tool. • Draw the car's wheels (see the next figure). • When finished, select File. • Select Exit and Return to Document. • Click Yes.

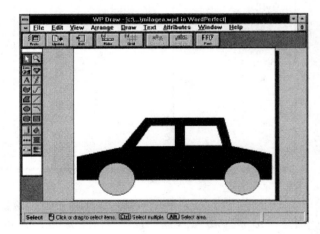

12. Resize and reposition the graphic as needed to fit within the table box. • Be sure to place the graphic on bottom side of your "divided highway" effect created with the graphic line (see the next figure).

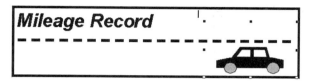

13. Click on Exit Template button. • Click Yes to save your template.

VARIATIONS

Car Repair: *Make some simple adjustments to this form and create a repair record detailing car repair work made to your vehicle, such as oil changes and replaced belts, battery, and spark plugs. This would be handy to have in your car's glove compartment for easy referral.*

MOVING TRACKING SHEET

MOVING TRACKING SHEET

Family Name: _____
Moving Company: _____
Moving From Address: _____
Moving To Address: _____
Moving Dates: _____

U-MOVE

ROOM	BOX #	CONTENTS	Packed	Loaded	Arrived	Unpacked
TOTAL BOXES						

If you've ever experienced the fun of moving, you know what an ordeal it can be keeping track of boxes. How about creating a form using WordPerfect for Windows that will help you detail what's in each box, what room it's from, whether it made it onto the moving van, and—most importantly—whether it made it to the destination. Here's a perfect way to create such a form, with an added graphic and an information text box.

PREPARATION

Start with a graphic.

1. Select Layout. • Select Page. • Select Paper Size. • Select the Letter Landscape size. • Click Select.

2. Select Layout. • Select Margins. • Margins: .5" all around. • Click OK.

3. Click on Draw button on WordPerfect Button Bar. • Click on Rectangle tool. • Select Attributes. • Select Fill. • Change the color options to the color or pattern desired. • Click OK.

4. With the Rectangle tool and the Polygon tool, begin building a box with flaps for the top. • Change the Fill colors (see the next figure) to create depth. • To edit any shape created, select the shape with the Select tool. • Select Edit. • Select Edit Points. • Use the mouse pointer to pull the edit points of the shape in different directions.

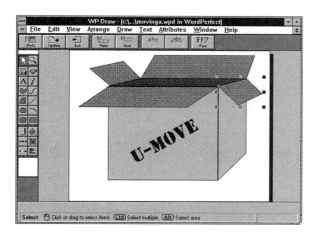

5. Click on Text tool. • Add a line of text above the box drawn. • Font Face: Braggadocio or Steamer. • Type: U-MOVE. • Select the text with the Select tool. • Select Edit. • Select Rotate. • Rotate the text slightly and move inside of box shape.

6. When finished, select File. • Select Exit and Return to Document. • Click Yes.

7. Place the graphic in the upper right corner of the page.

Add a text box with moving information.

8. Click on Text Box button. • Resize the box to fit the upper left portion of the page. • Click on Border/Fill button on Graphics Box Feature Bar. • Border Style: Single. • Click OK.

9. Font Face: Braggadocio or Steamer. • Font Size: 36. • Justification: Center. • Type: MOVING TRACKING SHEET. • Font Face: Times New Roman. • Font Size: 12. • Justification: Left. • Add the rest of the information, such as name, moving company, addresses, and so on (see the next figure).

Create a table.

10. Move the cursor beneath the text box and graphic. • Click on Table Create button. • Size: 7 columns and 14 rows.

11. Reposition the width of each row to fit the text you intend to place in the form. • Type in the text for each column or row (see the next figure). • Font Face: Arial. • Font Size: 12. • Click on Bold button. • Justification: Center.

ROOM	BOX #	CONTENTS	Packed	Loaded	Arrived	Unpacked
TOTAL BOXES						

12. Save and print your form.

VARIATIONS

Moving Labels: *Another idea is to create matching box labels to place on each box for easy identification. Use the same graphic and text box, make a few changes, and then print them out. Organizing has never been so easy! (If only moving were as easy.)*

PROJECT SCHEDULE

YUBBLES COLA CAMPAIGN

Client: Yubbles Cola, Inc.   **Contact:** Jake Cannon   **Phone:** (317) 000-0000
Ad Team: Willard-Williams   **Team Leader:** Rob Barber   **Accountant:** Lisa Bell   **Account Number:** 10929A
Campaign Date: 11-15-94
Media: Print, Radio, Television, Billboard

Project Stage	Team Leader	Account Executive	Senior Editor	Senior Art Dir.	Account Executive	Final Check
AD COPY DRAFT	10/5	10/7	10/12	10/12	10/12	❑
PRELIMINARY SKETCHES	10/7	10/12	10/13	10/13		❑
CLIENT PRESENTATION	10/15	10/15				❑
FINAL MOCK UPS						❑
FINAL COPY						❑
FINAL LAYOUT						❑
SHIP TO PRINTER						❑
PROOFS						❑

NOTES:

If your company or department works with a lot of project schedules, you might like to try this idea for creating a visual display that clearly shows a project's progress. Colored graphic lines are used to mark the progress of each project stage (like a scoreboard for deadlines). This idea can also be used for school and homework project assignments.

PREPARATION

Start with a text box.

1. Select Layout. • Select Margins.
   • Margins .5" all around. • Click OK.

2. Click on Text Box button on WordPerfect Button Bar. • Resize text box to fit upper portion of page, stretched across horizontally. • Click on Border/Fill button. • Border Style: Single. • Click OK.

3. Font Face: Swis721 Blk Ex BT. • Font Size: 40. • Type the title of your project. • Press Enter. • Font Face: Arial. • Font Size: 12. • Type in project information, dates, and so on (see the next figure).

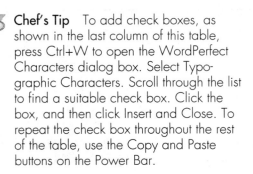

YUBBLES COLA CAMPAIGN

Client: Yubbles Cola, Inc.   Contact: Jake Cannon   Phone: (317) 000-0000
Ad Team: Willard-Williams   Team Leader: Rob Barber   Accountant: Lisa Bell   Account Number: 10029A
Campaign Date: 11-15-94
Media: Print, Radio, Television, Billboard

Insert a table.

4. Move the cursor beneath text box.
   • Click on Table button on Power Bar.
   • Set a table with 7 columns and 9 rows.

5. Font Face: Arial. • Add text to table.
   • Reposition column lines to fit text.

Chef's Tip To add check boxes, as shown in the last column of this table, press Ctrl+W to open the WordPerfect Characters dialog box. Select Typographic Characters. Scroll through the list to find a suitable check box. Click the box, and then click Insert and Close. To repeat the check box throughout the rest of the table, use the Copy and Paste buttons on the Power Bar.

Add the graphic lines to chart the progress of your project.

6. Select Graphics. • Select Custom Line.
   • Line Color: shaded color of your choice. • Line Thickness: .133".
   • Click OK.

Cook's Caution Be sure to choose a very light color when choosing a color for the graphic lines created in step 6. If you choose a light shade, any text beneath the line will be clearly visible.

7. Move the graphic line to the area of the table to track a project stage.
   • Resize the line to fill the space needed. • Repeat these steps for each graphic line (see the next figure).

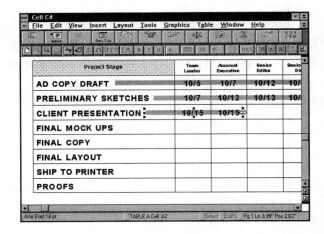

8. When finished tracking each project stage with a graphic line, save and print your form.

5 min.

Easy

SALES CONTACTS LISTING

Since this entire section of the book focuses on organizing, why not straighten up your paperwork at the office? Here's a very simple idea for making an attractive form that helps you keep track of sales contacts. Of course, you'll want to adapt your form with the information you and your company need to gather from prospective sales accounts. However, this idea is a good place to start. It may even motivate you to make more sales calls . . . well, it could.

PREPARATION

Start with a graphic logo and text box.

1. Select Layout. • Select Margins.
   • Margins: .5" all around. • Click OK.

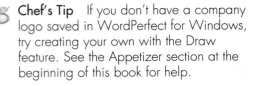 2. Click on Figure button on WordPerfect Button Bar. • Choose your logo from the list of graphic files. • Click OK.

Chef's Tip If you don't have a company logo saved in WordPerfect for Windows, try creating your own with the Draw feature. See the Appetizer section at the beginning of this book for help.

3. Resize the figure; place in upper right portion of page. • Click on Wrap button. • Setting: No Wrap. • Click OK.

4. Click on Text Box button. • Click on Border/Fill button. • Click on Customize Style button. • Under Select sides to modify, click the Left and Bottom check boxes. • Under Drop Shadow, change the Type and Color as shown. • Click OK.

5. Resize the text box to fill upper portion of form, including the figure added in step 1. • Font Face: Arial. • Font Size: 36. • Justification: Left. • Type form's title: SALES CONTACT LIST (see the next figure).

Insert a table.

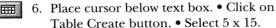 6. Place cursor below text box. • Click on Table Create button. • Select 5 x 15.

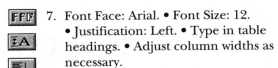 7. Font Face: Arial. • Font Size: 12. • Justification: Left. • Type in table headings. • Adjust column widths as necessary.

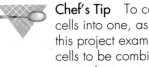 **Chef's Tip** To combine several column cells into one, as shown in the first row of this project example, first highlight the cells to be combined. Next, click the right mouse button on highlighted cells. Choose Join Cells. Now you have one big cell.

8. Select the top two rows. • Click on TblLineFill button on Table Button Bar. • Line Styles: all Button Bottom/1. • Click OK.

9. Save and print your form.

VARIATIONS

Give Me Some Room: *We left a lot of room at the top of this form anticipating that it would be attached to a salesperson's clipboard. There may be some other size considerations your sales force might apply for this type of form and how it is used—be creative!*

THINGS TO DO LIST

When it comes to organizing, there's nothing more practical than a To Do list. This project idea will show you how to make a list that incorporates TextArt and a graphic design. Depending upon how you're going to use this list, you may want to add a company logo, a school symbol, or an organizational motto. If you turn any of these elements into a shaded watermark, you've got an easy To Do list in a few simple steps.

PREPARATION

Begin with a custom box defining your To Do list size.

1. Select Layout. • Select Margins.
   • Margins: .5" all around. • Click OK.

2. Select Graphics. • Select Custom Box.
   • Select Figure. • Click OK.

3. Click on Size button. • Size settings, width: 5.32" and height: 8". • Click OK.

4. Click on Border/Fill button. • Border Style: Single. • Click OK.

5. Move the box to the left side of page.
   • Click on Wrap button. • Set No Wrap.
   • Click OK.

 Chef's Tip Why place the list on the left side of the page? So you can make a duplicate of everything and copy it to fit onto the right side of the page. That way, you can print out two copies of the list at once!

Set some lines.

6. Click inside the figure box. • Press Shift+Hyphen until you have as many lines filling the box as possible (see the next figure).

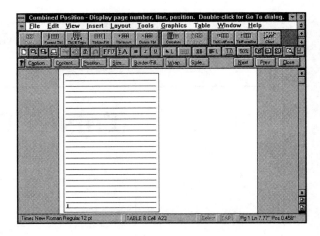

Add a watermark made of TextArt.

7. Select Layout. • Select Watermark.
   • Select Watermark A. • Click on Create button.

8. Click on TextArt button. • Font Face: Impact, Boulder, or a similar style.
   • Type: THINGS TO DO. • Click the wavy shape (upper right button). • Text Color: light gray. • Outline: No Outline.
   • Width: 5". • Height: 4" (see the next figure). • Select File. • Select Exit & Return to WordPerfect. • Click Yes.

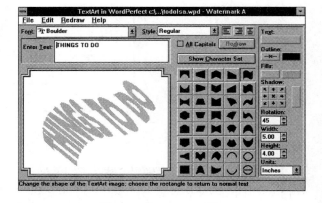

9. Reposition or resize the TextArt to fit in the upper left corner of box. • Click on TextArt button again. • Font Face: Boulder or a similar style. • Type: NOW! • Text Color: light gray. • Change Outline to none. • Width: 5". • Height: 4". • Select File. • Select Exit & Return to WordPerfect. • Click Yes.

10. Reposition or resize the TextArt to fit in the bottom right corner of box.

Add a graphic design to the watermark.

 11. Select the TextArt with word "NOW!" in it. • Click on Copy button.

 12. Click on Draw button. • Select Edit. • Select Paste. • Choose Select All. • Reposition the word "NOW!" into the center of drawing area.

13. Using a combination of lines in different colors, draw squiggles, zigzags, and other shapes around the pasted word. • When finished, select each part of the word, and press Delete until every letter is gone from the screen (see the next figure).

 Cook's Caution   Be sure to choose the lightest colors for the shapes you draw. Because the design is going to be used as a watermark, you need to keep the colors very light so the shapes can be written over when they become part of your To Do list.

14. Select File. • Select Exit & Return to WordPerfect. • Click Yes. • Position graphic over the exiting TextArt of the word "NOW!". • Click Close. • Click Close again to exit the watermark screen.

15. Save and print your list.

 Cook's Caution   Careful! You may have to experiment with the placement of the TextArt words in your watermark to get them positioned where you want on the page. To edit the watermark, select Layout Watermark. When the dialog box appears, click on the Edit button. Make your changes to the design.

VARIATIONS

The Professional Touch: *Take your To Do list design to a professional copier to have actual pads of paper made. This is a great gift idea for holidays, birthdays, and other occasions.*

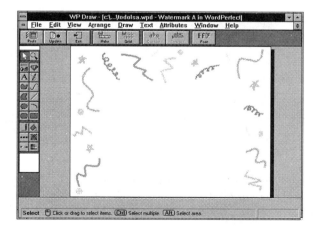

Advanced

WEEKLY CALENDAR

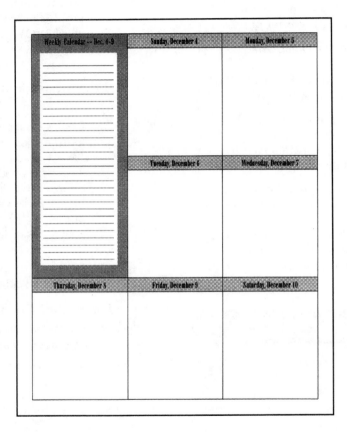

Tired of using the same preprinted, costly weekly calendars found in office supply and stationery stores? Use WordPerfect for Windows to design your own calendar to fit your weekly needs. Here's a simple weekly planner you can easily whip up and use or give to others to use. You'll find big open spaces in which you can record your own information for each day, plus an area for organizing notes.

PREPARATION

Create the table.

1. Select Layout. • Select Margins.
   • Margins: .5" all around. • Click OK.

2. Click on Table Create button. • Select 3 columns and 6 rows.

3. Font Face: Onyx BT. • Double-click on Font Size button. • Font Size: 16. • Click OK. • Justification: Center. • Type in the text for dates and the calendar title in the cells, as shown.

Weekly Calendar -- Dec. 4-10	Sunday, December 4	Monday, December 5
	Tuesday, December 6	Wednesday, December 7
Thursday, December 8	Friday, December 9	Saturday, December 10

4. In column 1, select the first four cells. • Click the right mouse button. • Select Join Cells (see the next figure).

5. While the joined cells are selected, click on TblLineFill button. • Fill Option: a dark gray color. • Click OK.

6. Select a date cell. • Click on TblLineFill button. • Fill Option: light gray. • Click OK. • Repeat the sequence for the remaining date cells.

7. In each remaining empty row, press Enter six times to add depth (see the next figure).

Add a text box with lines for organizing.

8. Click on Text Box button on the WordPerfect Button Bar. • Move box over first cell. • Click on Border/Fill button on Feature Bar. • Border Style: None. • Fill Style: 100%. • Foreground Color: white. • Click OK.

9. Resize text box to fit inside the cell. • Press Shift+Hyphen; fill the space with lines (see the next figure).

Weekly Calendar -- Dec. 4-10	Sunday, December 4	Monday, December 5
	Tuesday, December 6	Wednesday, December 7

10. Save and print your weekly calendar.

VARIATIONS

Beautify: *Use WordPerfect's graphic files and Draw feature to add artwork to your calendar. You can even insert a watermark in the background. Designate birthdays, holidays, and other events with graphics you create with WordPerfect. Pass your weekly calendars out to others who need them to keep track of your busy schedule.*

PART SIX

DESSERTS: FUN

Since I usually like to eat dessert before the main course, I was a little confused when my editor asked me to place this section *at the end.* Oh, well. No imagination.

Anyway, they say that good stuff comes to those who wait (why is that?), so here are some fun recipes that'll make you want to stay late just fiddlin' around: bumper stickers, door hangers, party games, gift tags, Halloween masks, and even a personalized storybook. There's more I could tell you about, but I don't want to spoil the fun. Dig in!

BUSINESS   ORGANIZATION   HOME   SCHOOL

Moderate

AWARD

Maybe Sally has just signed the biggest deal of the year. Or maybe Mikey has just completed his extracurricular reading course after three months of trying. Or maybe Junior has just mastered a two-wheel bike. Whatever the reason, show 'em they're special with an award designed just for them. Although WordPerfect comes with two award templates, this recipe will show you how to make your certificate a stand-out.

PREPARATION

Add an official-looking border.

1. Select Layout. • Select Page. • Select Paper Size. • Select Letter Landscape. • Click Select.

2. Click on GrphPgBrdr button on Design Tools Button Bar. • Select Classic. • Select Landscape. • Click OK.

Add some official-looking text.

3. Select Layout. • Select Page. • Select Center. • Select Current Page. • Click OK.

4. Font Face: Blackletter686 BT, Frankenstein, or similar font. • Font Size: 48. • Justification: Center. • Type: Certificate of Merit. • Font Size: 24. • Press Enter two times.

Cook's Caution You'll need to switch to 24 pt. text before pressing Enter to add blank lines throughout this recipe. If you don't, the amount of space between each line of text will vary, and the award will not look as nice.

5. Font Face: Shelley Volante, Dauphin, or some other elegant font. • Type: awarded to. • Press Enter twice.

6. Font Face: Times New Roman. • Font Size: 36. • Type name of recipient (see the next figure). • Font Size: 24. • Press Enter twice.

7. Font Face: ShelleyVolante, Dauphin, or similar font. • Type a description of the award. • Press Enter twice.

8. Font Face: Blackletter686 BT, Frankenstein, or similar font. • Font Size: 24. • Click on Date Text button.

Certificate of Merit

awarded to

Gwen DeLaJuen

Add an official-looking ribbon.

9. Click on Draw button on WordPerfect Button Bar. • Select File. • Select Page Layout. • Set dimensions to 2" x 2". • Click OK.

10. Click on Fill Color tool. • Select light gray. • Click on Ellipse tool. • Draw a circle.

11. Click on Fill Color tool. • Select a slightly darker gray. • Click on Polygon tool. • Clicking once at each point, draw starburst around first circle (see the next figure).

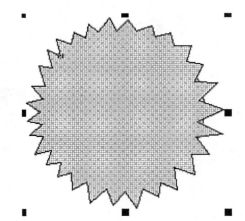

12. Click on the starburst. • Select Arrange. • Select Back.

13. Click on Fill Color tool. • Select light gray again. • Click on Polygon tool.

• Draw the left ribbon. • Draw the right ribbon (see the next figure).

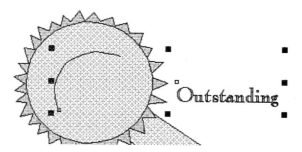

14. Press and hold the Shift key. • Click on Select tool. • Click on left ribbon. • Click on right ribbon. • Select Arrange. • Select Back.

Add some text to the ribbon.

15. Click on Curved Line tool. • Draw a curve.

16. Select Text. • Select Font. • Font Face: CaslonOpnface BT. • Font Size: 12. • Click OK. • Click on Text tool. • Click where you want to start typing. • Type: Outstanding. • Press Enter.

17. Click on Select tool. • Press and hold the Shift key. • Click on curved line. • Click on text. • Select Arrange. • Select Effects. • Select Contour Text (see the next figure). • Select Top Center. • Click OK.

18. Select Text. • Select Font. • Font Face: CaslonOpnface BT. • Font Size: 12. • Click OK. • Click on Text tool. • Click where you want to start typing. • Type: Quality. • Press Enter.

19. Click on Select tool. • Click on "Quality." • Select Edit. • Select Rotate. • Rotate text (see the next figure).

20. Click on Line tool. • Draw two lines above and below "Quality."

21. Select File. • Select Exit and Return to Document. • Select Yes.

22. Resize the ribbon as necessary. • Click the right mouse button. • Select Wrap. • Select No Wrap. • Click OK. • Drag ribbon into place.

23. Save and print your award.

VARIATIONS

Portrait Time: *Design an award that's oriented vertically by skipping step 1. In step 2, select Portrait.*

BIRTHDAY PARTY GAME

Tail

Pin the tail here.

Let's face it—birthdays are for kids. They were something to celebrate, in that innocent time when you couldn't even imagine being TWENTY or THIRTY. And never could you ever imagine getting to be as old as your PARENTS, or saying dumb things like, "OK, everyone, be quiet or we won't play this game!" or "If you do that one more time, your face will freeze like that." With this recipe, you'll create a nice game to keep the kids busy while you sneak away into the kitchen and suck down a gallon of ice-cream while trying to remember what it was like to be only six.

PREPARATION

Start up WordPerfect Draw.

1. Select Layout. • Select Margins. • All margins: .25". • Click OK.

2. Click on Draw button. • Select File. • Select Page Layout. • Set dimensions to 7.5" x 10". • Click OK.

Create a desert scene.

3. Select Attributes. • Select Fill. • Select Gradient. • Center Color: light tan. • Outer Color: white. • Click OK. • Click on Rectangle tool. • Draw desert floor.

4. Click on Figure tool. • Drag to create a figure box. • Select COYOTE.WPG (see the next figure). • Click Retrieve.

Add some cactus.

5. Select Attributes. • Select Fill. • Center Color: green. • Angle: 45. • Click OK.

• Click on Closed Curve tool. • Draw the cactus body (see the next figure).

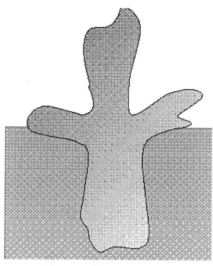

6. Click on Line tool. • Draw several vertical lines on cactus trunk. • Draw horizontal lines on cactus branches.

7. Select Attributes. • Select Fill. • Select Pattern. • Select the pattern of criss-crossing lines. • Click OK. • Click on Closed Curve tool. • Draw several nodes, branching off of the main cactus body (see the next figure).

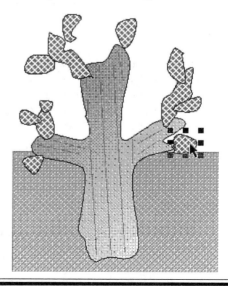

8. Select the entire cactus. • Select Arrange. • Select Group. • Select Edit. • Select Duplicate.

 Chef's Tip To select a group of objects in a drawing, drag with the Select tool over the objects you want to select. Those objects you select will then appear with handles.

9. Reduce the size of the duplicate. • Drag duplicate to upper right on the desert floor. • Select Arrange. • Select Flip Left/Right (see the next figure).

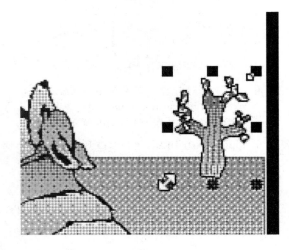

Shine on, moon.

 10. Select Attributes. • Select Fill. • Select Pattern. • Fill pattern: 100% Fill. • Foreground Color: light yellow. • Click OK. • Click on Closed Curve tool. • Draw a half moon.

 11. Click on Select tool • Double-click on coyote figure. • Click on tail. • Select Edit. • Select Cut.

12. Click on black hole left by tail. • Select Attributes. • Select Fill. • Select Pattern. • Fill pattern: 100% Fill. • Foreground Color: light gray. • Click OK.

13. Select File. • Select Exit and Return to Document. • Click Yes.

14. Click on the figure. • Right-click, and select Size. • Size: Full for both width and height. • Click OK.

 15. Press Enter to start a new page. • Click on Paste button. • Click on tail figure. • Right-click, and select Size. • Size: Full for both width and height. • Click OK.

16. Save and print your "Pin the Tail on the Coyote" game. • Cut out the tail on page two. • Make copies of the tail, one for each child.

VARIATIONS

Animal Kingdom: *Use a different animal if you like. WordPerfect comes with a horse (shown in the figure below), a cat, a cheetah, a tiger, a dog, and other graphics that might be suitable. Or you may want to try your hand at drawing something yourself, such as a dinosaur (see the place mat recipe in this section).*

BOOKPLATE

Property of

Glenn Valley High School
1245 Creek Side Drive
Green Valley, Ohio 45677

Return postage guaranteed

Have you ever loaned a book to someone and it was never returned? Well, I probably have it. It's not that I'm trying to steal myself a massive library one book at a time, but it takes me so long to find enough stolen moments to read a book that by the time I'm done with it, I can't remember who I borrowed it from. A bookplate would help; it's usually glued to the inside cover of a book, and it identifies the owner. With this recipe, you'll create a custom bookplate to stop your books from slip, slip, slippin' away.

PREPARATION

Start up WordPerfect Draw.

1. Select Layout. • Select Labels. • Select a 3.5" disk label appropriate to your printer (for example, Avery 5096). • Click Select.

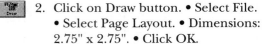 2. Click on Draw button. • Select File. • Select Page Layout. • Dimensions: 2.75" x 2.75". • Click OK.

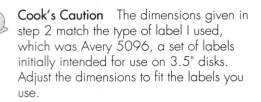 **Cook's Caution** The dimensions given in step 2 match the type of label I used, which was Avery 5096, a set of labels initially intended for use on 3.5" disks. Adjust the dimensions to fit the labels you use.

Draw some rectangles.

3. Select Attributes. • Select Fill. • Select Gradient. • Center Color: medium magenta. • Outer Color: white. • Click OK.

4. Click on Rectangle tool. • Draw a thin rectangle (see the next figure).

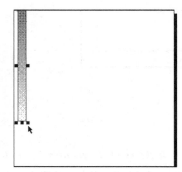

5. Select Attributes. • Select Fill. • Center Color: blue. • Click OK.

 6. Click on Rectangle tool. • Draw a thicker rectangle beside the first rectangle. • Draw a small rectangle at the bottom of the first rectangle (see the next figure).

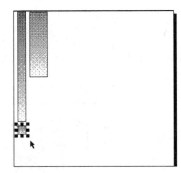

Add some text.

7. Select Text. • Select Font. • Font Face: Brush738 BT. • Font Size: 30. • Click OK. • Click where you want to start typing. • Type: Property of. • Press Enter.

8. With the Select tool, click on the text box. • Select Edit. • Select Rotate. • Rotate the text box to the left (see the next figure). • Drag the text box into place.

A 9. Select Text. • Select Font. • Font Face: Humanst521 Cn BT. • Font Size: 24. • Click OK. • Click on Text tool. • Click where you want to start typing. • Type your name. • Press Enter.

A 10. Select Text. • Select Font. • Font Size: 20. • Click OK. • Click on Text tool. • Click where you want to start typing. • Type the owner's address. • Press Enter. • Click where you want to start typing. • Type the owner's city, state, and zip. • Press Enter.

A 11. Select Text. • Select Font. • Font Size: 14. • Select Italic. • Click OK. • Click on Text tool. • Click where you want to start typing. • Type: Return Postage Guaranteed. • Press Enter.

Save it for later.

12. Select File. • Select Save Copy As. • Type a file name, such as BOOKPLT.WPG. • Click Save.

13. Select File. • Select Exit and Return to Document. • Click Yes. • Reposition the bookplate if necessary to center it on the first label.

Making more labels.

Figure 14. Click on the second label. • Click on Figure button. • Select your bookplate file. • Click OK.

15. Click on Border/Fill button. • Border Style: none. • Click OK. • Click on Close button.

16. Repeat steps 14–15 for additional labels.

17. Save and print your bookplate labels. • Affix a label to the inside front cover of each book.

VARIATIONS

Set Your Own Style: *A bookplate reflects the style of the book's owner. Use one of WordPerfect's graphics or other drawn art to reflect your mood. For example, combine the knight graphic with some arrows created in WordPerfect Draw. Or create a dramatic look with two different colored rectangles acting as the background.*

BUMPER STICKER

Americans are bombarded every day with so many messages, imploring them to "Buy Sudso Deluxe, now with extra whiteners," "Save the whale, the spotted owl, the middle class." So, why not toss your opinion into the maelstrom? With this recipe, you can create a bumper sticker to sell, making money for your organization or school. Or if you prefer to keep your opinions to yourself, you can create a single bumper sticker.

PREPARATION

Start up WordPerfect Draw.

1. Select Layout. • Select Page. • Select Paper Size. • Select Letter Landscape. • Click Select.

2. Select Layout. • Select Margins. • All margins: .25". • Click OK.

3. Click on Draw button. • Select File. • Select Page Layout. • Dimensions: 10.50" x 3.75". • Click OK.

Get your message across.

4. Select Text. • Select Font. • Font Face: Braggadocio, Swis721 BlkEx BT, Cupertino, or some other bold font. • Font Size: 78. • Click OK. • Click on Text tool. • Click where you want to start typing. • Type: Go Tigers! • Press Enter.

5. Select the text box. • Select Edit. • Select Rotate. • Rotate text to the left (see the next figure).

Add a tail.

6. Select Attributes. • Select Fill. • Select Gradient. • Center Color: white. • Outer Color: light orange. • Type: Linear. • Click OK.

7. Click on Closed Curve tool. • Draw the tail (see the next figure).

Cook's Caution   Drawing the tail is tricky, but just click several times to establish the curves of the bottom edge. When you reach the end, click along the top edge. Double-click when you're done.

8. Select the tail. • Select Arrange. • Select Back.

9. Click in the drawing area to unselect the tail. • Select Attributes. • Select Fill. • Select Pattern. • Fill pattern: 100%. • Foreground Color: black. • Click OK.

10. Click on Closed Curve tool. • Draw the tail stripes (see the next figure).

Cook's Caution   Be careful not to get the stripes too close to the text box, so your message will remain readable.

Add a tiger.

11. Click on Figure tool. •Drag to establish figure box. • Select TIGER_J.WPG. • Click Retrieve.

12. Select File. • Select Exit and Return to Document. • Click Yes.

Add the finishing touches.

13. Click on the figure. • Right-click, and select Size. • Size: Sized to Content for both width and height. • Click OK.

14. Save and print your bumper sticker original. • Then take to a printer to have made into bumper stickers.

VARIATIONS

Private Message: *If you have a small-scale project in mind, you can print your bumper stickers on 8 1/2" x 11" labels by Avery (#5165). In step 1, select Layout/Labels. Click Create, type a name, and then click Change. Click Wide Form, and then click OK twice. In step 12, save your bumper sticker as a file with the File/Save As command, and copy the figure twice onto each sticker. Print, cut the labels in half, and you have yourself two deluxe, custom labels!*

More Ideas? *WordPerfect comes with many graphics you can base a bumper sticker on. A Greenpeace message would look nice with the MARSH graphic, for example. Start with the BUBBLES graphic, add some colored circles, and you have a nice bumper sticker advertising a local festival. Just use your imagination!*

20 min.

BUSINESS   ORGANIZATION   **HOME**   SCHOOL

Advanced

DOOR HANGER

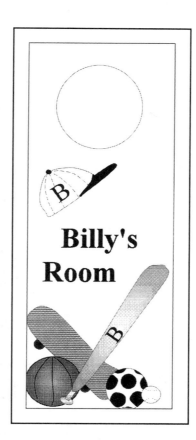

The first door hanger dates back to caveman times. Ogg, whose wife Bella was visiting her cavemother, realized he had a golden opportunity to goof off, so he quickly made up a sign that said, "Gone Pterodactyling." Of course, he had no intention of working up a sweat (and possibly losing several limbs) hunting the pterodactyl meat his wife loved. Instead, he was off to the Tarpit Sports Bar to suck down a few grogs, joke with his buddies, and watch the dinosaur races. Door hangers are still in use today, sometimes for more civilized purposes. You can create your own doorhanger with this recipe.

PREPARATION

Start up WordPerfect Draw.

 1. Click on Draw button.

2. Select File. • Select Page Layout. • Dimensions: 4" x 10.5". • Click OK.

 3. Click on Ellipse tool. • Turn object fill off by clicking on Object Fill On/Off button. • Draw a circle at top of door hanger.

Draw a baseball cap.

 4. Click on Closed Curve tool. Draw the cap body.

 5. Turn object fill on by clicking on Object Fill On/Off button. • Click on Fill Color tool. • Color: red. • Click on Ellipse tool. • Draw a button at top of cap.

 6. Click on Closed Curve tool. • Draw cap brim (see the next figure).

 7. Select Text. • Select Font. • Font Face: Times New Roman. • Font Size: 68. • Click OK. • Click on Text tool. • Click where you want to start tying. • Type your child's first initial. • Press Enter. • Drag into place.

 8. Click on Line Style tool. • Select the second dashed line style. • Click on Line tool. • Draw the cap lines.

9. Select Edit. • Choose Select. • Select All. • Select Arrange. • Select Group. • Select Edit. • Select Rotate. • Rotate the baseball cap (see the next figure).

Add your child's name.

 10. Click on Text tool. • Click where you want to start typing. • Type your child's name. • Press Enter. • Click where you want to start typing. • Type: Room. • Drag into place.

Add a skateboard.

11. Select Attributes. • Select Fill. • Select Pattern. • Foreground Color: gray. • Background Color: white. • Pattern: wide horizontal stripes. • Click OK.

 12. Click on Closed Curve tool. • Draw the skateboard.

 13. Select Attributes. • Select Fill. • Fill pattern: 100% Fill. • Click OK. • Click on Ellipse tool. • Draw the two wheels for the skateboard.

 14. Click on skateboard body. • Select Arrange. • Select Front.

Add a basketball.

15. Select Attributes. • Select Fill. • Select Gradient. • Type: Circular. • Center Color: light orange. • Outer Color: medium orange. • Click OK.

16. Click on Ellipse tool. • Draw the basketball.

 17. Click on Line Style tool. • Select a thin, solid, line style. • Click on Curved Line tool. • Add stripes to basketball (see the next figure).

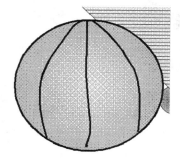

Add a baseball bat.

18. Select Attributes. • Select Fill. • Type: Linear. • Center Color: white. • Outer Color: light tan. • Click OK.

 19. Click on Closed Curve tool. • Draw the bat body. • Click on Rounded Rectangle tool. • Draw the bat handle. • Click on Ellipse tool. • Draw the bat end (see the next figure).

 20. Click on the bat end. • Select Arrange. • Select Back.

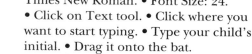 21. Select Text. • Select Font. • Font Face: Times New Roman. • Font Size: 24. • Click on Text tool. • Click where you want to start typing. • Type your child's initial. • Drag it onto the bat.

 22. Select the entire bat. • Select Edit. • Select Rotate. • Rotate the bat to the right.

 Chef's Tip To select a group of objects in a drawing, use the Select tool to drag over the objects you want to select. Selected objects appear with handles.

Add a soccer ball.

 23. Select Attributes. • Select Fill. • Select Pattern. • Fill pattern: 100% Fill. • Foreground Color: white. • Click OK. • Click on Ellipse tool. • Draw a soccer ball.

 24. Click on Fill Color tool. • Select black. • Click on Ellipse tool. • Draw a small circle on the soccer ball. • Click on Closed Curve tool. • Draw the remaining black circle-parts (see the next figure).

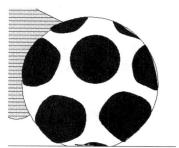

Add a baseball.

 25. Click on Fill Color tool. • Select white. • Click on Ellipse tool. • Draw a baseball.

26. Click on Line Style tool. • Select the
    sixth dashed line style. • Click on
    Curved Line tool. • Draw the two stitch
    lines (see the next figure).

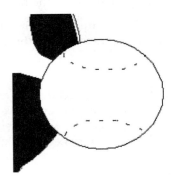

Final steps.

27. Select File. • Select Exit and Return to
    Document. • Click Yes.

28. Select the figure. • Right-click, and
    select Border/Fill. • Border Style:
    Single. • Click OK.

29. Save and print your door hanger. • Cut
    along border. • Laminate. • Cut out
    circle, and hang on door.

VARIATIONS

Multi-Purpose: *You can design a door
hanger for many purposes, such as the two
shown here. For the conference room door
hanger, rotate some block text, add a shadow
with the Attribute/Text command, and draw
a simple projector. Clever use of circular
gradient fills and lots of circles and closed
curves make this bear surprisingly easy to
create. Consider also creating door hangers to
mark a copy room, to warn people not to knock
while you're having a meeting, or to let other
teachers know that you're conducting a test.*

JOURNAL

Journal of Kate Scott

Knowing that I'm a writer by profession, you might think I keep a nice journal, forever immortalizing my every thought in a poetic tumble of words. Wrong. I can't even get around to sending my friends a card every now and then so they know I'm still alive and not in a ditch somewhere, not to mention a real handwritten letter, thank you very much. So a journal is, for me, out of the question, but it doesn't have to be that way for you, not with this nice recipe teaching you to create a great header, which, by the way, wastes a big third of EVERY PAGE, so you have less blank space staring you in the face, making you wonder if keeping a journal was such a great idea in the first place.

PREPARATION

Create a header.

1. Select Layout. • Select Margins. • All margins: .25". • Click OK.

2. Select Layout. • Select Header/Footer. • Select Header A. • Click Create.

 3. Click on Draw button.

4. Select File. • Select Page Layout. • Dimensions: 10.5" x 5". • Click OK.

Draw a vine.

 5. Click on Fill Color tool. • Select medium green. • Click on Curved Line tool. • Draw a curving vine.

 6. With the Curved Line tool, add stems for leaves at various points along the vine (see the next figure).

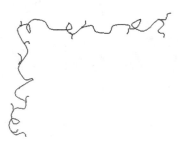

Add some leaves.

7. Select Attributes. • Select Fill. • Select Gradient. • Center Color: light green. • Outer Color: medium green. • Type: Rectangular. • Click OK.

 8. Click on Closed Curve tool. • Draw the vine leaves (see the next figure).

 9. Click on Line Color tool. • Color: dark green. • Click on Line tool. • Add a center vein to each leaf.

Add some flowers.

10. Select Attributes. • Select Fill. • Center Color: white. • Outer Color: light blue. • Click OK.

 11. Click on Closed Curve tool. • Draw the four petals for the first flower. • Click on Ellipse tool. • Draw the flower's center (see the next figure).

12. Repeat step 11 for additional flowers.

Personalize your journal.

 13. Select Text. • Select Font. • Font Face: ShelleyVolante BT. • Font Size: 48. • Click on Text tool. • Click where you want to start typing. • Type: Journal of. • Type your name. • Drag the two text boxes into place.

14. Select File. • Select Exit and Return to Document. • Click Yes.

15. Select the figure. • Right-click. • Select Size. • Select Sized to Content for both width and height. • Click OK.

16. Click on Close button on Header/Footer Feature Bar.

17. Save your journal. • After typing a journal entry, print your journal.

VARIATIONS

Other Art: *If you are allergic to flowers, use one of WordPerfect's graphics instead, such as a deer, cheetah, cowboy, or racehorse.*

Make Your Mark: *If you'd like a more subtle look, try adding your design as a watermark instead of as a header.*

LUGGAGE LABELS

Property of:

Dennis Blake
2113 West Boulevard
Indianapolis, In. 46250
(317) 456-7890

Sometimes, when I go on vacation, my luggage has a better time than I do. I board a plane to Ohio to visit an aunt, and my luggage gets a free ride to the Virgin Islands. I come back with a headache, and my luggage comes back with a tan, mon. Well, at least it comes back, thanks to the labels I put on my luggage at the last minute, at the insistence of the baggage handler who probably knew there was no way my luggage was going to go with me to a place called Ohio, not when it could get a free ride to someplace warm and sunny.

PREPARATION

Start WordPerfect Draw.

 1. Click on Draw button.

2. Select File. • Select Page Layout.
   • Dimensions: 3.5" x 2.5". • Click OK.

 3. Turn object fill off by clicking on Object Fill On/Off button. • Click on Ellipse tool. • Draw a small circle at the left-hand side of the label.

Add some lines.

 4. Turn object fill on. • Click on Line Color tool. • Color: medium cyan. • Click on Line Style tool. • Select the third line width. • Click on Line tool. • Draw a line at top of label.

 5. Click on Line Style tool. • Select the second line width. • Draw a line at bottom of label (see the next figure).

 6. Click on Line Color tool. • Color: light cyan. • Click on Line Style tool. • Select the first line width. • Draw a line above the other line at bottom of label (see the next figure).

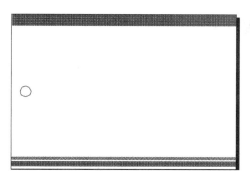

Add a few triangles.

 7. Click on Polygon tool. • Draw a large triangle at top of label. • Draw a smaller triangle at the lower right (see the next figure).

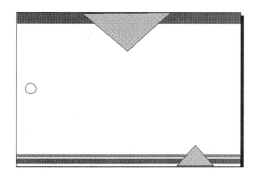

Add your name.

 8. Select Text. • Select Font. • Font Face: Humanst521 Cn BT • Select Italic. • Font Size: 18. • Click on Text tool. • Click where you want to start typing. • Type: Property of:

 9. Select Text. • Select Font. • Font Face: Humanst521 Cn BT. • Font Size: 24. • Click on Text tool. • Click where you want to start typing. • Type your name.

10. Select Text. • Select Font. • Font Size: 18. • Click on Text tool. • Click where you want to start typing. • Type your address.

11. Center each text box, using the large triangle as a guide.

Bon Voyage.

12. Select File. • Select Exit and Return to Document. • Click Yes.

13. Select the figure. • Right-click; select Border/Fill. • Border Style: Single.

14. Save and print your label. • Cut out along border. • Laminate and attach to luggage.

VARIATIONS

That's My Bag! *Design labels to identify your briefcase, or the backpack your kid takes to school. Add art or graphic designs to enhance your labels. This bunny was constructed with gradient closed curves. The "text" at the top was hand printed with the Freehand tool and a larger line width.*

PARTY INVITATIONS

Inside message ————

6:00 p.m.
November 24, 1994
Scott & Jennifer's
A celebration of thanks at

Come join us!

———— Front of invitation

Everyone loves a party, except maybe the hostess. When I give a party, I run around all weekend, cleaning the house, picking up decorations, planning the menu, cooking, cleaning again, and hoping everyone is late so I can get last minute things done, such as hiding the laundry and changing my outfit because I just spilled cranberry sauce on it. My husband doesn't understand my frantic behavior—there's a ball game on later and he has located the remote, so the party's obviously going to be a big success. Anyway, you can get your party off to a grand start with customized invitations created with this recipe. If you really want to drive yourself crazy making everything perfect, you can create matching place cards with the recipe that follows.

PREPARATION

Start WordPerfect Draw.

1. Select Layout. • Select Margins. • All margins: .25". • Click OK.

2. Click on Draw button. • Select File. • Select Page Layout. • Dimensions: 8" x 10.5". • Click OK.

Draw a turkey.

3. Click on Fill Color tool. • Select tan. • Click on Closed Curve tool. • Draw the turkey's body in the bottom right corner (see the next figure).

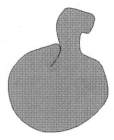

4. Click on Fill Color tool. • Select yellow. • Click on Polygon tool. • Draw the beak. • Draw the feet.

5. Click on Fill Color tool. • Select red. • Click on Closed Curve tool. • Draw the wattle (see the next figure).

6. Click on Fill Color tool. • Select black. • Click on Ellipse tool. • Draw the eye.

7. Select the entire turkey. • Select Arrange. • Select Group.

Chef's Tip   To select several objects at once, drag over them with the Select tool. The selected objects will appear with handles.

8. Select Attributes. • Select Fill. • Select Gradient. • Center Color: red. • Outer Color: light yellow. • Type: Circular. • Click OK. • Click on Closed Curve tool. • Draw the turkey feathers (see the next figure).

9. Click on the turkey body. • Select Arrange. • Select Front.

Add a nice border.

10. Click on Line Color tool. • Select red. • Click on Line Style tool. • Select the second line width. • Click on Curved Line tool. • Draw a curving border.

11. Click on Closed Curve tool. • Draw two large turkey feathers in the lower right-hand corner. • Draw smaller feathers on the border (see the next figure).

12. Select the two large turkey feathers.
• Select Edit. • Select Duplicate. • Drag
the copies to upper left-hand corner.
• Select Edit. • Select Rotate. • Rotate
the feathers so they are upside-down.

Add your invitation.

13. Select Text. • Select Font. • Font Face:
Arial. • Font Size: 58. • Click on Text
tool. • Click below turkey. • Type:
Come join us! • Select Edit. • Select
Rotate. • Rotate the text to the right.

14. Select Text. • Select Font. • Font Size:
32. • Click OK. • Click in upper left
corner. • Type: A celebration of thanks.
• Type your address and the date and
time information.

15. Select the text boxes. • Select Arrange.
• Select Group. • Select Edit. • Select
Rotate. • Rotate the text boxes so they
are upside-down.

Finishing touches.

16. Select File. • Select Exit and Return to
Document. • Click Yes.

Cook's Caution If you plan on making
matching place cards (see the next
recipe), save your figure in a file. Before
exiting, use the File/Save As command,
type a file name, such as TURKEY.WPG,
and press Enter.

17. Select the figure. • Right-click, then
select Size. • Select Sized to Contents
for both width and height. • Click OK.

18. Save and print your invitation.

VARIATIONS

Holiday Madness: *You can easily adapt
this recipe for various holidays, such as
Valentine's Day, Fourth of July, or The-Boss-
Is-Home-Sick-So-Let's-Take-The-Rest-Of-The-
Day-Off-Day. Just substitute the turkey with
some other symbol. For a birthday party, use
candles or balloons for the border, or incorporate the theme (dinosaurs, unicorns, and
so on).*

10 min.

Moderate

PLACE CARDS

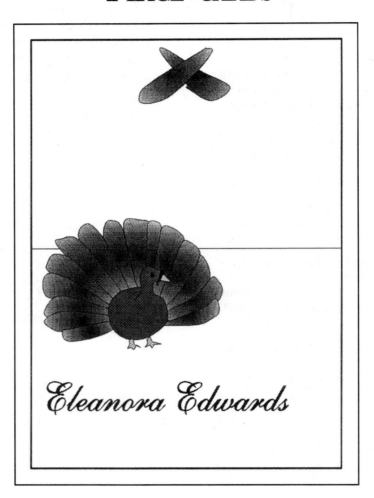

Eleanora Edwards

For a truly elegant affair, without fistfights, temper tantrums, or food fights, assign the perfect place for everyone at your dinner table with a fancy place card. Separate your two cousins who haven't spoken for years, separate Uncle Bill from the whiskey bottle he stashed last year in your floor plant, and separate your cares from your woes with this easy recipe.

PREPARATION

Start WordPerfect Draw.

 1. Click on Draw button. • Select File.
   • Select Page Layout. • Dimensions:
   3.5" x 5". • Click OK.

 2. Click on Line tool. • Draw a horizontal
   line marking the middle of the place
   card (see the next figure).

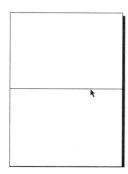

Add your turkey.

 3. Click on Figure tool. • Draw an area for
   the figure. • Select your turkey file.
   • Click Retrieve.

 Chef's Tip   If you didn't complete the
invitation recipe earlier, follow steps 3–9
in the previous recipe to create a turkey
for your place card.

4. Double-click on the figure. • Select the
   turkey (see the next figure). • Select
   Edit. • Select Cut.

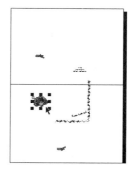

5. Select the remaining parts of the figure.
   • Press Delete.

6. Select Edit. • Select Paste. • Select the
   turkey. • Resize and drag into place
   (see the next figure).

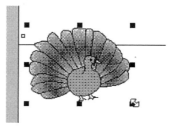

 Chef's Tip   Be sure that the turkey is
placed partly on top of the horizontal
line.

Add some feathers.

7. Select Attributes. • Select Fill. • Select
   Gradient. • Center Color: red. • Outer
   Color: light yellow. • Type: Circular.
   • Click OK.

 8. Click on Closed Curve tool. • Draw two
   upside-down turkey feathers at the top
   of the card (see the next figure).

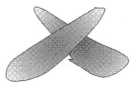

Add a name.

9. Select Text. • Select Font. • Font Face: ShelleyVolante BT. • Font Size: 42. • Click on Text tool. • Click where you want to start typing. • Type the name of a guest. • Press Enter.

10. Select File. • Select Exit and Return to Document. • Click Yes.

11. Select the figure. • Right-click, and select Border/Fill. • Border Style: Single. • Click OK.

Create additional place cards.

12. Click on the figure. • Click on Copy button. • Click in the document. • Click on Paste button. • Drag the copy to a new location on the page. • Double-click on the copy.

13. Double-click on the text box. • Select the text; replace it with another guest's name. • Press Enter.

14. Select File. • Select Exit and Return to Document. • Click Yes. • Repeat steps 12–14 for additional place cards.

15. Save and print your place cards. • Cut around the top of the turkey, around the feathers that are located above the horizontal line. • Fold the place card along the horizontal line. (The feathers you cut around will stick up, above the top of the place card.)

VARIATIONS

Other Reasons, Other Seasons: *Adapt this recipe for use in a formal meeting to identify your guests or to identify students in a training session (though you may not want to use the turkey).*

PLACE MAT FOR BIRTHDAY PARTY

Every birthday party needs decorations, so here's a practical, yet easy idea you can use: Make place mats for the birthday table using WordPerfect for Windows. There's no reason to go out and buy expensive place mats with the latest Disney movie characters. Good grief—make your own! You've got an expensive computer, you might as well put it to use. Besides, everybody just throws away the place mats anyway because they're covered with cake crumbs and drippy ice cream. The following steps show you how to design a place mat that can also be used in a coloring contest; the theme is dinosaurs, and I even added prehistoric balloons.

PREPARATION

Set up the page layout.

1. Select Layout. • Select Page. • Select Paper Size. • Select Letter Landscape from the list. • Click on Select button.

2. Select Layout. • Select Margins. • All margins: .25". • Click OK.

 3. Click on Design Tools Button Bar. • Click on GrphPgBrdr button. • Select Confetti. • Click OK (see the next figure).

Design the dinosaurs.

 4. Select the WordPerfect Default Button Bar. • Click on Draw button.

 5. Click on Freehand drawing tool. • Select Attributes. • Select Line. • Line Color: light blue. • Change Line Thickness to .15". • Click OK. • Draw a dinosaur body. • Use the other tools to add eyes, mouth, and toenails (see the next figure).

6. Once drawn, select Edit. • Choose Select. • Select All. • Choose the Edit menu again. • Choose Rotate.

 7. Click on Select tool. • Drag a rotating square; move dinosaur drawing so that it is tilted in drawing area (see the next figure).

8. Select File. • Select Exit and Return to Document. • Click Yes. • Place dinosaur in upper right corner of page.

 Chef's Tip   If you really, really like the dinosaur you drew, save it as a WordPerfect Graphic File. Select File. Select Save Copy As, give it a name, and click Save. Now that you've saved it, you can use it again and again in other documents.

9. Use Copy and Paste buttons to copy dinosaur drawing three times. • Place drawings in appropriate corners.

Chef's Tip To flip or rotate a drawing, right-click and select Feature Bar. Click on the Tools button and use the Flip or Rotate tools to adjust the figure.

Design prehistoric balloons.

10. Click on Draw button. • Click on Ellipse tool. • Select a fill color if desired. • Draw a circle. • Click on Polygon tool. • Draw a balloon end shaped like a triangle. • Click on Curved Line tool. • Draw a string attached to the balloon (see the next figure).

11. When finished, select File. • Select Exit and Return to Document. • Click Yes. • Place balloon drawing along the edges of place mat.

Chef's Tip What are prehistoric balloons? I don't know, I just made this up. My version of a pre-historic balloon is to use different shapes, such as a square or triangle—sort of a spin off of the invention of the wheel. The first wheels probably weren't the right shape, so maybe the first balloons weren't either. Just play along and use your imagination.

12. Repeat steps 10 through 11 to draw different balloon shapes (see the next figure). • Use the Edit Rotate command to tilt each shape as needed.

Chef's Tip You can also use the Copy and Paste buttons to place several of the same balloon shapes around the place mat.

Add the text.

13. Click on TextArt button. • Font Face: Braggadocia or Boulder, or similar style. • Type: Happy Birthday (name of child), three lines. • Click the 1st shape in the 4th row (see the next figure). • Select File. • Select Exit & Return to WordPerfect. • Click Yes. • Place TextArt in middle of page, resizing if needed to fill space.

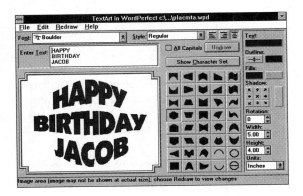

14. Save and print your place mats.

VARIATIONS

More Fun! *You can also add games to your place mats, such as crossword puzzles, word find puzzles, dot-to-dots, and more. Use the drawing feature and the Table Create commands to fill the place mats with fun activities suitable to the ages of your party children.*

Adult Place Mats: *Create theme-styled place mats for adults, too. Design your own for summer picnics, barbecues, holidays, and more. Print them on colored paper that coordinates with your napkins and other paper goods.*

CHRISTMAS CARD

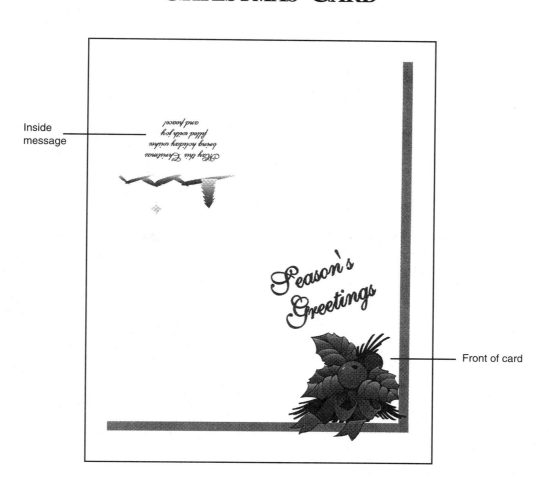

Inside message

Front of card

Forego those same old Christmas cards you buy every year along with everyone else. Why not make your own? You can personalize them, print them on brightly colored paper, glue on some glitter, and mail them off. Mind you, it takes some creativity with design, plus a spiffy saying or poem for the inside. But hey—if Hallmark can do it, why can't you?

PREPARATION

Start with setting up the page layout and guide rules.

1. Select Layout. • Select Margins. • All margins: .25". • Click OK.

2. Select Graphics. • Select Horizontal Line. • Move line to very center of page (see the next figure).

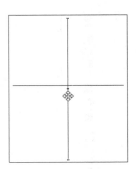

3. Select Graphics. • Select Vertical Line. • Move line to very center of page (see the preceding figure).

 Chef's Tip The rule lines are just to help you figure out how to fit things into the front or inside of the card. You'll delete these guide lines at the end of this project.

Add a Christmas graphic.

4. Click on Figure button. • Select CENTERPC.WPG. • Click OK.

5. Click on Border/Fill button. • Border Style: None. • Click OK.

6. Place graphic in lower right corner of page, resizing as needed (see the next figure). • Click on Wrap button. • Select No Wrap. • Click OK.

Add some TextArt.

 7. Click on TextArt button. • Font Face: ShelleyVolante BT, or a similar script style. • Justification: Center. • Type: Season's Greetings, two lines. • Text Color: red. • Outline Color: red. • Select a thicker outline. • Rotate text 25 degrees (see the next figure). • Select File. • Select Exit & Return to WordPerfect. • Click Yes.

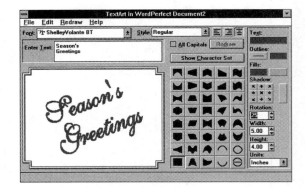

 Cook's Caution Never use a script style font with all capital letters. It will look just awful, and it's very hard to read. Script style fonts were meant to look like cursive writing with upper- and lowercase letters. Never fall victim to this professional no-no.

8. Resize the TextArt. • Place above graphic figure in lower right corner (see the next figure).

Add more graphic lines.

9. Select Graphics. • Select Custom Line. • Select Horizontal. • Line Color: shaded red. • Thickness: .255". • Click OK.

10. Place line below graphic figure, slightly overlapping (see the next figure). • Resize to fit entire width of document, margin to margin.

11. Select Graphics. • Select Custom Line. • Select Vertical. • Line Color: shaded red. • Thickness: .255". • Click OK.

12. Place the line to far right of graphic figure, slightly overlapping. • Resize to fit entire depth of document, margin to margin. • In bottom right corner, resize both overlapping lines until they form a precise corner (see the next figure).

Create the upside down inside card.

13. Click on Draw button. • Click on Text tool. • Select Text. • Select Font. • Font Face: ShelleyVolante BT. • Appearance: Bold. • Click OK. • Click inside of drawing area. • Type inside greeting of your card. • Center lines in middle of the drawing area.

14. Click on Closed Curve tool. • Select Attributes. • Select Fill. • Select Gradient. • Select a light color shade. • Click on Line Style button. • Select No Line. • Click OK. • Draw a Christmas scene as shown, creating drifts of snow, a tree, and a star—use different colors for each element (see the next figure).

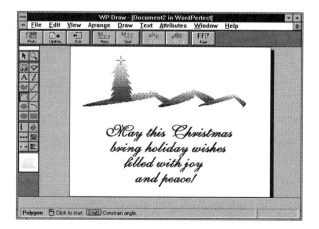

15. Select Edit. • Choose Select. • Select All. • Select Edit menu again. • Select Rotate. • Rotate upside down (see the next figure). • Select File. • Select Exit and Return to Document. • Click Yes.

Chef's Tip Why upside down? Because when you fold the card, that portion of the page will end up on the inside of the card itself. Really!

16. Place the graphic in upper left corner of page. • Size to fit as needed.

17. Click on horizontal guide line created in step 2. • Press Delete.

18. Click on vertical guide line created in step 3. • Press Delete.

19. Save and print your card.

20. Fold card from top to bottom and side to side, just like a fancy-schmancy store-bought card.

VARIATIONS

Other Kinds of Cards: *Use these project steps to create similar greeting cards for birthdays, other holidays, thank-you notes, or announcements. Print them on colored paper to add pizzazz. Glue on knickknacks, such as buttons, dried flowers, raffia string, and other interesting items to make your card a work of art.*

CHRISTMAS LETTER

Greetings Friends and Family,

    Our warmest wishes to you and yours during this holiday season. We hope all is well with you. We've had a very busy year, just like every other. The children are growing like weeds and need a good mowing. Caitlin turned five and Holly is now 1year old. Caitlin spent her first year in preschool and enjoyed it immensely. She has learned to ride her bicycle without training wheels, has taken up Barbie doll collecting, and talked us into adopting a kitten named Spiff. Holly, not to be outdone, has learned to walk, talk, and has adopted her own pet--a stuffed rabbit named Ralph. The girls are both learning to help Mom around the house, assist Dad with yardwork, and keep Grandpa and Grandma young at heart.

    Karl is still enjoying his work at NASA, being actively involved with the space shuttles. Every once and a while, he threatens to send the girls to the moon. I'm still very active with church, a Ladies Bible Study group, Caitlins preschool, and various crafts. This year, we're planning a two-week vacation in which we hope to stop and see everyone we know--we'll sure try to see you and your family. Of course, you're always encouraged to visit us at any time.

    It's not often that we stop and tell others how much they mean to us and our family, but we certainly want to extend our appreciation to you now. We've been blessed with so many cherished friends and relatives, we just want you to know that we're truly thinking of you in this Christmas season, and wishing you the very best. We look forward to hearing from each of you this year. Have a very Merry Christmas!

                           Love, the Federhart's
                         Stacey, Karl, Caitlin & Holly

Another good way to put your WordPerfect program to use around the holidays is to make a family Christmas letter. Everybody gets one of these from some distant cousin or aunt detailing the year's events, dental and plastic surgeries, children's ballet recitals, and other exciting happenings. I'm not too keen on these letters because they always seem so impersonal. So, why not improve upon the idea with nifty graphics you create using WordPerfect Draw? (It's up to you to write your own dynamic text to go with the artwork.) This particular project shows you how to make colorful ornaments to decorate the page, including a sprig of holly. Without a color printer (or a color book for that matter), you won't be able to appreciate this, but use your imagination!

PREPARATION

Set up the page layout.

1. Select Layout. • Select Margins. • All margins: .5". • Click OK.

Draw an ornament.

2. Click on Draw button. • Select Attributes. • Select Fill. • Fill Type: Gradient. • Center Color: a shade of red. • Type: Circular. • Y Offset: 100%. • Click OK.

Chef's Tip   To get rid of the line that surrounds the shape you're drawing, click on the Line button in the Fill Attributes dialog box. Then change the setting to No Line, and click OK.

3. Click on Ellipse tool. • Draw a large circle in the drawing area.

4. Click on Polygon tool. • Select Attributes. • Select Fill. • Color Settings: a shade of brown. • Click OK. • Draw top of ornament (see the next figure).

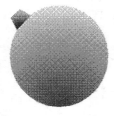

5. Click on Closed Curve tool. • Click on Fill/No Fill tool; change to no fill. • Draw a hoop as shown below.

6. Click on Curve Line tool. • Draw a hook shape (see the next figure).

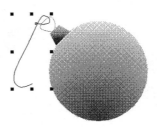

7. Select File. • Select Exit and Return to Document. • Click Yes. • Place ornament in top left corner of page. • Resize as necessary.

Add a TextArt line.

8. Click on TextArt button. • Font Face: BrushScript WP. • Type: Merry Christmas. • Text Color: green. • Outline: Green. • Select the wavy shape, last button on first row. • Width: 8". • Select File. • Select Exit & Return to WordPerfect. • Click Yes.

Cook's Caution   Never use a script style font with all capital letters. It will look just awful, and it's very hard to read. Script style fonts were meant to look like cursive writing with upper- and lowercase letters. To use it with all capital letters is a big No-No.

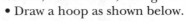

9. Place the TextArt next to the ornament graphic, resizing to fit as necessary.

Type the letter.

10. Move the cursor down below the graphic elements by pressing Enter. • Type in your Christmas letter text (three paragraph maximum). • Font Face: BernhardMod BT. • Font Size: 12. • Use ruler to adjust margins to fit nicely in width of page.

Add more ornaments and a sprig of holly.

11. Double-click on ornament to start WordPerfect Draw. Select Edit. • Choose Select. • Choose All. • Select the Edit menu again. • Select Duplicate. • Move the copy next to the first. • Repeat this to create four ornaments in a row, resizing as necessary to fit.

12. Click on Edit. • Choose Rotate command. • Change position each ornament. • Select an ornament circle that you want to change color. • Select Attributes. • Select Fill. • Change the color setting to another color. • Click OK to exit the Fill dialog box.

13. Click on Closed Curve tool. • Select Attributes. • Select Fill. • Color: green. • Click OK. • Draw a leaf pattern. • Duplicate the leaf and flip vertically. • Position leaves in bottom left corner, as shown in the next figure.

14. Click on Ellipse tool. • Select Attributes. • Select Fill. • Color: a shade of red. • Click OK. • Draw three circles for the holly berries. • Select Arrange • Select Front. • Place holly sprig elements to front of drawing.

Chef's Tip Sending art elements to the Front or Back lets them overlap without showing through. Select the item to be moved. Select Arrange, and choose Front or Back, depending on how you want to overlap.

15. When finished, select File. • Select Exit and Return to Document. • Click Yes. • Place graphic at very bottom of page, resizing to fit as needed.

16. Save and print your letter.

VARIATIONS

What Else?   *There are a hundred zillion ways to create a Christmas letter, and this is just one. Making ornaments is fairly easy, but you should also try your hand at Christmas trees, stars, angels, and other associated artwork. Of course, you can also personalize each letter in the text instead of resorting to the tacky run-off-several-generic-copies-and-mail-'em-to-everyone approach. Be inspired, instead!*

BUSINESS   ORGANIZATION   **HOME**   SCHOOL

10 min.

Easy

GIFT TAGS

Have you begun to notice how much money we're saving you by showing you how to make creative paper products using your WordPerfect for Windows program? Quite a lot. Here's another one: make your own gift tags. It's simple.

PREPARATION

Make a box.

1. Select Graphics. • Select Custom Box. • Select Figure. • Click OK.

2. Click on Size button on the Feature Bar. • Size: 3" by 2". • Click OK.

Draw a flower.

3. Click on Draw button. • Select Attributes. • Select Fill. • Select Gradient. • Center Color: a light pink shade. • Outer Color: an even lighter pink or white shade. • Type: Circular. • Click on Line Style button. • Click the No Line check box. • Click OK.

4. Click on Closed Curve tool. • Draw one petal at a time, starting at back of flower. • Change the Fill Attributes Offsets settings from petal to petal to achieve different degrees of color (see the next figure).

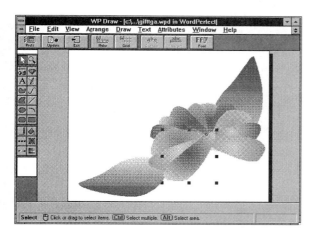

5. Add leaves to the background using green colors. • To place leaf behind flower, select the leaf with the Select tool. • Select Arrange. • Choose Back.

6. Select File. • Select Exit and Return to Document. • Click Yes.

7. Place flower in lower right corner of box (see the next figure).

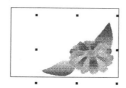

 Chef's Tip Add color to your gift tag flower later with paints, markers, or crayons (unless you happen to have a color printer, in which case, you don't need to read this tip).

Insert two graphic lines.

8. Select Graphics. • Select Custom Line. • Select Horizontal. • Set the line color to a pink shade. • Change the thickness slightly. • Click OK.

9. Place the line inside the top of the box, resizing to fit (see the next figure).

10. Select Graphics. • Select Custom Line. • Select Vertical. • Line Color: a pink shade. • Change thickness slightly. • Click OK.

11. Place line inside box to left, resizing to fit.

Add text.

 12. Move cursor inside box. • Font Face: CalsonOpnface BT. • Font Size: 20. • Type: To:. • Press Enter. • Type: From: (see the next figure).

13. Save and print your gift tag.

VARIATIONS

Flower Power: *If you're really into placing flowers on your gift tag, try this tulip design with a row of TextArt bullets. Use the Closed Curve tool in the Draw feature to create three shaded petals, two leaves, and a stem (see the next figure).*

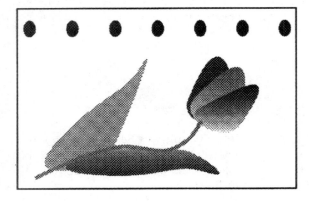

Coordinate: *Use this recipe and coordinate it with the next one, which shows you how to make giftwrap. Then, you'll have a great gift-giving combo designed especially by you. (Why spend the money on costly giftwrap that just gets torn off and thrown away? Use your computer paper instead.)*

GIFTWRAP

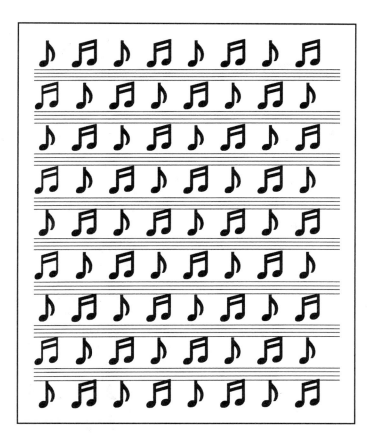

You can whip up a simple one-page giftwrap sheet using your WordPerfect for Windows program. True, it won't wrap a large present, however, it can certainly be put to use for those little surprise gifts. (Actually, you could wrap large presents, just run off several copies of the pattern and tape them together.) This particular idea uses a black and white pattern that looks pretty jazzy.

PREPARATION

Start with the symbols.

1. Select Layout. • Select Margins.
   • All margins: .25". • Click OK.

2. Place cursor at top of page. • Select
   Insert. • Select Character. • Select
   Iconic Symbols. • Select the note
   symbol (see the next figure). • Click
   Insert and Close.

3. Press Spacebar; repeat step 2, but this
   time choose the other musical note
   symbol.

4. Keep repeating between two symbols
   until entire first row is filled (see the
   next figure).

Chef's Tip   To access the WordPerfect
Characters dialog box more quickly,
press Ctrl+W. Another way to duplicate
the notes over and over again is to use
the Copy and Paste buttons on the Power
Bar.

Repeat the row.

5. Select the entire row of symbols. • Click
   on Copy button. • Move cursor to next
   line down. • Click on Paste button.
   • Continue pasting until entire page is
   filled with symbol lines (see the next
   figure).

Chef's Tip   To stagger the symbols, as
shown in the example, set up another row
that alternates the symbols. Then, copy
and paste both rows to fill the page.

Insert graphic lines.

6. Move cursor back to top of page.
   • Select Graphics. • Select Horizontal
   Line. • Move line directly below first
   row of symbols (see the next figure).

7. Repeat step 6, moving new line slightly below first horizontal line. • Keep repeating step 6 until four horizontal lines are placed in between the two text lines, as shown in the next figure.

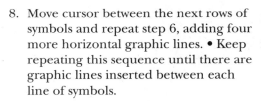
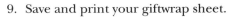

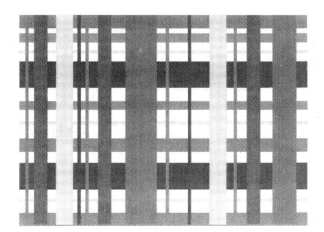

8. Move cursor between the next rows of symbols and repeat step 6, adding four more horizontal graphic lines. • Keep repeating this sequence until there are graphic lines inserted between each line of symbols.

9. Save and print your giftwrap sheet.

VARIATIONS

Get Graphic: *Another idea you can try is designing a plaid giftwrap sheet made up entirely of graphic lines, both horizontal and vertical. The lines should vary in thickness and color shades. Coordinate with a plaid gift tag.*

HALLOWEEN MASK

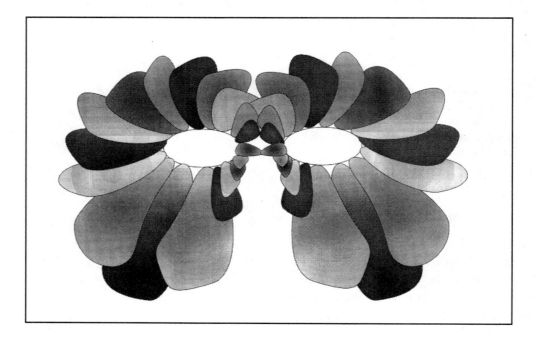

Paper Halloween masks are a great idea for school or home. Using WordPerfect Draw, you can design simple face masks that can be cut out and attached to hand-held sticks (opera-style) or tied with elastic bands or string. The tricky part is measuring to fit. Your kids will come up with all sorts of interesting designs, both scary and funny. This is also a good idea for a masquerade ball for adults!

PREPARATION

Start with the eye holes.

1. Select Layout. • Select Page. • Select Paper Size. • Change to Letter Landscape. • Click Select.

2. Click on Draw button. • Click on Ellipse tool. • Draw two ovals in the drawing area, about 1" apart (see the next figure).

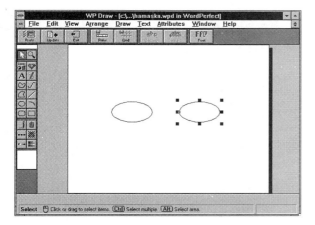

Build the mask shapes.

3. Select Attributes. • Select Fill. • Fill Type: Gradient. • Select a color for the Center Color. • Type: Circular. • Click OK.

4. Click on Closed Curve tool. • Draw an elongated shape attached to the left eye hole, as shown in the next figure.

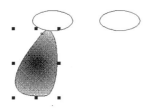

5. Click on Select tool. • Select the shape. • Select Edit. • Select Duplicate. • Move the duplicate shape over and select Arrange. • Select Flip Left/Right. • Then attach the shape to right eye hole (see the next figure).

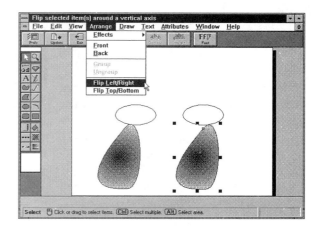

6. Repeat step 4, drawing a new shape with a different fill color (see the next figure).

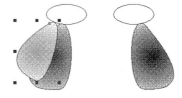

7. Follow step 5, creating a duplicate and flipping it to mirror the first. • Then attach it to the right eye hole. • Keep repeating steps 4 and 5 until you've drawn shapes of varying sizes and colors all around the eye holes (see the next figure).

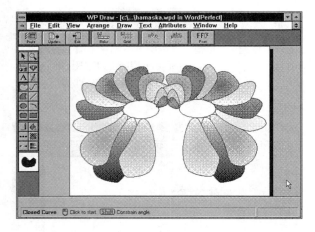

8. When finished, select File. • Select Exit and Return to Document. • Click Yes. • While the graphic is selected, click the right mouse button. • Select Size. • Size: Full. • Click OK.

9. Save and print your mask.

10. Attach a stick for holding the mask to your face (I used a chopstick), or use string or elastic bands to hold the mask onto your face.

Chef's Tip   You may have to resize your final design several times to get the eye holes just right for the person who will be wearing the mask. Be patient, though—it will work!

VARIATIONS

Class Contest: *Have your class make a contest out of who can design the neatest mask, scariest mask, funniest mask, and so on. After they are printed, color or paint them. Then attach hand sticks (opera-style) for holding or string for tying them on.*

15 min.

Moderate

NEEDLEWORK DESIGN

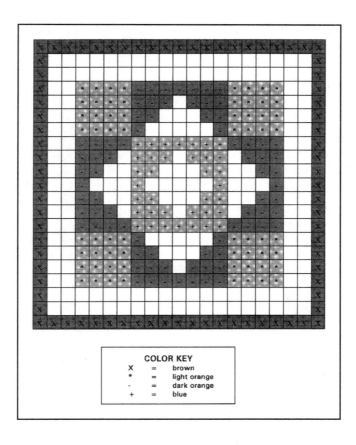

COLOR KEY

X	=	brown
*	=	light orange
-	=	dark orange
+	=	blue

For all of you crafty people out there, this idea is a real stitch. It's a needlework design you can make for cross-stitch projects. If you're tired of purchasing those expensive pattern books, then why not try making your own—yes, you can teach your computer to sew! With a Table and Fill patterns, you can design all sorts of cross-stitch projects. The following design shows a simple quilt-style pattern that can be made into a pillow, bookmark, wall hanging, or just about anything. (You'll probably come up with some nifty ones yourself.) I've also included a key box on the pattern page that shows what color the stitches are.

PREPARATION

Set your table.

 1. Click on Table Create button. • Table Size: 21 columns and 21 rows.

Make your pattern with shaded fill colors.

 2. Select top row of table. • Click on TblLineFill button. • Fill Options: 60% Fill Style. • Foreground Color: brown. • Click OK.

3. Repeat steps 2 and 3, select the other three sides of design; change fill pattern.

 4. Select table cells D4 through G7. • Click on TblLineFill button. • Fill Options: 40% Fill Style. • Foreground Color: light orange. • Click OK.

5. Repeat step 5 for table cells O4 through R7, D15 through G18, and O15 through R18 (see the next figure).

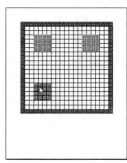

 6. Select table cells H4 through N4. • Click on TblLineFill button. • Fill Options: 80% Fill Style. • Foreground Color: orange. • Click OK. • Repeat sequence for rest of pattern as shown in example.

 7. For center pattern, click on TblLineFill button. • Fill Options: 20% Fill Style. • Foreground Color: light blue. • Click OK. • Repeat sequence for entire remainder of center pattern.

Add letters to indicate what thread colors to use.

  8. For the different patterns, type characters into each table cell to indicate what color of thread to use. • Font Face: Times New Roman. • Font Size: 12. • Click on Bold button. • Justification: Center (see the next figure).

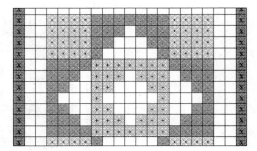

 Chef's Tip I used different characters for each pattern. For example, on the outer edges, I typed in an X for the color brown. Then on the design key box set in step, I designated what X stood for. On the center pattern, I used +'s. You can come up with your own color coding system.

Add a key telling which stitch is what.

 9. Click on Text Box button on the WordPerfect Button Bar. • Move box below table. • Click on Border/Fill button. • Style: Single Border. • Click OK.

10. Type in the key text. • Font Face: Arial.
• Font Size: 12. • Resize box when
finished (see the next figure).

11. Save and print your needlework design.

VARIATIONS

Change Pattern Sizes: *You can easily create
a smaller pattern by changing the Font Size
used in the table. Select the entire table, click
on the Font Size button, and choose a smaller
size. This will reduce the size of the table on
the page.*

PARTY DECORATIONS

If you're going to throw a party, you'd better have decorations—it's the proper way to set the mood. With WordPerfect for Windows you can make party banners, place mats, place cards, and masks (see these projects elsewhere in the Desserts section). Just to inspire you, I'll show you how to make a party hat. What party would be complete without goofy hats worn by the participants? This is an incredibly easy project to make with the computer. The tricky part comes in assembling the hat. However, all that takes is a piece of tape, so jump right in.

Preparation

Set up the page.

1. Select Layout. • Select Page. • Select Paper Size. • Select Letter Landscape. • Click Select.

2. Select Layout. • Select Margins. • All margins: .25". • Click OK.

Add some TextArt.

3. Click on TextArt button on WordPerfect Button Bar. • Font Face: Blackletter, Bazooka, or a similar style. • Type: HAPPY. • Press Enter. • Type: BIRTHDAY!. • Justification: Center (see the next figure). • Select File. • Select Exit & Return to WordPerfect. • Click Yes.

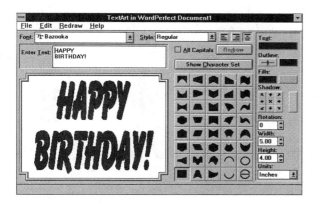

4. Move TextArt to middle of page, resizing as necessary (see the next figure).

5. Select the TextArt. • Click on Copy button.

Open the Draw program.

6. Click on Draw button. • Select Edit. • Select Paste. • Move TextArt text to middle of drawing area.

7. Using the Curve Line, Ellipse, and Line tools, draw various colored and shaded shapes around the TextArt text (see the next figure). • Draw zigzag lines. • Draw filled circles. • Draw stars. • Draw wavy lines (see the next figure).

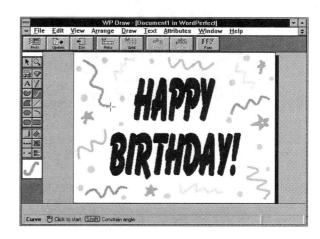

8. When finished, select the TextArt text.
• Delete the TextArt text completely
(see the next figure).

9. Select File. • Select Exit and Return to
Document. • Click Yes.

10. Resize graphic to fill entire page,
enclosing TextArt (see the next figure).

11. Save and print your project. • Color it
in, if necessary.

Turn a flat page into a hat.

12. Curve the short edges of the page so
they meet. • Curve the paper so that
the top of the page forms a point,
looking like a funnel. • Tape the edges
together. • Tuck in and fold any
bottom edge to make an even line so
that the hat can sit flat on a table.
• Attach string or ribbon if needed.

VARIATIONS

King or Queen for a Day: *Another variation using the Draw feature is to create a
crown. Use the Polygon tool to make points
and gemstones. Print out the page and attach
to a wide paper band that can be turned into
a head band. Then cut out the crown to really
look like a king or queen.*

PERSONALIZED STORYBOOK

Need a rainy day project for kids? Let them create their own storybooks using WordPerfect. This is also a great class project idea. Let them write a story first. They can personalize it for themselves or for someone they're going to give it to. Have them illustrate and type the text for each page using the computer (with adult guidance, of course). When finished, have them design a book cover, such as these project steps show.

PREPARATION

Start with a border.

1. Change to Design Tools Button Bar. • Click on GrphPgBrdr button. • Select Fancy. • Click OK.

Open WordPerfect Draw.

2. Click on Draw button on WordPerfect Button Bar. • Select Attributes. • Select Fill. • Change to Gradient. • Colors: shades of blue. • Click OK.

3. Click on Rectangle tool. • Draw the base of castle and towers. • Click on Polygon tool. • Draw edge of castle and tiny towers. • Fill Color: shades of green. • Draw the rooftops (see the next figure).

4. Fill Color: yellow. • Click on Polygon tool. • Draw the flags. • Fill Color: shades of pink and yellow.

5. Click on Ellipse tool. • Draw a large circle. • Select the circle. • Select Arrange. • Select Back (see the next figure).

6. Click on Insert Figure tool. • Draw a small box to the left of the castle. • Select HORSE_J.WPG. • Click Retrieve.

7. Select the figure. • Resize as needed. • Select Edit. • Select Rotate. • Rotate horse. • Click on Closed Curve tool. • Add a wing to the horse. • Click on Freehand tool. • Add feathers.

8. Click on Curve Line tool. • Draw three curved lines trailing the horse, each in a different color.

9. Select File. • Select Exit and Return to Document. • Click Yes.

10. Resize to fit in center of page (see the next figure). • Click on Wrap button. • Select No Wrap. • Click OK.

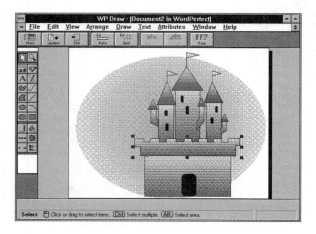

Add TextArt.

11. Click on TextArt button. • Font Face: ShelleyVolante BT, or other script style. • Type: Once Upon a Time... • Set in a curved arch shape. • Change width to 8" (see the next figure). • Select File. • Select Exit & Return to WordPerfect. • Click Yes.

12. Resize to fit above the graphic (see the next figure).

Add the author's name.

13. Move cursor to bottom of page. • Font Face: Chelmsfordbook or BernhardMod. • Font Size: 38. • Click on Bold button. • Justification: Center. • Type the author's name.

14. Save and print your storybook.

15. Assemble the book by stapling the pages together. Or using a hole punch, bind the pages with colored yarn or string.

VARIATIONS

More Fun Stuff: *Another idea is to have kids create their own activity books. Fill the book with crossword puzzles, word-find games, mazes, coloring pages, dot-to-dots, riddles and jokes, and other fun stuff. All of these things can be created with WordPerfect for Windows. Add a cover page and an answer page to complete the book. Have the kids exchange books and try the activities.*

PUZZLE

Another good rainy-day project for kids (or for very bored adults) is to make a WordPerfect puzzle. Using WordPerfect's graphics, you can design all kinds of puzzle scenes, print them out, and cut them into pieces to be reassembled again. This particular project shows you how to combine two graphics into one and add a few extra touches.

PREPARATION

Set up your page.

1. Select Layout. • Select Page. • Select Paper Size. • Select Letter Landscape. • Click Select.

2. Select Layout. • Select Margins. • All margins: .25". • Click OK.

Insert the first graphic figure.

3. Click on Draw button on WordPerfect button bar. • Click on Insert Figure tool. • Draw a large box inside the drawing area where the graphic is to be inserted. • From the list of clip-art files, select WINDMILL.WPG. • Click Retrieve.

4. Click on Select tool. • Resize graphic to fill drawing area.

5. Select Edit. • Select Edit Figure. • Click on Select tool. • Select a blue cloud band. • Select Attributes. • Select Fill. • Colors: shades of green to make the cloud into trees. • Click OK. • Repeat sequence for second cloud (see the next figure).

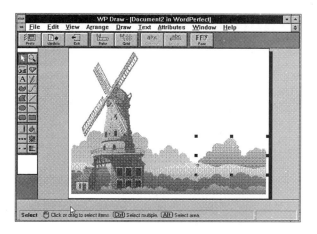

Add another graphic figure.

6. Click on Insert Figure tool. • Draw another box inside drawing area. • Select HOTAIR.WPG. • Click Retrieve.

7. Click on Select tool. • Select the new figure. • Select Edit. • Select Edit Figure. • Delete each landscape band, leaving only the hot air balloons in the figure (see the next figure).

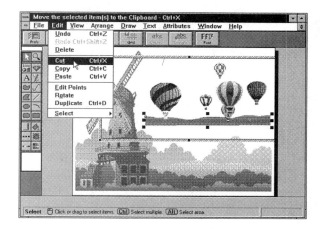

Chef's Tip There are two ways you can remove selected items. One way is to open the Edit menu and choose Cut. Another way is to just press Delete. Both accomplish the same thing; just make sure you have something selected with the Select tool before you try to delete.

8. Resize the graphic to fit nicely inside the first graphic (see the next figure).

Draw a few clouds.

9. Select Attributes. • Select Fill. • Color: light shades of blue. • Click on Line button. • Select No Line. • Click OK.

10. Click on Closed Curve tool. • In the remaining areas of the combined figures, draw some clouds. • Click on Freehand tool. • Draw puzzle pieces (see the next figure).

11. When finished, select File. • Select Exit and Return to Document. • Click Yes.

12. Resize the graphic to fill the page.

Finish up.

13. Save and print your puzzle.

14. Add color with markers, paints, or crayons. • Cut the picture into puzzle pieces.

Chef's Tip For a sturdier puzzle, glue picture to poster board before cutting out pieces.

VARIATIONS

Puzzle Invitations: *Use similar steps to create puzzle invitations for children's parties. Design your invitation in WordPerfect with time, date, and other party information. Add some spiffy graphics. Print it out and cut the invitation into puzzle pieces. Mail them to your guests, who then have to put the puzzle together to read the invitation! (This would be a fun idea for adult parties as well!)*

TRAVEL GAMES—CHECKERS

Before you start this year's family vacation, get yourself ready by designing some travel games for the kids. Your computer can help you. Rather than field those "How long till we get there?" questions every five minutes in the car, have some handy-dandy games ready to keep those little hands and minds busy. Design your own dot-to-dots, puzzles, word find games, and even a game of checkers. The following steps show you how to create a simple paper checkers game. The pieces can then be cut out and used to play (or bring along a pair of safety scissors and let the kids cut out the pieces).

PREPARATION

Create the page.

1. Select Layout. • Select Page. • Select Paper Size. • Select Letter Landscape. • Click Select.

2. Select Layout. • Select Margins. • All margins: .25" all sides. • Click OK.

3. Press Enter several times to move cursor down two or three lines.

4. Select View. • Select Ruler. • Ruler margins; left: 2", right: 9" (see the next figure).

Insert a table.

 5. Click on Table Create button. • Size: 8 columns and 8 rows (see the next figure).

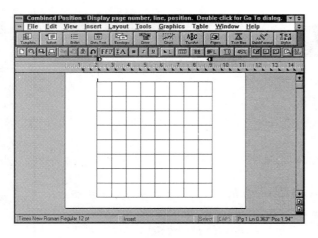

6. Insert cursor in first cell of each row. • Press Enter three times.

7. Select the first table cell. • Click on TblLineFill button on the Tables Button Bar. • Fill Style: 80%. • Foreground Color: dark black or grey. • Click OK.

8. Repeat the fill sequence in step 7 for alternating squares in table (see the next figure).

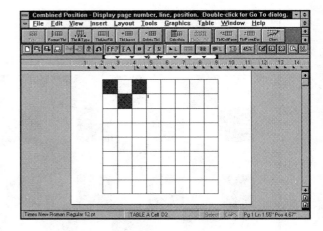

9. When entire table is done, save and print the checkerboard. • Glue checkerboard to poster board for sturdier game.

Design checker pieces.

 10. To open a new file, click on New File button.

11. Select Layout. • Select Page. • Select Paper Size. • Select Letter Landscape. • Click Select.

12. Select Layout. • Select Margins. • All margins: .25". • Click OK.

 13. Click on Draw button on WordPerfect Button Bar. • Select Attributes. • Select Shadow. • Click the Shadow On check box. • Click OK. • Make sure Fill/No Fill tool is on the fill setting.

14. Click on Ellipse tool. • Draw a circle.
• Click on Select tool. • Move circle to upper left corner of drawing area (see the next figure).

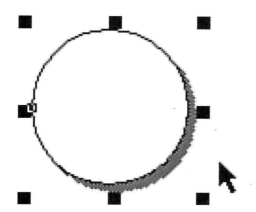

15. Select Edit. • Select Duplicate. • Move duplicate circle below first circle.
• Keep copying the circle until you have 12 playing pieces drawn (see the next figure).

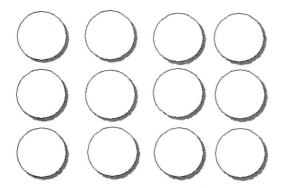

16. Select File. • Select Exit and Return to Document. • Click Yes. • Resize the graphic to fit in upper 1/4 of the page (see the next figure).

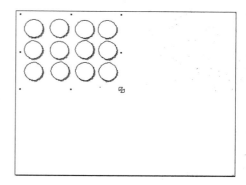

17. Repeat steps 13 through 16 to draw the second set of playing pieces (see the next figure). • Fill Color: a shade of red.
• Place graphic in lower 1/4 of the page.

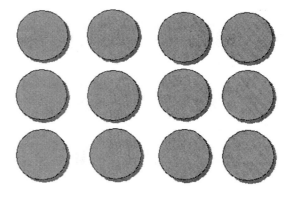

18. Save and print the pieces. • Glue to poster board. • Cut them out; use them to play checkers on table designed at beginning of the project.

VARIATIONS

More Games: *There are many travel games you can design with WordPerfect. How about a bunch of tic-tac-toe sheets? Or what about Hangman forms? You can even design your own versions of the License Plate game (where players look for other state license plates while traveling), or the Alphabet game (where players look for letters of the alphabet on road signs and billboards). Be creative with your computer!*

PART SEVEN

BASIC KITCHEN SKILLS

Used to be, all you needed to know to get along in life was how to tie your shoes, how to add one and one, and how to get out of doing the dishes. That was before computers came along. Now, you need to know how to select commands, navigate dialog boxes, and use buttons. As if that weren't enough to remember, your little word processor asks you to be skilled at drawing, bending text, handling graphics, and merging files (yech). If your memory needs a little jogging, this section's for you. You won't find every little thing about WordPerfect here, just the essentials you need to get along in life and to complete the projects. After all, this book is about fun, not work.

Basic Kitchen Skills

Things You Need to Know to Complete the Recipes in This Book

This section of the book presents some basic skills for using the WordPerfect for Windows 6.0 program. You'll find information about using menus, dialog boxes, Button Bars, and other regular old WordPerfect features. Plus, you'll find out how to use advanced features, such as WordPerfect Draw and mail merge. Just flip to the topic you need to know more about, read a brief description about the topic or how to use it, and then get back to your recipe.

Starting the Program

To start WordPerfect for Windows, you must first start the Windows program. To start Windows:

1. At the DOS prompt (which looks like C:> or C:\>), type WIN.

2. Press Enter.

Once Windows is running, the Program Manager screen should be displayed. Locate the WordPerfect for Windows program group icon, a small picture with the label "WPWin 6.0" below it. To open the WordPerfect for Windows program group:

1. Move the mouse pointer directly over the icon.

2. Double-click the left mouse button.

When the program group opens, it will display more WordPerfect program icons in the program group window. Locate the WordPerfect for Windows icon.

To start WordPerfect for Windows:

1. Move the mouse pointer directly over the program icon.

2. Double-click the left mouse button.

WPWin 6.0 Program group window

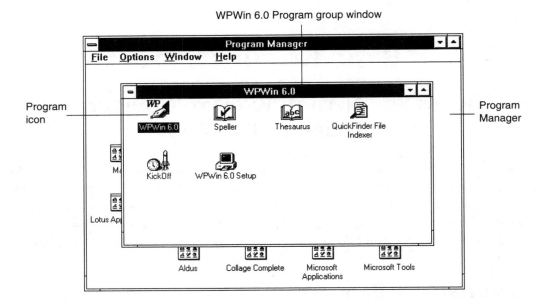

Program icon

Program Manager

Exiting the Program

When you've finished working on a project in WordPerfect for Windows, and you've already saved and printed the file, you're ready to exit the program. To exit WordPerfect for Windows:

1. Select the File menu.

2. Select Exit.

If you try to exit without saving the document you were working on, a dialog box appears, asking you whether you want to save your changes. Click on the appropriate button. If you click on Yes, another dialog box may appear, in which you can name and save your file. If you click on Cancel, you will be returned to the program. If you select No, you'll exit directly to the Windows Program Manager, and your file will not be saved.

Chef's Tip   A faster way to exit WordPerfect is to double-click on the Control-menu box located in the upper left corner of the window. (It's a little gray box with a dash in it.)

WHAT'S ON YOUR SCREEN?

The WordPerfect for Windows screen contains features that are typical of all Windows programs. If you're not too familiar with what those are, here are brief descriptions. At the top of the screen is a *Title Bar* that shows the name of the file you are working on. Beneath that is a *Menu Bar* that lists the names of various menus you can use. Underneath the Menu Bar are the *Button Bar* and the *Power Bar*. Their buttons (which you'll learn more about under the topic "Bars") provide shortcuts to frequently used commands.

Also on your screen, you can find *scroll bars*. They're located on the right side and bottom of the screen, and they allow you to view different parts of your document. At the very bottom of the screen, you see another bar called the *Status Bar*. It shows information about the text you type and where the cursor is located.

The open white space on your screen is the typing area. This is where you enter your text or figures. The *cursor* marks the place in the document where text will be inserted. Move the cursor (with the arrow keys or by clicking inside the typing area) to insert text at a different location.

The minimize and maximize arrows in the upper right corner of the screen make your window larger or smaller (icon-size). The *Control-menu box* contains a menu of window commands, such as Close (which can be used to exit WordPerfect).

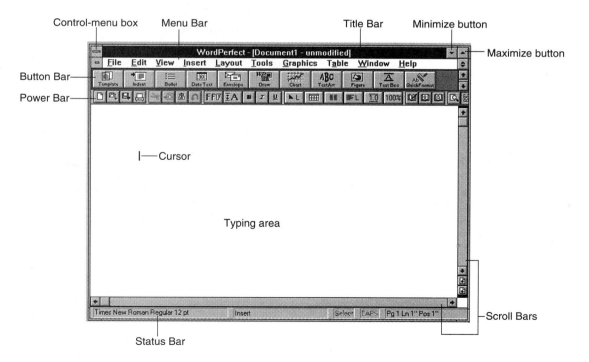

WORKING WITH THE MOUSE

If you're new to computer programs, you'll want to learn all you can about using the mouse. It's essential for accomplishing any computer task, especially the recipes in this cookbook.

The *mouse* allows you to move around on the computer screen, make selections, and activate commands. In this book, you'll also use the mouse to draw, resize, and reposition various elements. You roll the mouse around on a mouse pad, and a mouse pointer on the screen corresponds with the movement. Therefore, when you move the mouse to the right, the mouse pointer on-screen moves to the right, simultaneously.

There are five essential mouse skills to master:

Point   Roll the mouse on the desk until the tip of the mouse pointer on-screen is directly on top of the item you want to select.

Click   Point to the desired item on-screen, and then press and release the left mouse button. Whenever you tap the mouse button, you hear a soft clicking noise.

Double-click   Point to the desired item on-screen, and press and release the left mouse button quickly twice. These two quick taps of the button must be in rapid succession.

Right-click   Click the right mouse button instead of the left. Right-clicking displays QuickMenus that allow you to choose commands quickly.

Drag   While pointing at an item, hold down the left mouse button and move the mouse to a new position. When you have reached your destination, release the mouse button.

MENUS

Menus display commands that tell WordPerfect for Windows what to do. The commands are displayed in a list that drops down from the Menu Bar. By moving the mouse pointer or the keyboard arrow keys up and down the list, you can highlight the different command names and make a selection.

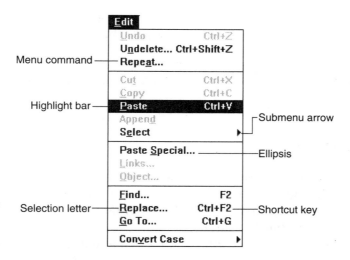

There are several distinguishing features in a menu.

Ellipsis   Commands that are followed by three dots, called an ellipsis, will reveal a dialog box when selected.

Submenu arrow   Commands that have an arrow at the end of the word will reveal another menu list to view when selected.

Grayed text   Commands that are displayed in shaded gray text are not available for selection at the present time.

Shortcut keys   Press the shortcut keys to activate a command without opening the menu.

Selection letters   Press the selection letter (the underlined letter in a command) to select a command when the menu is open.

To select a menu command:

1. Move the mouse pointer to point at a menu name on the Menu Bar.

2. Click the left mouse button to open the menu.

3. Move the mouse pointer to the menu item you want to select.

4. Click the left mouse button again.

To use the keyboard to select a menu command, first press the Alt key and the selection letter of the menu name you want to pull down. For example, press Alt+F to open the File menu. From the displayed menu list, type the selection letter of the command you want to choose.

Chef's Tip To quickly see what a menu command does without actually selecting it, use the arrow keys to move the highlight bar over the command name. Then look up at the Title Bar for a brief description of what the command does. If you've accidentally opened a menu, press the Esc key to close it, or click anywhere outside the menu.

DIALOG BOXES

A *dialog box* is a separate window that appears on-screen when WordPerfect needs more information from you in order to carry out a task. Where do dialog boxes come from? They show up in a variety of circumstances. For example, clicking on a Button Bar or Power Bar button often opens a dialog box. Selecting a menu command that is followed by an ellipsis will open a dialog box. Numerous buttons on a Feature Bar access dialog boxes. Some dialog boxes also have buttons inside their windows that open up yet another dialog box.

Although each dialog box is different, they all share common elements. It's a good idea to familiarize yourself with what those elements are and how to use them.

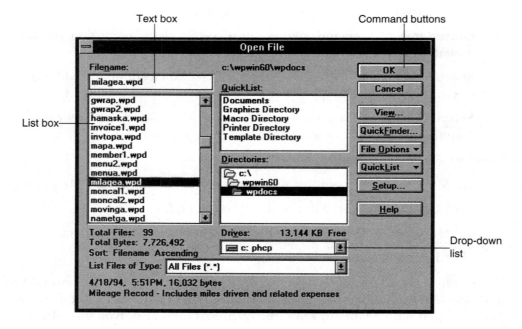

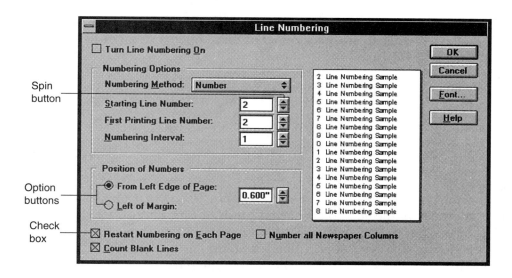

Text box   Type information pertaining to the task you are performing into this box.

List box   Click on an item in the displayed list to select that item.

Drop-down list   Click on the down arrow to open this list, and then click on an item in the list to select it.

Command buttons   Click on OK to execute your selections, or click on Cancel to return to WordPerfect without doing anything. Other command buttons, such as View, QuickList, and so on, will reveal either another dialog box or a list in which you can make selections. Click on Help for help completing a particular dialog box.

Option buttons   Click on an option to select it from the group. Only one option button in a group can be selected at any time; the option you select will be displayed with a filled dot.

Check box   Click on a check box to turn an attribute on or off with an X. You can select several check boxes in a group.

Spin buttons   Click on the up or down arrow to change the value and choose from a range of numbers, higher or lower.

To make a selection in a dialog box, simply click on the item you want with the mouse, or press Alt and the underlined selection letter on the keyboard. Pressing the Tab key will move you from item to item, as will the keyboard arrow keys. In some dialog boxes, you can also click on a button to open a visual display of styles or colors.

 Chef's Tip If you've accidentally opened a dialog box, you can close it without making any changes. Just click on the Cancel button or press Esc.

BARS

WordPerfect for Windows lets you use many kinds of *bars*. There's a Title Bar that's located at the very top of the WordPerfect screen that shows the name of the file you are working on. Beneath that is a Menu Bar that lists the names of various menus you can use. At the very bottom of the screen, you see another bar called the Status Bar. It shows information about the text you type and where the cursor is located. At the bottom and right sides of the screen are scroll bars that allow you to move up and down or right and left on the document page.

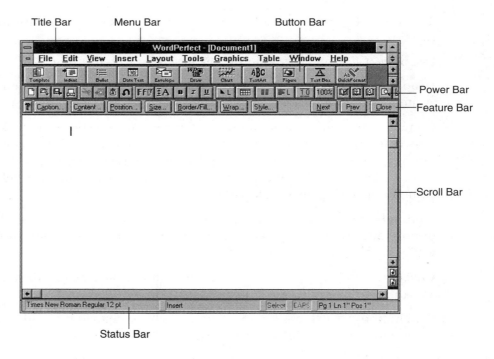

Besides these bars, there are three other kinds of bars that you'll use for practically every recipe you'll do in this book: Button Bars, a Power Bar, and Feature Bars. These bars are filled with buttons that quickly activate commands or carry out tasks. Each bar contains a different set of buttons to use. The buttons are illustrated with tiny icons or pictures that relate to what the button does.

BUTTON BARS

The *Button Bar* is located at the top of the screen below the Menu Bar. It displays buttons that activate frequently used commands or tasks. These commands can also be activated through the menus, but you'll find that clicking on a Button Bar button is much faster than pulling down menus and selecting from the lists. There are 12 predefined Button Bars, including the default bar that appears whenever you use WordPerfect (which is called the WordPerfect Button Bar, by the way). Each Button Bar has a different set of buttons you can click to select; however, you can only display one Button Bar at a time.

To select a Button Bar button:

1. If necessary, click on the up or down arrow at the end of the Button Bar to display the button you want to select.

2. Point at the button with the mouse pointer.

3. Click the left mouse button.

 Chef's Tip   If you want to find out what a button does before selecting it, point to the button with the mouse pointer and look at the Title Bar to see a brief description.

Most of the recipes in this book use the default (WordPerfect) Button Bar. When new Button Bars are called for, they are identified in the instructions. To change to another Button Bar, just click the right mouse button in an empty area on the current Button Bar, and choose another Button Bar from the QuickMenu list that appears.

WordPerfect Button Bar buttons:

![Template button]	Lets you open a WordPerfect template.
![Indent button]	Indents a paragraph by one tab stop.
![Bullet button]	Inserts bullets or numbers into a document.
![Date Text button]	Inserts the current date into your document.

Creates an envelope.

Starts the drawing program.

Makes charts with the drawing program.

Lets you create special effects for text.

Retrieves a graphic file.

Creates a floating text block.

Copies formatting from one selected block to another.

Creates, edits, and applies formatting styles.

Chef's Tip   You can also design your own Button Bar by selecting File Preferences, double-clicking on the Button Bar icon, and choosing from the available bars or creating a new one with the buttons you use most.

POWER BAR

Beneath the Button Bar is another bar with smaller buttons, called the *Power Bar*. These buttons are also quick shortcuts to commands found on the menu lists; they allow you to perform such tasks as printing or opening a new file. However, unlike the many Buttons Bars, there is only one Power Bar.

To select a Power Bar button:

1. Point at the button with the mouse pointer.
2. Click the left mouse button.

Some commands selected on the Power Bar, such as Cut, activate a task right away. Other commands, such as Print, open a dialog box where other options can be selected.

Chef's Tip   If you want to find out what a button does before selecting it, point to the button with the mouse pointer and look at the Title Bar to see a brief description.

Power Bar buttons:

Starts a new document.

Opens an existing document.

Saves the current document.

Prints the document.

Cuts selected text or graphic to the Clipboard.

Copies selected text or graphic to the Clipboard.

Pastes items from the Clipboard into a document.

Undoes the last edit made.

Changes the font.

Changes the font size.

Bolds text.

Italicizes text.

Underlines text.

Specifies tab stops and positions.

Creates a table.

Creates columns.

Aligns text.

Specifies line spacing of text.

Zooms the page view in or out.

Checks the spelling in your document.

Opens a thesaurus for finding words.

Checks the grammar in your document.

Displays the entire document page.

Displays or hides the Button Bar.

Feature Bars

Feature Bars appear beneath the Power Bar when certain program features are at work, for instance when you're manipulating graphics or creating watermarks. Like the other bars, they contain buttons that activate commands. However, these buttons do not show icons; they have words on them instead.

Graphics Box Feature Bar

To select a Feature Bar button:

1. Point at the button with the mouse pointer.

2. Click the left mouse button.

Feature Bars, such as the Graphics Box Feature Bar, must be closed before you can continue working on the rest of your document. Just click on the Close button on the Feature Bar to continue with your regular work. To make a Feature Bar appear (so you can work with a specialized item, such as a graphic, header, or footer), select the item, right-click, then select Feature Bar from the QuickMenu.

Files

Files are the basis for any computer program. Files are where you keep your work, start new work, or summon up old work. Files are part of the organizational structure of a computer that keeps everything accessible. Files that you save can be stored on your computer's hard disk drive (a storage device located inside your computer) or floppy disks (those flat plastic things that come in two sizes). Files are organized into different directories. WordPerfect files saved on your hard disk are saved in the WordPerfect directory unless you specify otherwise.

Whenever you start WordPerfect for Windows, a new file is opened and ready to go. WordPerfect even gives it a name, DOCUMENT1. However, when you save the file, you must give it a new name. WordPerfect files can be named just about anything, using up to eight character letters, such as MEMO1 or REPORT. File extensions can be added to the end of the file name to further describe what kind of file it is. For example, the clip art files (graphics) that come with WordPerfect all have a file extension of .WPG (stands for WordPerfect Graphic). Document files have an extension of .WPD (WordPerfect Document).

OPENING A FILE

To open a file you have previously saved:

1. Select File, then select Open, or click the Open File button on the Power Bar.

2. In the Open File dialog box, scroll through the list of file names and click on the one you want to open, or type the name of the file in the text box.

 Chef's Tip To switch to a different directory, select one from the QuickList.

3. Click OK.

SAVING A FILE

To save a file:

1. Select File, and then select Save. Or click on the File Save button on the Power Bar.

2. In the Save As dialog box, type in a file name for the document in the Filename text box.

3. If necessary, change the directory, drive, or file type.

4. Click OK.

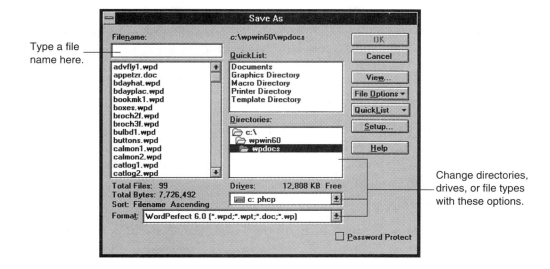

Type a file name here.

Change directories, drives, or file types with these options.

Printing a File

To print a document:

1. Select File, then select Print. Or click on the Print button on the Power Bar.

2. In the Print dialog box, change any printing options as desired.

3. Click on Print button.

Change any printing options before clicking on Print.

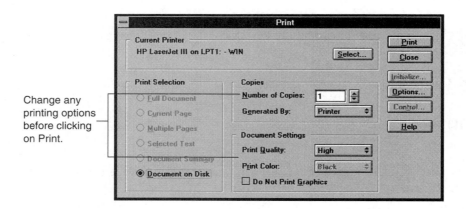

Closing a File

Closing a file isn't the same as *exiting* the program. Closing a file just removes it from your screen. To close a file or document you were working on:

1. Select File, then select Close.

2. If you haven't saved the file, a dialog box will appear asking you if you want to save. Make a selection by clicking on the appropriate button.

Zooming In and Out

Depending on what kind of project you're doing, you may need a different page view of your document. WordPerfect has a *zoom* feature that lets you view a page up close or far away. This feature will be used a lot in creating the recipes in this book, so make sure you know how to use it.

To use the zoom feature:

1. Click on the Zoom button on the Power Bar. A list of percentages appears.

2. Choose a page view based on percentages. Just select the view you want.

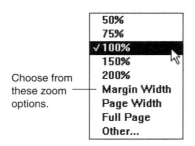

Choose from these zoom options.

```
    50%
    75%
  √ 100%
   150%
   200%
   Margin Width
   Page Width
   Full Page
   Other...
```

A Full Page zoom lets you see the whole page, but text will be illegible. A 100% view is the default view that WordPerfect normally uses. You can also set your own percentage of a view by using the View menu and selecting Zoom. For a fast full-page view, click on the Page Zoom Full button on the Power Bar.

WORKING WITH TEXT

When working with text, there are a variety of things you can do to control the way words appear or where they are placed. This is called *formatting*. You can format text before you begin typing, or afterward (called editing). When you first start WordPerfect for Windows, a document file opens, and you're all set to start typing text. The cursor, which indicates where typed characters will appear, is ready to go at the top of the page.

As type is entered, the cursor, also called the *insertion point*, moves to the right, advancing automatically to the next line when the current line is full (this is called *word wrapping*). Press the Enter key *only* when you want to begin a new paragraph. The *cursor* can be moved to new positions in the text by clicking within the typing area, or using the arrow keys on the keyboard.

SELECTING TEXT

An important skill in editing what you type is learning how to select text. Selecting text means to *highlight* it, causing a solid black bar to appear around the text. When text is selected, it can be deleted, formatted (such as changing fonts and sizes), moved to a new location, realigned (such as centered or fully justified), and more.

To select text with the mouse:

1. Point to the first letter of the text block you want to select.

2. Press and hold down the left mouse button, and drag the mouse pointer to the last character of the block you want selected.

3. Release the mouse button, and the text block is selected.

SANDWICHES (served with potato chips and pickle)

Roast Beef with cheese (your choice bread)	$3.50
Turkey (choice of bread)	$3.50
Pastrami (choice of bread)	$3.50
Bologna (your choice of bread)	$3.00
Ham with Swiss or American (choice of bread)	$3.50
Corned Beef (choice of bread)	$3.50
Salami (choice of bread)	$3.50
Chicken Salad (choice of bread)	$3.50
Tuna Salad (choice of bread)	$3.50

Selected text is highlighted with a black bar.

In the left margin of your screen is an invisible Selection Bar (trust me, it's there). Here you can click to the left of a line to highlight it quickly. To select a whole paragraph, just double-click in the left margin next to the paragraph you want to highlight.

 Chef's Tip To quickly select a word, move the pointer anywhere over the word, and double-click. To select a sentence, triple-click anywhere in the sentence.

To select text with the keyboard:

1. Use the arrow keys to move the pointer to the first letter of the text block you want to select.

2. Press F8.

3. Press the arrow keys to move the cursor to the last character of the block you want selected.

 Chef's Tip To quickly select text with the keyboard, hold down the Shift key and press the arrow keys to highlight the text. To select words, hold down the Shift key and the Ctrl key, then press the arrow keys.

FONTS

Fonts are sets of characters that share a particular design style. There are a variety of fonts that come with WordPerfect for Windows. Most word processing and desktop publishing programs come with fonts. Even Windows comes with fonts. If you have several of these types of programs installed on your computer, you have access to many different fonts.

Some fonts are block styles, others are more elegant. Some look like cursive writing, others look like billboard letters. It's good to have a variety, because this book features a myriad of recipes you can use these different fonts in.

To choose a font with the Power Bar button:

1. Click on the Font Face Button on the Power Bar. A list of fonts appears.

2. Scroll through the list of fonts and click on the one you want.

 Chef's Tip You can also choose a font by double-clicking on the Font Face button to open the Font dialog box. Here you can choose a font, a size, and make changes to its appearance (such as bold or underline) all at once. To exit the box, click OK.

FONT SIZES

You can set your text to different sizes, ranging from small to large. Each font comes in many different sizes that are measured in points. One point is equal to 1/72 of an inch.

To set a font size with the Font Size button on the Power Bar:

1. Click on the Font Size button. A list of font sizes appears.

2. From the list of sizes, click on the one you want to set.

JUSTIFICATION

Justification refers to the positioning of text on a page (also called alignment). By default, WordPerfect for Windows sets everything flush left to the left margin, meaning everything lines up on the left side of the page. But, you can also center text, flush it to the right margin, or justify it so that it lines up on both the left and right margins.

To set text justification:

1. Click on the Justification button on the Power Bar.

2. From the list of options, select the one you want.

You'll also find indentation controls that allow you to indent text, as well as tabs for aligning columns. Use the Indent button on the Button Bar to indent text, and the Tab Set button on the Power Bar to set tabs.

MARGINS

You can control a page's margins by opening the Margins dialog box. You can also use the Ruler to set margins as well. Margins are changed at the current insertion point and are in effect until you change them again.

To open the Margins dialog box:

1. Select Layout.

2. Select Margins.

3. Make any changes to the margin settings in the Margins dialog box.

4. Click OK to exit the box.

 Chef's Tip   If the Ruler Bar is displayed on your screen, you can quickly access the Margins dialog box by double-clicking on a margin marker.

THE RULER

Use the Ruler Bar to help you set tabs and margins quickly. The Ruler Bar is not displayed until you turn it on.

To view the Ruler Bar:

1. Select View.

2. Click on Ruler Bar. A check mark next to the command means the ruler will be visible. If there's no check mark, the Ruler Bar is hidden.

To set a margin with the Ruler Bar, click and hold the mouse button while pointing to a margin marker (the markers at either end of the Ruler). Then, drag the marker to a new setting and release.

To change the margins for a paragraph, use the paragraph margin markers (the inner markers on the Ruler). To change a paragraph's indent, drag the upper paragraph margin marker on the left.

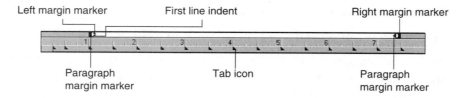

To set a tab with the Ruler Bar, click on the ruler where you want the new tab stop to appear. To move an existing tab stop, click on the icon and drag it to a new position. To delete a tab stop, click on the tab icon and drag it below the Ruler Bar. To quickly access the Tab Set dialog box, just click the right mouse button while pointing on the ruler. This will display a QuickMenu from which you can select the Tab Set command.

CUTTING, COPYING, AND PASTING

Stand-out features that make word processing programs so easy to use are the *Cut*, *Copy*, and *Paste* commands. With these, you can move, delete, and copy text and graphics, and paste everything into a new position.

To cut text or graphics:

1. Select the text or graphic to be cut.

2. Click on the Cut button on the Power Bar.

To copy text or graphics:

1. Select the text or graphic to be copied.

2. Click on the Copy button on the Power Bar.

3. Click the cursor at a new location.

4. Click on the Paste button on the Power Bar.

Chef's Tip   You can quickly copy or move text by dragging it. Select the text, then drag it to its new location. To copy text, press Ctrl while dragging.

To paste text or graphics:

1. First follow the procedure for cutting or copying a selected item.

2. Click the cursor where you want the item pasted.

3. Click on the Paste button on the Power Bar.

Of course, all of these commands can also be used through the Edit menu.

Chef's Tip   Everything you cut disappears into an invisible holding area called the Windows *Clipboard*. The Clipboard keeps the very last item you cut or copied. Always remember to paste right away, or you might forget and replace the item with something else you cut or copy. You can also use the Clipboard to cut and copy things in and out of other Windows programs to share with other programs.

WORKING WITH GRAPHICS

WordPerfect for Windows has many graphic features for you to use. In word processing programs, graphics are the secret ingredient used to jazz up an otherwise boring document. A *graphic* is anything that is treated like a piece of artwork by the program. A graphic can be a clip art file (a premade drawing), a picture you create using the Draw feature, a border, special effects for text (called TextArt), or even a floating Text Box. Basically, anything that's not typed in as text is a graphic.

Inserting a Figure (Graphic)

Use the Figure button on the default Button Bar to insert a WordPerfect graphic file (clip art) or a drawing you've saved in the Draw feature. You can also use the Figure button to insert a page border.

To insert a figure (graphic):

1. Click on the Figure button on the Button Bar.

2. From the list of graphic files, choose the file you want to insert.

3. Use the View button to preview the file before actually inserting it.

4. Click OK when the graphic file is chosen.

Once a figure has been placed in your document, you can resize it, move it, and use the Graphics Feature Bar to change other options.

Selecting Graphics

Once you have inserted a graphic element into your document, you must select it in order to edit it, move it, or delete it. To select a graphic, just click anywhere on it. When selected, small black boxes, called handles, appear on all corners and sides of the graphic.

Moving and Resizing Graphics

To move a graphic element, just click on the item. When the pointer becomes a four-headed arrow, drag the graphic to a new location. To resize the graphic, click on one of the small black boxes that appear around the element. When the mouse becomes a two-headed arrow, drag the mouse to resize the graphic.

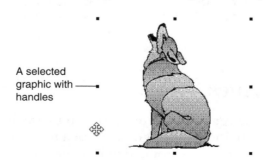

A selected graphic with handles

BORDERS

Borders are the lines or graphics that are placed around the edges of a page or a graphic or text box. You can access page borders by clicking on the GrphPgBrdr button on the Design Tools Button Bar, or by using the Layout menu. Page borders can also be selected with the Figure button that accesses the WordPerfect graphics files (clip art).

To select a border for a document page with the Layout menu:

1. Select the Layout menu.

2. Select Page.

3. Select Border/Fill.

4. In the Page Border dialog box, choose the border style you want to use from the drop-down list. Or click on the Border Style button and click the style.

5. Click OK to exit the dialog box and insert the border.

To change the borders of a graphic or text box:

1. Click on the box to select it.

2. Right-click, then select Border/Fill.

3. Select the desired border options.

4. Click OK.

GRAPHIC LINES

You can set ruled lines of varying thicknesses both horizontally and vertically in your document. *Graphic lines* can be set to specific sizes, or run the length or depth of your page. (But don't confuse these with a text underline.)

To set a line:

1. Select Graphics.

2. Select Custom Line.

 Chef's Tip   To create a graphics line that runs the length of the page, select Horizontal or Vertical Line at step 2.

3. In the Create Graphics Line dialog box, set the line options you want, such as type of line, measurement, color, thickness, and so on.

4. Click OK.

Like any other graphic, ruled lines can be moved about and resized. Just select the line, and follow the tips for resizing graphics in this section.

TEXTART

The *TextArt* feature is great, especially for cooking up the recipes in this book. With it, you can create all kinds of special effects for text headlines. You can arch words, set them at an angle, turn them into a circle, and create all kinds of other interesting shapes.

To insert TextArt:

1. Click on the TextArt button on the WordPerfect Button Bar. The TextArt dialog box appears.

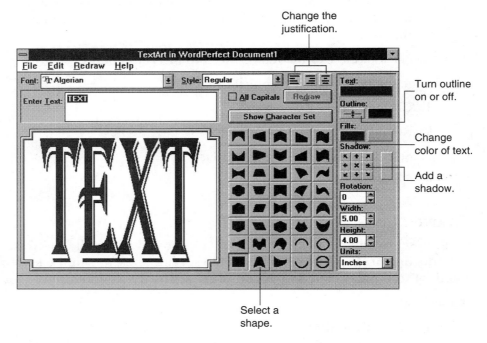

Change the justification.

Turn outline on or off.

Change color of text.

Add a shadow.

Select a shape.

2. In the TextArt dialog box, type in the text to use.

3. Choose from the many options for changing Font, shape, outline, color, size, rotation, and more.

4. When finished, select File.

5. Select Exit & return to Document.

6. Click Yes to embed the object into your document.

You can edit your TextArt at any time. Just select the item and double-click. This will open the TextArt dialog box again where you can then make your edits. Once a TextArt element has been placed in your document, you can resize it, move it, and use the Graphics Feature Bar to change other options, such as adding a border or changing the fill.

TEXT BOX

The *Text Box* feature allows you to insert floating boxes that can hold text, or nothing at all. Use them to create boxed text with borders, a fill pattern, or other graphic options.

To insert a Text Box:

1. Click on the Text Box button on the Button Bar.

2. A text box with a default border will appear in your document.

3. Use the Graphics Box Feature Bar commands to change the border or size; or resize the box with the mouse pointer.

4. To type in text, double-click inside the box and a cursor appears, then type in text. You can apply formatting to the text at any time.

To edit your Text Box, just select the box, and double-click to edit your text; or make changes to the options with the Graphics Feature Bar. Once a Text Box element has been placed in your document, you can also resize it or move it.

 Chef's Tip   You can Cut, Copy, and Paste graphics just as you can with text. Refer to the Cutting, Copying, and Pasting section under "Working with Text" for information about using these commands.

USING WORDPERFECT DRAW

The *WordPerfect Draw* feature is an essential ingredient to many of the recipes in this book. With it, you can design company logos, illustrate text, or just doodle. Like other drawing programs, it features various tools for making lines, circles, squares, and other strange shapes. Once opened, the drawing program displays a drawing area, a Menu Bar, a Button Bar, and drawing tools. Use the menu items for controlling drawing features and setting special effects, such as rotating. Use the Button Bar buttons to quickly access commands or tasks. Use the drawing tools for creating your graphic designs.

To access the Draw feature:

1. Click on the Draw button on the Button Bar.

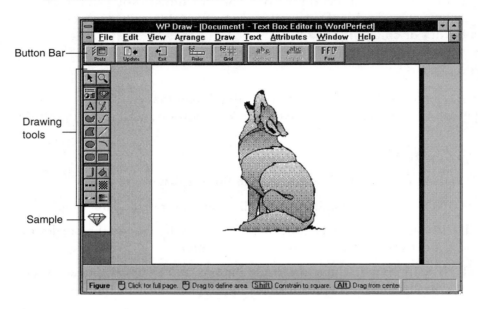

2. Choose any of the tools and begin drawing. See the table on the next page to learn what each tool does.

To exit the drawing program:

1. Select Fle.

2. Select Exit and Return to WordPerfect.

3. Click Yes to save the drawing and place it in the document.

Once the drawing is in your document, you can resize it, move it, and use the Graphics Box feature Bar to change other options.

 Chef's Tip You can also save your drawing as a file to reuse in other documents. Select File Save As, type a name, such as LOGO, then click OK. Follow the steps above to exit the drawing program.

The Drawing tools:

	Select	Selects parts of your drawing.
	Zoom	Enlarges portions of your drawing.
	Chart	Creates a data chart.
	Figure	Retrieves a graphic figure from the WordPerfect graphic files.
	Text	Changes the mouse pointer into a cursor for typing text.
	Freehand	Draws free-form lines, like a pencil or paintbrush does.
	Closed Curve	Draws closed curve shapes.
	Curved Line	Draws curved lines.
	Polygon	Draws polygon shapes.
	Line	Draws straight lines.
	Ellipse	Draws circles and ovals.
	Elliptical Arc	Draws a section of an ellipse.
	Rounded Rectangle	Draws round-cornered rectangles.
	Rectangle	Draws squares and rectangle shapes.
	Line On/Off	Outlines objects when the pen is at the right of the box.
	Fill On/Off	Fills objects with colors or patterns.
	Line Style	Controls thickness of lines; outlines.
	Pattern	Controls fill patterns.
	Line Color	Controls the color of a line.
	Fill Color	Controls the color or shading.

Watermarks

A *watermark* is a graphic or text that appears as a shaded background on a page. Watermarks, such as an elegant company logo on stationery, always appear behind the text in your document. You can create some pretty cool things with watermarks. You can have more than one on a page, and they can even alternate between pages.

To set a watermark:

1. Click on the Grph Wtrmrk button on the Design Tools Button Bar, or select the Layout Watermark command.

2. In the Watermark dialog box, select either Watermark A or B.

3. Click on the Create button to open a screen for designing your watermark. Here, you'll find a Feature Bar with options for inserting graphics, controlling placement, and more.

4. Design your watermark; you can use graphic elements or text. You can even use Draw to create a watermark.

5. When finished, click on the Close button on the Feature Bar and you'll be returned to your document page.

 Chef's Tip   To edit a watermark, open the Watermark dialog box and click on the Edit button. Make your changes, then click Close. To delete a watermark, click on the Discontinue button in the dialog box.

Tables

Every WordPerfect chef needs to know how to set a nice table. *Tables* are great for organizing information. Arranged in a grid of boxes, called *cells*, tables are set up in rows and columns. Columns are designated by character names, such as A, B, and so on. Rows are designated by numerical names, such as 1, 2, and so on. Each cell in a table has a name based on its location in the intersecting columns and rows. For instance, the very first cell in a table is A1, because it's in the first column (A) and the first row (1).

Tables can be formatted with colors, shading, and ruled lines, and are perfect for creating forms. Such options are accessed through the Table Button Bar that appears when a table is selected.

To set a small table:

1. Click on the Table button on the Power Bar.

2. In the drop-down grid, select how many columns and rows your table will have. Just drag the pointer over the size of your table.

3. Release the mouse button, and your table appears in the document.

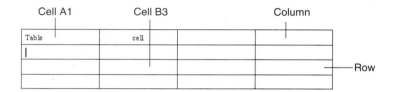

To set a larger table, select the Table menu and choose Create. A Table dialog box will appear where you can enter the size of the table. Click OK to create the table.

TEMPLATES

Templates are premade documents that come with your WordPerfect for Windows program. Since they are ready-made, all you have to do is open one up and enter your own text. Everything has already been formatted and designed for you. (Actually, every time WordPerfect starts a file, it's based on a template with default fonts, sizes, and positioning. These styles remain in effect until you change them.)

Templates are easy to use and often quite the time-savers. You'll find many different kinds for making letters, reports, forms, and more. In the recipe sections you'll learn how to customize the WordPerfect templates by adding your own text, graphics, and so on.

To select a template for a document:

1. Click on the Template button on the Button Bar.

2. From the list of available templates, select the one you want.

3. Click OK.

 Chef's Tip   In the Templates dialog box, you can also choose other options, such as editing an existing template, deleting a template, or creating a new template.

MERGING

WordPerfect has a *merging* feature that allows you to create form letters, envelopes, and other mass-mailing materials. The merge feature takes a data file that contains names and addresses, and merges it with a form file that contains a letter or memo. By merging the two files, a personalized document is created.

MAKE A DATA FILE

Start by creating a data file. *Data files* are databases that contain complete records of each item in the database, such as name, address, and phone number. The information is broken down into fields. For example, an address is a field. This detailed organization of information is what makes a data file unique from regular word processing files.

To make a data file:

1. Select Tools.

2. Select Merge.

3. In the Merge dialog box, click on the Data button.

4. Select the New Document Window option.

5. Click OK.

6. In the Create Data File dialog box, type the name of the first field in your record. For example, type: First Name.

7. Press Enter or click on the Add button to add this field to the list of Field Names.

8. Repeat steps 6 and 7 until you've entered all the fields you need for your data file.

9. Click OK.

10. In the Quick Data Entry dialog box, fill in the information needed for each record. Click on the New Record button to type another record.

11. When you've complete all of the records needed, click Close.

12. Give the data file a name, such as CLIENTS, and click OK.

MAKE A FORM FILE

Next, you must create a form file. A *form file* is the text and graphics you designed for your mass mail project. A form file can be a letter, a memo, or other form.

To make a form file:

1. Select Tools.

2. Select Merge.

3. In the Merge dialog box, click on the Form button.

4. Click on the New Document Window option.

5. Click OK.

6. In the Create Form File dialog box, type the file name of the data file you want to use. If you don't have that completed, select the None option button.

7. Click OK.

8. Design your form, entering text, graphics, and formatting as needed.

9. To insert information from the data file (such as a name or address), select the Insert Field command from the Feature Bar.

10. In the Insert Field Name or Number dialog box, select the field you want to insert from the list of field names.

11. Click Insert. The field name and its merge code will appear in your form.

12. Repeat steps 9 through 11 to insert any other fields into your form.

13. When finished, click on the Close button in the dialog box.

14. To insert a date code into your form, click on the Date button on the Feature Bar.

15. To save the form file, select the File menu, then choose Save. Give the file a name and click OK.

Merge

Once the data file and form file have been created, you're ready to *merge*. When merged, all of the fields specified in your form should be filled with information you typed into the data file, personalizing the form itself.

To merge the files:

1. Select Tools.

2. Select Merge.

3. Click on the Merge button in the Merge dialog box.

4. In the Perform Merge dialog box, fill in the names of the files you want to merge, based on the file names you gave them above.

5. Click OK to begin the merging process. When everything is complete, a new file is created with all of your information merged.

INDEX

Q-R

S